COORDINATING HEALTH CARE
Explorations in Interorganizational Relations

Volume 17, Sage Library of Social Research

D1739291

POLICY RESEARCH SERIES

Sponsored by the Center for Policy Research, Inc., (New York)

Series Editor: Amitai Etzioni

Policy research is concerned with developing solutions to societal problems by taking into account both effects and costs on a long- and short-term basis. Unlike "applied" research, policy research is broader and more encompassing—as well as being less abstract than basic research, and more willing to recommend changes and specific courses of action. Policy research also offers alternative lines of approach to the conception and solution of fundamental problems, and to the advancement of major social programs.

Coordinating
Health Care

**Explorations in
Interorganizational Relations**

Edward W. Lehman

Foreword by AMITAI ETZIONI

Volume 17
SAGE LIBRARY OF
SOCIAL RESEARCH

SCHOOL OF
CALIFORNIA PROFESSIONAL
PSYCHOLOGY
LOS ANGELES

SAGE PUBLICATIONS   **Beverly Hills**   **London**

For information address:

SAGE PUBLICATIONS, INC.
275 South Beverly Drive
Beverly Hills, California 90212

SAGE PUBLICATIONS LTD
St George's House/44 Hatton Garden
London EC1 8ER

International Standard Book Number: 0-8039-0512-2 (p)
0-8039-0442-8 (c)
Library of Congress Catalog Card Number: 75-691

First Printing

FOR BUNNIE

CONTENTS

COORDINATING HEALTH CARE
Explorations in Interorganizational Relations

Volume 17, Sage Library of Social Research

FOREWORD

A wit once referred to the entangled webs of organizations which carry out our society's domestic missions as a "crazy quilt." True, added another observer, but a multi-dimensional one. There are in each community in this land, scores of agencies, private and public and semi-public, local, branches of state, and arms of federal ones, pure and mixed agencies, supervisory and regulating, and others. They vary in competence, justification and size. Some disregard all others; others try to cooperate; others — created to provide coordination — add to that which must be coordinated.

Attempts have been made to conceptualize the relationships among these various agencies in neat models, whose main virtue is the economy of the conception. However, Lehman wisely assumes that such simplifications are too far from the socio-political reality to serve us. Hence, he opens his theoretical concept widely and develops a matrix which is more complex but also much more incisive than simpler approaches.

While Lehman deals with health organizations, essentially the same issues are faced by educational, welfare, and practically any other domestic service area. No one interested in organizational analysis, especially interorganizational linkage, will want to miss this volume.

Amitai Etzioni
Professor of Sociology, Columbia University
and Director of The Center for Policy
Research

PREFACE

This monograph operates on three levels. First, it is an exercise in the sociological theory of interorganizational relations. Its principal contribution here is to suggest that analogies to the development of international political communities further our understanding of interorganizational processes. The implications of such a perspective are developed throughout the monograph, but the main points are summarized in chapter 1 in a "paradigm for the analysis of interorganizational relations." The central element of this paradigm is a typology of control configurations. The four types (in order of complexity) are feudal, mediated, imperial, and corporate.

A second purpose is to examine the extant materials about the degree of coordination among health care units in the United States using the four types of fields as a theoretical backdrop. A word of caution is called for here. Our coverage inevitably is only partial. This is so first, as we note in chapter 2, because key cases tend to go unreported. It also is true because there is an unavoidable time lag between the completion of a monograph such as this and its publication. Rather than try to append each new development in an ad hoc fashion, we have decided that it would be better simply to claim that our report represents interorganizational relations in the American health system as of mid-1972. Some later events are mentioned, but we make no claim of systematic coverage. Hence, the most recent governmental initiatives (or noninitiatives) as well as the latest efforts to organize consumers may not be included. Yet, we suggest that real changes have been minimal, and that the picture drawn in the following pages, although not entirely up-to-date, remains substantially correct.

The third and most important purpose of the monograph is to consider the contemporary American health care "crisis" insofar as it is affected by types of coordination among health delivery agencies. Four areas of strain in our present system are pinpointed: an inability to deliver comprehensive care (its ineffectiveness); a failure to control costs (its inefficiency); a tendency to ignore the demands of rank-and-file professionals as well as clients (its unresponsiveness); and a propensity toward disregarding the psychosocial needs of patients (its insensitivity). Particular chapters of the monograph explore how feudal, mediated, imperial, and corporate fields exacerbate or ease these strains. The monograph concludes with policy recommendations on how to help reduce the deficiencies in each particular type of field and thus enhance the overall viability of our health care system.

This report was made possible by HEW Grant MH 17159-0151 to the Center for Policy Research, Inc. I wish to acknowledge the advice, encouragement, and suggestions of Robert Alford, Sally Hillsman Baker, Nancy Castleman, Amitai Etzioni, Gail Freedman, Eliot Freidson, Ruth Gable, Harry Greenfield, Wolf Heydebrand, Ethna Lehman, Murray Milner, Jr., Patricia Moberg, David Rogers, Suhasini Sankaran, and D. Anthony Vice.

January 1974   *Edward W. Lehman*
                              New York University and
                              The Center for Policy Research

INTRODUCTION

All known human societies have had people who diagnose sickness as well as those who provide methods for managing it (Freidson, 1971: 3). Presumably, one of the fruits of modernization, professionalization, and the concomitant growth of scientific and technological knowledge has been the everexpanding efficacy of man's capacity to diagnose and to treat illness. However, today we are confronted by the apparent paradox that in the most modern, industrialized, and scientifically advanced society in history, the existing practice of medicine is under attack as never before. "Ranged behind a banner reading Health Care Crisis," says Harry Schwartz, "a large and vociferous group of critics claims that the nation's medical system is woefully deficient in so many major respects that it must be radically reorganized — and quickly" (1971: 14). Those who advocate that there is a "crisis" encompass a broad political spectrum and advance proposals ranging from mild reform of the present system to what amounts to medical, and even political, revolution. They range all the way from a conservative Republican president of the United States to the new "health radicals" who crusade to shift "medical power to the people" (Bazell, 1971: 506-509).

Those who proclaim that there is a health crisis point to three primary foci of discontent with our delivery system: (1) its ineffectiveness; (2) its inefficiency; and (3) its lack of responsiveness.

Attacks on the effectiveness of the system denigrate the quality of its "output" and often center on the unfavorable comparison between the U.S. health statistics and those of the industrially advanced societies of Western Europe, and go further. A major target is the organization of the health system. Its critics contend that the present system produces too few physicians and other health professionals whom it then endows with excessive zeal for solo practice. As far as nonhuman resources are concerned, the system is marked by gaps and duplications of services. The result, it is claimed, is the fragmentation of services. Patients are divided into discrete diagnostic and treatment categories, which precludes an overall capacity for coordination in the health system.

In short, much of the onslaught by critics with regard to the system's alleged ineffectiveness has dealt with its failure to provide *comprehensive care;* that is, care in which the resources and personnel of diagnosis and treatment are coordinated in such a way as not to fragment services to the patient. (Our use of the term "comprehensive" thus encompasses the concept of continuity of care because fragmentation may entail the disjointed service at any given point over time as well as disjointed services in time.)

Obviously, comprehensive care entails more than just coordinating the activities of solo practitioners or streamlining their referral networks. Rather, if the American health delivery system is to become truly comprehensive, coordination must be macroscopic as well as microscopic; that is to say, it must focus on the articulation of activities of health care units (complex organizations) and not just on individual practitioners. This macroscopic articulation is becoming increasingly important because clinics, hospitals, medical centers, medical schools, and so on are where the funds, equipment, and personnel capable of altering the system are to be found. The aim of this book (discussed in detail later) is to consider the various patterns of linkages among health care organizations in the United States, as well as their significance for transforming the health system.

The health delivery system has been attacked not only for its ineffectiveness, but for its inefficiency as well. The critics of the present system are dissatisfied not only with the system's output but with the costs per unit of output. They charge that the nation's medical bill is increasing more rapidly than is the quality of medical care. For example, Harry Greenfield has shown that when compared to the overall Consumer Price Index, hospital daily service charges increased 3.3 times faster in 1966, 6.6 times faster in 1967, 3.1 times faster in 1968, 2.4 times faster in 1969, and 2.1 times faster in 1970 (1972: 1). Once more, critics insist that the allocative system that distributes personnel and resources in a hit-or-miss manner is at fault. Some even suggest that the entire health crisis can be solved by introducing the criteria of operating efficiency from the business sector to the relations among organizations in the health field (see chapter 5). In any event, economic inefficiency, whether or not it is viewed as the whole problem, generally is regarded as a major factor in the American health crisis.

While interorganizational coordination is thought of by some as a possible solution for the system's ineffectiveness and inefficiency, the growing bureaucratization of the health field, in turn, is attacked as a major source of its unresponsiveness. Health radicals, such as those at Health-PAC (see chapter 4), allege that "within the institutions that make up the American health system – hospitals, doctors, medical schools, drug companies, health insurance companies – health care does not take top priority. Health is no more a priority of the American health industry than safe, cheap, efficient, pollution-free transportation is a priority of the American automobile industry" (Health-PAC: 1970: vi). Consequently, these critics argue that the existing providers of health services no longer ought to be left alone to make policy. Rather, if the health delivery system is to have some authentic interest in health, then the recipients of services must have some say in the decision-making process. It is assumed that only when the interests of the consumers are formally built into the medical system can that system be counted on to be responsive to their interests. Some critics extend this argument and suggest that rank-and-file professionals (including nonphysicians) as well as nonprofessional staff also must be consulted and considered.

Yet, in the face of this massive disaffection, "counterrevolutionary" advocates have come forth to argue that the health crisis is largely a myth. (See, for example, Fuchs, 1970; Ginzberg with Ostow, 1969; and Schwartz, 1971, 1972). They note that the objective performance of America's health delivery system has improved markedly in the past decade (more doctors, more beds, lower infant mortality rates, more public funds spent on health), and they agree generally with Harry Schwartz, one of their more articulate spokesmen, that: "We have every reason to suspect that if the revolutionary proposals for transforming American medicine are adopted and implemented, medical care in this country will cost more while providing less satisfaction and poorer treatment for millions" (1971: 55).

What the health "counterrevolutionaries" fail to grasp is that their pleas that there is no real health crisis are a little like someone's having said in 1776 that George III was not such a bad fellow or in 1789 that Louis XVI was clearly an improvement over his predecessors. Students of political revolutions have long noted that these events often occur not at the point of maximum deprivation but only after things have begun to improve a bit, setting off a "revolution of rising expectations." Societal improvement generates revolution because only then is the basic malleability of the system, and hence, its potential for transformation, made visible. Thus, improvements do not so much preclude a crisis, as they are, in effect prerequisites for one!

Indeed, a major cause of the crisis is that America and its health system have changed so much over several decades rather than not at all. Before 1920, the majority of Americans lived on farms and in small towns rather than in and around urban centers. Medical needs were taken care of mostly by solo practitioners who were a part of the same communities as their patients. Because the technological and pharmacological revolutions in medicine were just beginning, hospitals, medical centers, and drug companies all played relatively minor roles. However, as America urbanized, as the focus of treatment shifted from the doctor's office to the clinic and to the hospital and private practitioners fled the inner city, there developed an everwidening discrepancy between what was going on in the health field and America's traditional health values that had stressed the intimate solo practitioner-patient bonds. Those values suggested that the doctor, unlike the businessman, should be professionally disinterested: that is, profit should be a secondary motive and the physician's primary interest should be the welfare of his patients. What urbanization and the bureaucratization of health essentially did was to destroy or to render irrelevant those institutional features of preurban America that had reinforced the traditional medical values. What was left was the value of disinterestedness or collectivity-orientation — minus the mechanisms for insuring that health practitioners would be collectivity-oriented. Hence, the key component of the contemporary health revolution is the search for new institutional mechanisms that will make sense of traditional medical values within the framework of today's society.

THE PRESENT STUDY

We begin this study with the assumption that in a society such as ours, the coordination of activities among organizations dealing in the delivery of health services may play a decisive role in coping with the crisis. Specifically, the purpose of this study is to explore the types of *lateral* relationships that have developed among health care units in the United States. We focus on lateral bonds because we regard the articulation of interests among the producers of services to be of central importance. We do not disparage the significance of hierarchic bonds (for example, a state department of health and its subsidiaries), but we feel that the topic is sufficiently broad to warrant a separate monograph. However, while we eschew the systematic study of hierarchically arranged health structures, our treatment makes it apparent that several kinds of lateral linkages cannot be fully understood unless they are viewed within some superordinate-subordinate context. Likewise, we do not deal here with another aspect of the structuring of health care units — namely, their stratification (that is, their relative position in the distributive system that differentially allocates the valued material and nonmaterial resources relevant to the health sector).

In sum, we are concerned fundamentally with the relations among units whose principal outputs are health services to clients or patients. We do not consider dyadic superordinate relations (that is, the relationships of one controlling agency to one controlled health care unit) unless they can be shown to have implications for lateral ties among health care units. We include the following kindred units under the headings of health care organizations: (1) units with an inpatient population, such as medical centers, general hospitals, specialty hospitals (for example, mental, cancer), and nursing homes; and (2) units providing ambulatory health services, such as O.P.D.s, community clinics, and so on. Not treated as health care units are such entities as narcotics treatment programs, social service agencies, community welfare councils, antipoverty projects, and so on. We exclude these latter groupings, not because they may not have a strategic bearing on the health of our citizens, but for heuristic reasons; that is, because our study is exploratory and the field is so large, it seems to make sense to restrict ourselves initially to units whose outputs are unequivocally of a health or medical nature. Moreover, because work on the so-called Health Maintenance Organizations is so new, we will not deal systematically with the extremely complex issue of group practice in this book.

In the course of this study, we: (1) generate a *typology* of configurations of interorganizational relations; and (2) consider whether these theoretical constructs are actually *empirically exhaustive.* In other words, we consider the "goodness of fit" between our typology and the real configurations existing among health care units. However, our enterprise moves beyond a simple typologic exercise and represents a preliminary attempt at a *paradigm for interorganizational analysis.* A paradigm is more than a typology in that it is inherently multidimensional. While it is more than a typology, a paradigm is less than a theory; the latter specifies the relationship among a predetermined set of variables. Rather, a paradigm provides a series of related questions — that is, a set of dimensions, variables, or a "language" — that illuminates a particular problem area.[1] At the outset, we must make it very clear that in this study we will be raising many more questions about health in America than we will be answering.

This study is paradigmatic because it moves beyond the issue of control configurations and asks some further questions about four aspects of content of interorganizational relations (see chapter 1). Here, too, we shall consider the utility of our proposed categories for analyzing the empirically observed patterns of interaction among health care units.

Let us stress that in all stages of our paradigm-building, the fitting of data to concepts is largely. *exploratory* as opposed to descriptive or explanatory. The available data (described later) cannot be treated as encompassing the entire universe of health care units, because no statement exists about the nature of such a universe. Moreover, we have little ground even for asserting that

the sources from which we draw most of our data are
representative of such a universe — if for no other reason than that
these data probably are "biased" toward a *formalistic*
characterization of the field to the relative detriment of informal
patterns (which are more likely to go underreported). Hence, our
argument throughout this monograph is that: the empirical
evidence appears to yield numerous "rich" illustrations of our
theoretical constructs and none of significance that fall outside;
consequently, that future interorganizational analyses would
profit by further experimentation with the paradigm. Further, we
feel that the use of this paradigm helps us understand several
facets of our health care crisis.

Our methodology basically has been one of secondary analysis.
We have largely, although not exclusively, focused on the study of
available data regarding interorganizational relations as they are
reflected in the published literature and at central data
repositories. More precisely, data collection has moved along six
fronts:

1. Hospital administration literature. An exhaustive review was conducted
of hospital, public health, and medical journals. Many of these reports
were highly qualitative in nature and largely concerned with formal
structure. This body of cases proved to be the richest source of data.

2. National organizations. Letters were sent to all federal and private
national health agencies to determine if they had any material bearing
upon interaction of health care units with which they dealt. The few
usable responses that were obtained are in the form of public relations
literature or personal letters that explain the officially defined goals of
their organizations.

3. Social science literature. The major sociological studies that touch on
interorganizational relations in the health field were examined.

4. Medical policy makers. We wrote to or conducted interviews with
representatives of a dozen agencies that make, advise, or seek to influence
or criticize policy. We collected literature from these agencies that explains
their official goals. We also examined the hospital policy-making literature.
As opposed to the materials in item (1), these data are largely prescriptive
rather than descriptive. A few of these articles, however, yielded data we
found useful for our purposes.

5. Nonmedical press. We also surveyed nonmedical newspapers and
popular magazines. Our richest source of leads here proved to be The New
York Times, which yielded information about cooperative practices not

reported elsewhere, as well as supplementary data from other sources, including material on trends in the area of medical policy.

6. Unpublished sources. We tried to find out who is currently working in this field and to contact them. In this way, we received several progress reports or drafts concerning studies whose published results are still forthcoming.

PLAN OF THE BOOK

Our paradigm for the analysis of interorganizational relations is developed in chapter 1. As we have noted, the core element of that paradigm is the typology of control configurations. We suggest that there are four analytically distinct types: feudal, mediated, imperial, and corporate. There are numerous examples of each in the health field, although the more complex the type (feudal is the most basic), the greater its potential policy implications for the health crisis.

Chapters 2 through 5 then treat each of the four patterns and discuss their relevance to the delivery of health services. The reader should be warned that the picture that emerges is, to say the least, not unduly optimistic. Consequently, we conclude (in chapter 6) with some suggestions of how interorganizational collaboration can reduce the ineffectiveness, inefficiency, and unresponsiveness of current delivery systems.[2]

NOTES

1. The reader will note that we do not use the term "paradigm" in the inclusive manner suggested by Kuhn (1962). Rather, for present purposes we are subscribing to the older, more circumscribed meaning of the term in Robert K. Merton's two well-known sociological paradigms: one on structural-functional analysis, the other for the sociology of knowledge (1968: 422-438 and 510-547). We regard Etzioni's paradigm for the study of political unification of equal importance for our work because it has had a direct, substantive influence on our paradigm (see 1965: 2-64).

2. For the moment, the classification of the crisis points for the health system in terms of ineffectiveness, inefficiency, and unresponsiveness will suffice. In chapter 5, we introduce a fourth dimension, insensitivity, which is closely linked to, but distinct from, the question of unresponsiveness.

REFERENCES

BAZELL, R. J. (1971) "Health radicals: crusade to shift medical power to the people." Science (August): 506-509.

ETZIONI, A. (1965) Political Unification. New York: Holt, Rinehart & Winston.

FREIDSON, E. (1971) Profession of Medicine: A Study of the Sociology of Applied Knowledge. New York: Dodd, Mead & Co.

FUCHS, V. R. (1970) "Why more physicians?" New York Times (December 19): 21.

GINZBERG, E. with M. OSTOW (1969) Men, Money, and Medicine. New York: Columbia Univ. Press.

GREENFIELD, H. I. (1972) Hospital Efficiency and Public Policy. New York: Center for Policy Research.

HEALTH POLICY ADVISORY CENTER [HEALTH-PAC] (1970) The American Health Empire: Power, Profits, and Politics. New York: Random House.

KUHN, T. S. (1962) The Structure of Scientific Revolutions. Chicago: Univ. of Chicago Press.

MERTON, R. K. (1968) Social Theory and Social Structure. 3d ed. New York: Free Press.

SCHWARTZ, H. (1971) "Health care in America: a heretical diagnosis." Saturday Review (August): 4-17, 55.

–––(1972) The Case for American Medicine: A Realistic Look at our Health Care System. New York: David McKay.

CHAPTER 1

A PARADIGM FOR THE ANALYSIS OF
INTERORGANIZATIONAL RELATIONS

This chapter presents a theoretical framework for the analysis of interorganizational relations.[1] The paradigm developed here is used throughout the remainder of the study for an understanding of the types of *lateral* interactions among health care units in the United States. The aim of the study is to describe the prevailing kinds of collaborative practices and to understand better what makes some health care networks more successful than others in coordinating their activities.

As we see it, existing interorganizational models suffer from one of two deficiencies. Some writers tend to employ an implicit utilitarian-pluralist perspective that leads them (1) to view the adaption of organizations to one another largely in terms of the needs and self-interests of *individual* organizations; and hence, (2) mostly to be concerned with explaining the performances of the single organizations rather than of the total network of which these units are a part.[2]

Other writers have become more aware of the interorganizational field as an emergent entity. This new understanding is stimulated in part by increased interest in how interdependent units make joint policy, as well as by concern over how such decisions can be made most effectively. However, these recent efforts are somewhat oversimplified because many have offered models of interorganizational relations that are built on the degree of conformity to or departure from some intraorganizational, rationalistic prototype (either bureaucratic or management science in nature).[3] In the course of our discussion, we suggest that other models, based in part on analogies to the development of national and international political communities, at times may be more fruitful.[4] The principal advantage of these "political" analyses is that they focus on the state of a multimember field in its own right while not committing themselves to the imagery of bureaucratic control. In other words, the overall adaptation of a system (and not just of one member) is studied, but centralized, hierarchic control is viewed as just one of several modes of potentially successful coordination.

CONFIGURATION AND CONTENT OF RELATIONS

Social relationships — whether microscopic (that is, among individual actors) or macroscopic (that is, among collectivities) — can be analyzed along at least five analytically distinct dimensions which, to some degree, vary independently of each other; the first deals with the configuration of the relationship and the latter four with its content. In a sense, configuration is the form of a relationship and content refers to its substance. In the present study, the concept of configuration points to the sociometric map of interorganizational control. We use the concept of content of interorganizational relations primarily to focus on the kinds of resources involved in the transactions among health care units. However, we also talk about how germane particular transactions are for health care systems (that is, their salience), whether transactions are all in one direction or whether there is some degree of reciprocity (that is, their symmetry), and whether transactions involve one, few, or many different kinds of resources (that is, their scope).

Because we focus on a multiplicity of dimensions and not just one, our efforts are more than typologic; they represent a preliminary attempt at a paradigm for interorganizational relations.

A TYPOLOGY OF INTERORGANIZATIONAL CONFIGURATIONS

The paradigm's central elements are *control configurations* that characterize different interorganizational fields. The special focus on control seems appropriate because of our concern with how pluralities of organizations coordinate their activities. We suggest that the success of coordination is explained in large part by the efficacy of control. Hence, we first offer a value-added typology of interorganizational control configurations. It is value-added because: (1) the configurations listed first are more "simple" and reflect less conscious control of an interorganizational field, while subsequent ones are progressively more "complex" and contain more deliberate patterns of control; and (2) each succeeding pattern contains all of the elements of the preceding ones plus at least one "added" factor. Thus, the value-added approach differs radically from the "property-space" strategy more commonly employed in sociology (although neither probably is so frequently used as are ad hoc typologies). In the property-space approach, each type is analytically "air tight" and differs from every other type in terms of two or more logically distinct attributes. On the other hand, what is especially important about a value-added typology is that all the values of a preceding type are present in a subsequent one; that is, nothing from a preceding level is lost but something "new" is added on. (The most extensive use of the value-added approach has been made by Smelser, 1963.)

We suggest that, theoretically, there are three broad patterns of control configurations and that the list is logically *exhaustive.* The three categories are: (1) a field of laterally linked organizations; (2) mediated interorganizational relations; and (3) guided interorganizational relations. In turn, our typology is cross-cut by three dimensions: (1) the degree to which interorganizational contacts entail procedures simply to inform or to consult one another versus the degree to which such contacts entail arrangements for actual co-decision-making about the future state of the field; (2) the degree to which the resources necessary for the wielding of systemic power (that is, for deciding upon joint goals, for pursuing them, and for implementing them) remain in the hands of the member organizations; and (3) the extent to which the responsibility for wielding systemic power is attributed to the individual member organizations versus the extent to which it is centered in an agency acting in the name of the entire field. (On the concept of systemic power, see Lehman, 1969).

A LATERALLY LINKED FIELD: INTERORGANIZATIONAL FEUDALISM

We here suggest an analogy between the most simple forms of interorganizational configurations, on the one hand, and the feudal societies of medieval Europe, as well as some aspects of contemporary international relations, on the other hand. For present purposes, European feudal societies may be characterized as macroscopic social systems. In these systems, the foci of identification and integration for member units (for example, fiefs, baronies, duchies, and so on) were largely internal rather than directed toward some center of systemic power. Furthermore, such systems lacked a strong controlling overlayer (for example, a Napoleonic state) that could exercise effective systemic power in either the market or political sector. Even where there was some collectivity-orientation, both the responsibility for wielding systemic power and the control of the requisite resources tended to be localized largely in the member units themselves. In any event, joint decision-making was only intermittent, and interaction consisted mainly of informing or consulting one another. (The classic characterization of feudalism is to be found in Bloch, 1931.)

Similarly, just because the U.S.S.R. and the United States today have become part of an interdependent international field (for example, "global system"), one cannot assume that these nation-states cooperate in regular, effective joint decision-making, or that they have surrendered significant portions of their claims to and resources for wielding systemic power to some supraagency. To the extent to which these two nations are not in conflict, their cooperation consists mainly of sending one another sufficiently clear signals about their own interests and intentions to prevent nuclear confrontation. Even proposed programs for further cooperation appear to be mainly along these lines. These programs suggest activities such as increasing international exchange (that is, in economic trade, tourism, cultural exchanges) or "defusing" the Cold War, which also often represents a form of exchange insofar as the transactions frequently proposed are devices such as mutual deescalation of the arms race.

There is more than a superficial similarity between these two cases and configurations found in some interorganizational fields. The simplest form of interorganizational control configuration resembles medieval feudalism and U.S. — Soviet relations because: (1) the activities of the member units are more heavily oriented to mutual information and consultation than to joint decision-making; (2) the member units retain control of the field's strategic resources; and (3) the responsibility for wielding systemic power is dispersed among the administrative centers of the member organizations. Obviously, there is considerable internal variation within this category of configuration. The degree to which contacts among organizations are intermittent or sustained and the varying quality of interaction (that is, the kind of resources involved, the salience, the direction of the flow, the scope) are two possible ways to discriminate among different types of interorganizational feudalism. However, from a policy-research perspective, how often units merely inform and consult one another versus the degree to which they also co-decide is probably the most important aspect of internal variation. Nonetheless, because our model is value-added, the issue is not simply one of informing and consulting versus co-deciding, but rather, informing and consulting plus progressively more intensive modes of co-deciding; that is, units that set and pursue common goals and cooperate in this pursuit and implementation inform and consult one another by definition. On the other hand, if we accept the proposition put forward by some authors that supramembership goal-setting, pursuit, and implementation are more effective and efficient than most comparable intermember mechanisms, then we would expect the range of co-decision-making in a feudalistic field to remain quite restricted because key resources are bound to member organizations and specialized centers of systemic power are absent (see Etzioni, 1968; Gamson, 1968; and Lehman, 1969). Thus, in contrast to the subsequent rungs in the model, we anticipate that interorganizational feudalism would involve more informing and consulting and less intense co-deciding.

MEDIATED INTERORGANIZATIONAL CONFIGURATIONS: A "COORDINATED" FIELD

The next rung in our typology involves a situation in which formal units exist to coordinate the articulation of several organizations. A useful analogy here is between such an interorganizational field and the role played by the international inspection teams set up under the Korean armistice and the 1954 Geneva agreements on Vietnam. The proposed function of neutral on-site inspectors in the U.S.S.R. – U.S. disarmament arrangements also fits into this analogy. In all of these actual or proposed international procedures, a coordinating unit (for example, inspectors) exists to facilitate the agreements and the transfer of information between nation-states. However, such units are fundamentally of a "service" character. Insofar as co-decision-making occurs, the requisite centers of control are still localized in the participating nation-state. The service units do not guide relations; at best, they "coordinate" them.

An interorganizational field with a mediated configuration consists of a plurality of organizations, each unit of which has its own set of goals and collaborates periodically with the others. Collaboration among the organizations is facilitated by an agency that funnels resources, communications, and services. Harrison's study of the American Baptist Convention indicates that it was first organized strictly for such a mediating role; key resources and controls were initially in the hands of local congregations. Only gradually did the central administrative structure acquire a relatively independent resource-base, greater control over intracongregational activities, and a capacity to set denominationwide policy. Hence, Harrison presents us with an illuminating picture of how a mediated configuration evolved out of a more feudalistic one and how, in turn, pressures arose that transformed it into a guided configuration (see Harrison, 1959).

In sum, the mediated configuration adds two factors not found on the feudalistic level. First and foremost, it introduces a new type of unit, which is not present in the simple feudal field. However, this unit provides coordination and services to the other units in the field rather than guidance. Second, the ratio of purely informing and consulting activities to co-deciding activities is likely to be more greatly weighted toward the latter than in a feudal context. Nonetheless, in light of the aforementioned hypothesis about supramembership control and effective wielding of systemic power, we suggest that co-decision-making in a mediated field is still largely on an ad hoc basis and most of the operative goals are simply those of each participating organization.

GUIDED INTERORGANIZATIONAL CONFIGURATIONS: EMPIRES AND CORPORATIONS

The final rung on out typology is reserved for guided configurations. These patterns are specifically concerned with co-decision-making and they presume that control is exercised by an agency acting for or on the system as a whole. We distinguish between two main subtypes of guided configurations based on whether the agency is a "member-elite", that is, one of the units participating in the interorganizational field, or a "system-elite," that is, an administrative unit to some degree external to the field. We label these patterns "empires" and "corporations" respectively.

The similarity is striking between an interorganizational field dominated by a member-elite unit and those political systems often referred to as empires. Empires tend to be characterized by at least one core "metropolitan" unit (for example, Britain) that is strongly identified with the entire system, both by itself and in the opinion of others (for example, the Roman Empire, the British Empire). Etzioni (1965: 79) characterizes such political systems in the following way:

> There was a mixture of exploitation and responsibility in the orientation of the core country of empires to those subordinated to it; the orientation of bloc "superpowers" to other bloc members tends to be governed primarily by expediency. The core-countries used to view the empire as an extension of their own politics; they often attempted to assimilate the subordinate units into the core country. . . . The modern bloc superpower, on the other hand, views the bloc as a limited partnership with outsiders. (The Soviet system comes closer to an empire than a bloc from this viewpoint.) At least some local elites in the subordinate countries responded by identifying with the empire, a phenomenon less intensively reproduced in the attitudes of members of blocs to the superpowers.

While the major thrust of this quotation is to distinguish empires from mere blocs in the field of international relations, the more crucial distinction for the interorganizational analyst is between "empires," that is, systems guided by member-elites, and cases of simple feudalism. Because supramembership identifications, normative bonds, and comprehensive control tend to be weaker among organizations than among countries, what we call interorganizational "empires" in actuality probably fall somewhere between Etzioni's categories of empires and blocs. Although it may be useful to place different guided configurations along such a continuum (that is, empire versus bloc), we suggest that it is more important to distinguish member-elite guidance from ordinary lateral linkages. A close examination of many situations apparently composed merely of laterally linked, autonomous units may reveal that one of the members controls the "lion's share" of resources and frequently is attributed the right to act in the name of the system as a whole. To treat such configurations as cases of interorganizational feudalism would be as misleading as regarding the relationship of the Soviet Union and Czechoslovakia as if both had equal leverage in the system they form.

Member-elite units represent one vehicle through which guidance may be exercised over an interorganizational field. The major alternative to this arrangement occurs when guidance is offered by a superordinate administrative agency that makes policy for some set of organizations in a given field, that is, a system-elite. A good intersocietal analogue of this corporate configuration is the case of the European Economic Community (E.C.C.) – the Common Market. This enterprise began as a supranational organization intended to make policy about coal and steel output by the six Western European member-countries. Although the guidance it originally exercised was highly limited in scope, especially when viewed within the context of the totality of interaction among these states, this zone has gradually grown to encompass more and more of the shared economic life of the societies involved, and has even begun to spill over into the political sector.

Municipal health departments probably represent one interorganizational analogue of the Common Market. Thus, participating health and welfare units are all subject to policies and programs formulated within some administrative overlayer. However, this example can be misleading, because city health departments tend to make rather inclusive decisions and exercise some form of final authority over the member units. Comparison to the Common Market sensitizes us to the fact that among corporate configurations, both the scope of the joint decisions and the degree of social control that the administrative overlayer is able to exert over participating organizations may vary markedly. The previously mentioned case of the American Baptist Convention is possibly more representative of corporately guided interorganizational bonds. Here, although there is a systemic power overlayer, the latter's decision-making capabilities are far from comprehensive, and member congregations still retain considerable autonomy compared, let us say, to the Catholic Church.

THE CONTENT OF INTERORGANIZATIONAL RELATIONS

The four other dimensions of our prospective paradigm focus on the content (as opposed to the configuration or form) of interorganizational relations. We begin here by asking about the substance of the transactions occurring in the field, that is, what are resources that provide the basis for articulation? It should be obvious that efforts to characterize resources in terms of some set of meaningful sociological categories can take a variety of alternative directions. For instance one can classify resources by what kinds of social relationships they are likely to promote (for example, whether they are normative, utilitarian, or coercive), or which of society's functional problems they most help to solve (for example, whether the resources are geared primarily toward adaptation, goal-attainment, integration, or pattern-maintenance). On the other hand, we find it particularly useful to examine resources in terms of their primary significance for the organizations that utilize them.

In all organizations, resources may be classified as being either relevant primarily for the implementation of the organization's goals, or dealing with some necessary but ancillary (that is, non-goal) problems the organization faces. It is clear that this is a *relative* classification of resources. That is, a resource that is primarily goal-relevant in one setting may have ancillary significance in another, or vice versa. For example, the presence of an x-ray machine in a hospital contributes to that unit's ability to deal successfully with its treatment goals, whereas the same machine in the New York Telephone Company's medical office is oriented toward an ancillary need of the Bell System.

In a heterogeneous interorganizational field, the goal relevance of particular resources possibly may vary markedly from organization to organization. Thus, in the articulation between a hospital and a professional linen service, sheets, pillow cases, lab coats, and so on are ancillary resources for the former and goal-relevant resources for the latter. Fortunately for us, this problem is not so acute, because our focus is primarily on the networks created among health care units as we have narrowly defined them. Therefore, because of the homogeneity of the kind of fields we are looking at, a goal-relevant resource and an ancillary one, for the most part, retain the same labels from one organization to the next throughout the study. We began our investigations with the following provisional cataloguing of major resources in the health field.

1. Goal-relevant resources:
    a. health-relevant facilities and equipment
    b. professional, semiprofessional, and technical staff
    c. "consumers," (that is, clients, patients, and so on)
    d. medical and diagnostic communications, information, advice, ideas, and so on.

2. Ancillary resources:
    a. facilities and equipment of an administrative or service sort
    b. administrative and all other nonprofessional personnel
    c. administrative communications, information, advice, ideas, and so on
    d. standardized procedures (that is, two or more units agree to use compatible administrative routines)

This initial classification of resources, for the most part, proved to be a useful mode of categorizing the substance of interorganizational relations. Nonetheless, without further supplementation, a simple enumeration of the kinds and frequencies of resources yields at best a highly partial picture of the content of interorganizational relations. To begin with, one also would like to know how intensive the transactions are; that is, how many *different* kinds of resources are employed in the joint activities of particular organizations. This aspect of content we label the "scope" of interorganizational relations. In fields whose scope is narrow, participating organizations transact only a limited amount of joint business, depending on one or a few types of resources. Organizations in fields whose scope is broad share or exchange several kinds of activities that involve a plurality of resource-types.

However, two different interorganizational fields may share roughly an equal number of activities and still differ considerably in the nature of their transactions. Hence, the examination of the content of interorganizational relations profits not only from an understanding of the types of resources involved and the scope of relationships, but also from a grasp of the *salience* of the transactions for the overall system. For example, health care units that share only a joint billing procedure and common laundry obviously have different interactions from those that share an E.E.G. technician as well as radiotherapy equipment but nothing else. A major difficulty is how one best judges and compares the salience of particular transactions for the state of a system. The issue would be infinitely more complicated if the participating units were highly heterogeneous and had markedly divergent goals. However, by restricting ourselves to fields made up of health care units, this problem can be largely bracketed in the present study. Because goal activities and ancillary activities are roughly the same from organization to organization in our study, we can safely assume that the exchange involving only the former is more salient than the exchange of only the latter. Thus, in the preceding example, the sharing of the E.E.G. technician and the radiotherapy equipment is presumed to be a more salient interaction, although formally no broader in scope, because it deals with goal-activities, while joint billing procedures and a common laundry have to do with ancillary tasks.

The question of salience comes close to the one about the types of resources involved. However, by treating the issues as analytically distinct, we remind ourselves that the relevance a transaction may have for some state of a multiorganizational field may be different from its significance for the goal attainment of any particular organization.

We of course recognize that there may be significant variation in salience within both goal-relevant and ancillary activities. We begin our investigations assuming that, all other things being equal: (1) the sharing or exchange of treatment facilities and equipment as well as of professional, semiprofessional, and technical personnel is more salient for a field than the referrals of patients or clients and the sharing and exchange of medical communications, and so on; and (2) the sharing or exchange of administrative equipment and personnel and all other nonprofessional personnel is more salient than the sharing or exchange of administrative communications, and so on, as well as the use of standardized routines.

Finally, a fuller appreciation of the content of interorganizational relations benefits from an understanding of what resources flow in which directions in the interactions; that is, the *symmetry* of transactions. From what sociologists know about exchange, dependence, and power, it seems important to determine not only what kinds and how many resources the units are sharing or exchanging, but also whether one organization is exclusively a supplier and another a recipient or whether there is, in fact, some authentic reciprocity inherent in the relationship; and if the latter is the case, what is the precise ratio of that reciprocity. (see Blau, 1964 and Emerson, 1962). For one thing, such knowledge would appear to be indispensable for ascertaining whether or not there was a member-elite unit in a field whose systemic power situation previously may have been obscure.

SUMMARY: SOME INGREDIENTS OF A PARADIGM FOR THE STUDY OF LATERAL INTERORGANIZATIONAL BONDS

The purpose of this study is to explore the types of relationships that have developed among health care units in the United States. In the process of this examination, we wish to better understand what makes some interorganizational fields flourish and others founder. The foregoing discussion focused on the several dimensions that we feel illuminate such an analysis. These dimensions may be treated as a provisional paradigm for the study of interorganizational relations. The paradigm is provisional in the sense that no paradigm is ever complete because additional theoretical and empirical work inevitably offers new or revised dimensions. Also, the paradigm is partial to the degree that it concerns basically lateral bonds and is intended neither for the study of primarily hierarchical relationships among organizations nor their stratification. With these limitations in mind, let us briefly review the dimensions of our paradigm:

1. The Basic Ingredient of Interorganizational Relations
   a. Control configurations
   b. Content
      1. resource-types
      2. scope
      3. salience
      4. symmetry
2. The Fundamental Issues of a Typology of Control Configurations
   a. The topic(s) of control
      1. only informing and consulting
      2. informing and consulting plus varying degrees of co-deciding
   b. The locus of the requisite resources for wielding systemic power
      1. dispersed among the member organizations
      2. in the hands of some elite unit
   c. The locus of responsibility for exercising systemic power
      1. in the hands of the member organizations
      2. in the hands of a supramembership agency
3. A Value-Added Typology of Control Configurations
   a. A laterally linked multiorganizational field: interorganizational feudalism
   b. A mediated interorganizational field
   c. A guided interorganizational field
      1. guidance by a member-elite: "empires"
      2. guidance by a system-elite: "corporations"
4. Types of Resources
   a. Basic Query: What is the most fruitful way to classify resources involved in interorganizational processes?
   b. A Suggestion: Classification of resources on the basis of the type of organizational activities they contribute to:
      1. goal-relevant resources
      2. resources focused on ancillary activities

    c. Major Difficulty: How applicable is such a classification in studies of highly heterogeneous interorganizational fields (that is, where there is a low correlation between what is a "goal-relevant" activity from organization to organization)?

5. The Scope of Interorganizational Relations: How many different kinds of resources are involved?

    a. Narrow scope — interorganizational fields in which transactions are limited to one or a few types of resources

    b. Broad scope — interorganizational fields in which transactions entail several types of resources

6. The Salience of Interorganizational Relations: How germane is (are) the resource(s) being shared or exchanged for the state of the interorganizational field?

    a. Basic Query: What is the most fruitful way to talk about salience of resources?

    b. A Suggestion: Classify salience in the same way as resources in general:

        1. most salient — goal-relevant resources

        2. least salient — resources focused on ancillary activities

    c. Major Problems:

        1. applicability to heterogeneous interorganizational fields (as in 4c above)

        2. how can we deal in some consistent way with the fact that neither all goal activities nor all ancillary activities are equally salient?

7. The Symmetry of Interorganizational Relations: In which direction(s) do resources "flow" among organizations?

    a. The degree of symmetry in the sharing or exchange of resources may be classified by the extent to which it is either:

        1. one way, or

        2. reciprocal

    b. Basic Query: What is the relationship between symmetry, power, and dependence in a given interorganizational field?

As in all paradigms, the ultimate test of the fruitfulness of ours is in the questions it helps to raise and to order in some theoretically meaningful way. In the last analysis, of course, "fruitfulness' is not enough. A paradigm should offer alternative answers to the questions it has raised. It is only through empirical research that the validity of the alternative answers can be assessed. Hence, although a paradigm is not an hypothesis, a proposition, or a theory, it too must face the scrutiny of empirical data. There is the implicit assumption in every paradigm that questions must be answered and not just posed. The remainder of this monograph represents a preliminary effort in this direction.

NOTES

1. The theoretical framework presented in this chapter originally appeared in Lehman (1971), a paper presented at the American Sociological Association meetings in Denver on August 31, 1971. To my knowledge, it is the first time that the notion of "control configuration" has been applied to the description of interorganizational fields. Haas and Drabek (1973: 228-232) subsequently have used the term and generated a typology in much the same way I first did.

2. See especially Blau and Scott (1962: chps. 3 and 8); Caplow (1964: 201-228); Clark (1956: 327-336); Cyert and March (1963: 4-6, 11); Elling and Halebsky (1961: 185-209); Emery and Trist (1965: 21-32); Evan (1966: 173-191); Levine and White (1961: 583-601); Levine, White, and Paul (1963: 1183-1195); Litwak and Hylton (1962: 395-420); March and Simon (1958: 131-135); Perrow (1961: 335-341); Reid (1970: 84-101); Simpson and Gully (1962: 344-351); Terreberry (1968: 590-613); Thompson (1962: 309-326; 1967); Thompson and McEwen (1958: 23-31).

3. See Dill (1962: 131-161); Guetzkow (1966: 13-44); Litwak (1969); Marrett (1971: 83-99); Mott (1968; 1970: 55-69); Starkweather (1970: 4-44); Thompson (1970: 156-167); Turk (1970: 1-19); and Warren (1967: 396-419; 1970: 114-129). The works of Litwak and Warren represent the most significant advances here.

4. Our work is especially influenced by Etzioni (1965). See also Deutsche et al. (1957); Haas (1958); and Rosenau (1969: 44-63).

REFERENCES

BLAU, P. M. (1964) Exchange and Power in Social Life. New York: John Wiley.
——— and W. R. SCOTT (1962) Formal Organizations. San Francisco: Chandler.
BLOCH, M. (1931) "Feudalism, European," pp; 203-210 in vol. 6 of Encyclopedia of Social Sciences. New York: Macmillan.
CAPLOW, T. (1964) Principles of Organization. New York: Harcourt, Brace & World.
CLARK, B. R. (1956) "Organizational adaptation and precarious values." Amer. Soc. Rev. 21 (June): 327-336.
CYERT, R. M. and J. G. MARCH (1963) A Behavioral Theory of the Firm. Englewood Cliffs, N.J.: Prentice-Hall.
DEUTSCH, K. et al. (1957) Political Community and the North Atlantic Area. Princeton, N.J.: Princeton Univ. Press.
DILL, W. R. (1962) "The impact of environment on organizational development," pp. 131-161 in Sydney Mailick and E. H. Ness (eds.) Concepts and Issues in Administrative Behavior. Englewood Cliffs, N.J.: Prentice-Hall.
ELLING, R. H. and S. HALEBSKY (1961) "Organizational differentiation and support: a conceptual framework." Adminstrative Sci. Q. 6 (September): 185-209.

EMERSON, R. M. (1962) "Power-dependence relations." Amer. Soc. Rev. 27 (February): 31-40.

EMERY, F. E. and E. L. TRIST (1965) "The causal texture of organizational environments." Human Relations 18 (February): 21-32.

ETZIONI, A. (1965) Political Unification. New York: Holt, Rinehart & Winston.

——— (1968) The Active Society. New York: Free Press.

EVAN, W. M. (1966) "Organization-set: toward a theory of interorganizational relations," pp. 173-191 in James D. Thompson (ed.) Approaches to Organizational Design. Pittsburgh: Univ. Of Pittsburgh Press.

GAMSON, W. A. (1968) Power and Discontent. Homewood, Ill.: Dorsey.

GUETZKOW, H. (1966) "Relations among organizations," pp. 13-44 in Raymond V. Bowers (ed.) Studies on Behavior in Organizations. Athens: Univ. of Georgie Press.

HAAS, E. B. (1958) The Uniting of Europe. Stanford, Calif.: Stanford Univ. Press.

HAAS, J. E. and T. E. DRABEK (1973) Complex Organizations: A Sociological Perspective. New York: Macmillan.

HARRISON, P. M. (1959) Authority and Power in the Free Church Tradition. Princeton, N.J.: Princeton Univ. Press.

LEHMAN, E. W. (1969) "Toward a macrosociology of power." Amer. Soc. Rev. 34 (August): 453-465.

——— (1971) "Toward a paradigm for the analysis of inter-organizational relations." Paper read at the annual meetings of the American Sociological Assoc. Denver (August 31, 1971).

LEVINE, S. and P. E. WHITE (1961) "Exchange as a conceptual framework for the study of interorganizational relationships." Admin. Sci. Q. 5 (March): 583-601.

——— and B. D. PAUL (1963) "Community interorganizational problems in providing medical care and social services." Amer. J. of Public Health 53 (August): 1183-1195.

LITWAK, E. (1969) "Toward the theory of coordination between formal organizations." Unpublished paper. Ann Arbor: Univ. of Michigan School of Social Work.

——— and L. F. HYLTON (1962) "Interorganizational analysis: a hypothesis on coordinating agencies." Admin. Sci. Q. 6 (March: 395-420.

MARCH, J. G. and H. A. SIMON (1958) Organizations. New York: John Wiley.

MARRETT, C. B. (1971) "On the specification of interorganizational dimensions." Sociology and Social Research 56 (October): 83-99.

MOTT, B. (1968) Anatomy of a Coordinating Council. Pittsburgh: Univ. of Pittsburgh Press.

——— (1970) "Coordination and inter-organizational relations in health," pp. 55-69 in U.S. Department of Health, Education and Welfare, Public Health Service, Health Services and Mental Health Administration, Inter-Organizational Research in Health: Conference Proceedings. Washington, D.C.: U.S. Government Printing Office.

PERROW, C. (1961) "Organizational prestige: some functions and dysfunctions." Amer. J. of Sociology 66 (January): 335-341.

REID, W. J. (1970) "Inter-organizational cooperation: a review and critique of current theory," pp. 84-101 in U.S. Department of Health, Education and Welfare, Public Health Service, Health Services and Mental Health Administration, Inter-Organizational Research in Health: Conference Proceedings. Washington, D.C.: U.S. Government Printing Office.

ROSENAU, J. N. (1969) "Toward the study of national-international linkages," pp. 44-63 in James N. Rosenau (ed.) Linkage Politics: Essays on the Convergence of National and International Systems. New York: Free Press.

SIMPSON, R. L. and W. H. GULLY (1962) "Goals, environmental pressures, and organizational characteristics." Amer. Soc. Rev. 27 (June): 344-351.
SMELSER, N. S. (1963) Theory of Collective Behavior. New York: Free Press.
STARKWEATHER, D. B. (1970) "Health facility merger and integration: a typology and some hypotheses," pp. 4-44 in Paul E. White and George J. Vlasak (eds.) Inter-Organizational Research in Health: Proceedings of the Conference on Inter-Organizational Relationships in Health. Washington, D.C.: Department of Health, Education and Welfare.
TERREBERRY, S. (1968) "The evolution of organizational environment." Administrative Sci. Q. 12 (March): 590-613.
THOMPSON, J. D. (1962) "Organizations and output transactions." Amer. J. of Sociology 68 (November): 309-326.
— — — (1967) Organizations in Action. New York: McGraw-Hill.
— — — (1970) "Thoughts on inter-organizational relations: a conclusion," pp. 156-167 in U.S. Department of Health, Education and Welfare, Public Health Service, Health Services and Mental Health Administration, Inter-Organizational Research in Health: Conference Proceedings. Washington, D.C.: U.S. Government Printing Office.
— — — and W. J. McEWEN (1958) "Organizational goals and environment: goal-setting as an interaction process." Amer. Soc. Rev. 23 (February): 23-31.
TURK, H. (1970) "Interorganizational networks in urban society: initial perspectives and comparative research." Amer. Soc. Rev. 35 (February): 1-19.
WARREN, R. L. (1967) "The interorganizational field as a focus of investigation." Administrative Sci. Q. (December): 396-419.
— — — (1970) "Alternative strategies of inter-agency planning," pp. 114-129 in U.S. Department of Health, Education and Welfare, Public Health Service, Health Services and Mental Health Administration, Inter-Organizational Research in Health: Conference Proceedings. Washington, D.C.: U.S. Government Printing Office.

CHAPTER 2

LATERALLY LINKED HEALTH CARE UNITS: INTERORGANIZATIONAL FEUDALISM

On the face of it, feudal fields should be of little interest to policy researchers seeking more viable and productive patterns of collaboration among health care units. By definition, feudal fields are networks that have minimal levels of actualization and the lowest potential for action in concert. Nonetheless, the study of feudal fields has both a theoretical and a practical importance. Theoretically, feudalism is important because it is the "core type" of control configuration and all of our other types represent elaborations of the feudal through additions to it. The study of feudal bonds has practical significance because, although we do not possess a statistically accurate count, feudalism is far and away the most common form of collaboration.

THE OBSERVATION OF FEUDAL FIELDS

Once a social researcher moves beyond the explicitly microsociological (for example, the study of small groups) to the more macrosociological realm of complex organizations (both of the *intra-* and *inter*-varieties), he is confronted by the fact that, methodologically speaking, it becomes far simpler to observe the formal and the deliberately created than it is the informal and "spontaneous." Considerable energy has been expended by intraorganizational analysts to move beyond the formal structure presented in tables of organization and in other blueprints to reveal the informal or "real" structures that lie behind them. Comparable progress has not been made to date in the interorganizational domain. Empirical observations in the latter area have tended to focus heavily on legally or quasi-legally created bonds among organizations. Even the more discursive, qualitative reports (for example, in *Hospitals* — the official journal of the American Hospital Association) suffer not only from the fact that their data are "soft," but because they, too, render an unduly formalistic picture. That is, these works commonly describe only officially generated arrrangements while ignoring unofficial accommodations. Furthermore, they are prone to accept uncritically the behavior prescribed in the arrangements as accurate descriptions of actual practices.

The study of interorganizational relations is then, in the words of an overused simile, somewhat like an iceberg; that is, the published materials largely reflect the visible formal arrangements, while the informal, less visible, "silent majority" of cases remains submerged. This dilemma is probably most acute in the area of feudalistic configurations. At the moment, it is impossible to assess the magnitude of the informal, unmediated, unguided contacts among health care units that operate in a common interorganizational field. When these patterns consist exclusively of arrangements for the sharing of information and in consultative practices (versus co-decision-making), they have an especially low visibility. It is only when the substance of such contacts is deemed "newsworthy" that they are likely to reach print. In these eventualities, the informal configurations are rarely systematically explored but must be deduced from "reading between the lines."

For example, on February 10, 1970, the *New York Times* reported a "new fever virus" that had killed three of the five Americans who were proven to have been infected (Altman, 1970). In recounting this episode, the news item inadvertently and vividly illuminated the informal configurations linking virological researchers at Yale University to physicians at Columbia-Presbyterian Medical Center concerned with tropical diseases — thus exposing an interorganizational web that would otherwise have gone unnoticed.

The disease, called Lassa Fever, had been contracted by three

American missionary nurses stationed in Nigeria and by two laboratory staff members at Yale University. Two of the nurses and one of those at Yale died. The last event the *Times* reported prompted American doctors to stop their research on the virus for the present.

The virus is named (by medical custom) for the place from which it came, the Nigerian village of Lassa, situated 150 miles south of the Sahara Desert, with a population of about 1,000. There, the first of the three missionary nurses became ill. After the two deaths, when a third nurse, Miss Lily Pinneo, developed symptoms, doctors had her flown to Lagos. Miss Pinneo spent four days there in a hospital, cared for by a U.S. Public Health Service physician who arranged for her transportation to Columbia-Presbyterian Hospital. When she arrived in the U.S., a blood sample was obtained from her. Columbia-Presbyterian sent this sample, along with those previously taken from the two dead nurses, to the Yale Arbovirus Research Unit. At Columbia-Presbyterian, Miss Pinneo was isolated after her doctors ruled out all known tropical diseases. But for the diagnosis of the new disease they looked to the Yale laboratory. In the meantime, she received no specific treatment, except, in the words of *Times*, "for excellent nursing care. . . ."

At Yale, the researchers isolated the virus and studied its effects on experimental animals. Only three staff members were permitted to work with the virus. After several months, one of the investigators, Dr. Tordi Casals, became ill. Dr. Casals entered Columbia-Presbyterian, where physicians suspected a laboratory-acquired infection by the Lassa virus. In order to save his life, the staff asked Miss Pinneo to fly back to Columbia-Presbyterian from her home in Rochester. There, she donated two units of blood from which plasma with still active antibodies was extracted. The virus stopped circulating in Dr. Casals' blood almost immediately after the injection of plasma.

Several months later, a Yale lab technician died of the disease while on Thanksgiving holiday in York, Pennsylvania. From the blood samples Dr. Casals obtained in York, the Yale researchers identified the Lassa virus. At the time the article appeared in the *Times,* however, they had not learned how the virus was transmitted to the technician.

This page-one story was intended primarily to tell readers about the Lassa Fever and about "the hazards of virology research which has led to at least 2,700 cases and 107 deaths from laboratory acquired infections over the years." But for the sociologist, it provides an unexpected and fleeting but still informative glimpse of the articulation between two giant medical centers — information usually offered only by a research project specifically designed to tackle that problem. The article tells us of recurrent contact between tropical disease specialists at Columbia-Presbyterian and virological researchers at Yale. It tells us these contacts appear to be geared basically toward informing and consulting rather than toward co-deciding, and that they are to some degree reciprocal. Further, the article makes clear that these bonds are largely unmediated and unguided and that each unit retains its autonomy. Fundamentally, what is exchanged is medical intelligence and medical material (for example, specimens). Thus, the substance of their transaction appears to be highly salient. However, the story also hints that exchange may become considerably more complex than that — as the hospitalization of a Yale researcher, Dr. Casals, at the Columbia-Presbyterian facility seems to imply. Unfortunately, because the manifest "news value" of this item and its interorganizational significance are so radically different, large "chunks" of data regarding the latter are absent. For example, the *New York Times* story gives us no appreciable information about the scope, the regularity, or the precise content of the transaction and nothing at all about the history of the relationship.

THE BLUMBERG REPORT

This is not to say that there is a total dearth of information about all feudalistic configurations. For example, Blumberg's *Shared Services for Hospitals* (1966) represents a milestone effort to chart such waters. The purpose of this study, performed between July 1963 and June 1964, was to provide a "preliminary review of the present status of shared services in hospitals." His report contains 147 references. As in our own inquiry, Blumberg's did not attempt to obtain definitive statistical data. Instead, he offers one or more "illustrative examples" for the types of services shared by hospitals. Blumberg treats the types of services under 12 topical chapter headings:

1. hospital administration services and consultation 2. business services 3. areawide planning and coordination 4. personnel activities 5. training and education 6. medical staff 7. laboratory, x-ray and related diagnostic services 8. medical records 9. purchasing and supplies 10. laundry 11. food services and 12. other.

This last category apparently is residual; not because of any judgment about its relative salience, but rather because of the relatively infrequent sharing of the services included under it (that is, nursing services, housekeeping, engineering and plant maintenance, pharmacy, blood banking, ambulance services, emergency or disaster services, "miscellaneous").

Even a rapid perusal of Blumberg's headings makes one aware that the scope of his inquiry does not coincide exactly with our effort to characterize feudal configurations. Blumberg's monograph is an invaluable guide to interorganizational collaboration in the health field. But his principal concern is with delineating the types of resources shared or exchanged by hospitals. Hence, although the bulk of his work is about feudal bonds (insofar as they are probably the most common ties), the reader must be alert to the fact that it is not Blumberg's intention to differentiate feudalism from mediation and guidance. Indeed, insofar as his concern is with content, Blumberg reports several instances of the latter configuration types.

For example, Blumberg reports that beginning in 1947, a group of 35 Seattle hospitals developed and adopted 12 standard medical forms (1966: 47). This case is probably fairly representative of the feudal types that tend to predominate in his monograph. On the other hand, he tells us about the Detroit Hospital Council's success in "persuading" area hospitals to merge obstetrical facilities (Blumberg, 1966: 20); and he also gives us examples of commercial test laboratories that provide groups of hospitals with evaluations of supplies being considered for purchase (Blumberg, 1966: 52). Whereas the first example clearly deals with feudalism, the other two are at least mediated fields, and the Detroit case contains hints of some degree of guidance. However, their special characteristics are never delineated, because Blumberg's monograph zeroes-in on the content of articulation — that is, the types of services shared by hospitals — and brackets the question of the variations in control configurations. Ours takes the latter as its starting point and as the framework within which issues associated with content are handled.

In addition, Blumberg's work is forced to focus on one class of services at a time. Hence, we are unable to consider the issue of how they hang together; that is, whether sharing one type of resource is associated with other kinds of sharing patterns. Of course, this deficiency is largely the fault of the available literature, which tends to report one cooperative practice at a time (for example, a story about computer sharing), with little or no hint about whether broader scope articulations exist. Our monograph, employing similar data, also has great difficulty in systematically dealing with the relative scope and salience of interorganizational relations.

What Blumberg's work does make extremely clear is that, although we may be tapping only the surface of feudal configurations (and perhaps not a very representative surface at that), there is an ample number of cases in the literature to permit us to talk about such control patterns without having to rely totally on theoretical speculations. Indeed, even if we suppose that the great majority of feudalistic bonds is still submerged (that is, unreported), the literature still offers a considerable diversity under this general heading.

There are at least seven different dimensions along which variations within the feudalistic category may be analyzed; six of these, we have already spoken of in the preceding chapter. These six are:

1. whether articulation entails only mutual consulting and informing or whether it also includes some co-decision-making
2. whether contact among the organizations is intermittent or sustained
3. how narrow or broad in scope linkages are
4. whether goal activities, ancillary activities, or both are involved
5. whether bonds are of high or low salience
6. in what direction(s) interactions tend to flow (that is, reciprocal or asymmetrical)

We here add a seventh item that we feel is especially important to consider when health care units are in "face-to-face" contact — that is, when they form an unmediated and unguided interorganizational field. We call this variable the "intricacy" of the relationship. The most basic form of feudalism is the dyadic bond. But as we shall see, the pattern can become extraordinarily more elaborate than that. By intricacy we mean not only that the number of participating units can increase, but that with this increase, the number of possible different combinations of interactions increases even more. Thus, the size of a feudal field can increase almost indefinitely, and beyond the dyadic bond it becomes even more problematic whether each organization in the field interacts with all the others. Hence, in a three-unit setting, unit A may interact with B and C or only with B or only with C. Units B and C face similar alternatives. Consequently, at one extreme we have a feudalistic field where all units are mutually interacting; while at the other, we have a situation where the only thing several units share is that they all interact with the same unit, although not with each other.

Perhaps a couple of microsociological analogies may clarify the picture. The case of a basketball team coming down court, passing the ball back-and-forth among the five players preparatory to shooting at the basket probably represents a good instance of "total" interaction. In contrast to this, we have the case of four people queuing up at the same time each morning to buy subway tokens from the same agent without ever acknowledging each other's existence. This represents a field in which the ratio of actual to potential interactions is extremely low. Given the nature of our data, we use size of field as our major indicator of intricacy, but this discussion should have made clear the fact that the concept implies more than the sheer number of units.

Ideally, of course, one would like to study how variation in each of these seven variables constrains the variation in some or in all of the others. Indeed, any adequate theory of interorganizational relations (or at least of feudalistic ones) must provide such a formulation. However, in light of its exploratory nature, this study can only at best lay the groundwork for this form of specification, while itself remaining within the realm of paradigm-building and illustration.

As an alternative strategy to multivariate analysis, we present the variations in feudal patterns by combining as many of the seven variables as possible under two subheadings — *simple feudal* and *complex feudal* — and then illustrating both species and some of their variants. Our hunch as to what makes a feudal field simple or complex emerged originally from a perusal of the literature. However, in light of the crucial question of representativeness, we here use such a classification basically for heuristic purposes. This presentation does not claim to offer an ideal-type construction (in the Weberian sense), although there may be good theoretical grounds for the affinity among elements. Also, because of the nature of our data, the simple-versus-complex schema cannot be regarded as an empirical generalization or even as well-grounded hypotheses about the actual empirical clustering of our variables. Nonetheless, theoretical insight and "peeking" at the data lead us to suggest that some of the seven sets of variables lend themselves more readily to dimensions of a simple-versus-complex rubric than do others.

For example, bonds that entail merely mutual consultation and informing are probably more "simple" than those directed to some degree of co-deciding. Similarly, articulations in which only one or a few types of resources are shared or exchanged — that is, those narrower in scope — may be treated as "simpler" than those enmeshed in a multiresource field — that is, those with broader scope. Third, interactions that are more irregular or intermittent suggest a less "complex" relationship than those where contacts are sustained. Finally, interorganizational fields with few member units are, all other things being equal, relatively simple. Other polarities are more difficult to categorize. Thus, questions of whether relationships deal with goal activities and, hence, are highly salient seem to cut across the issue of how complex an interorganizational field is. In much the same way, one cannot say that a field in which most of the resource flows emanate from one center — that is, an asymmetrical setting — is necessarily more complex or more simple than a field with multidirectional flows — especially because the question of symmetry seems to be so inexorably intertwined with the issues of power, dependence, guidance, and so on.

In sum, we are suggesting that a simple feudalistic field contains fewer participants, entails basically informing-consulting functions, has narrower scope, and involves only intermittent contact among member units. Conversely, a complex feudal field has more member units who have sustained interactions of broader scope that involve some co-decision-making. In the following sections, we illustrate each of these types as well as some strategic empirical departures. Throughout the chapter, we also attempt to deal with the topics that do not fit neatly into the simple-complex rubric: (1) the issue of whether articulation is goal-relevant and highly salient or ancillary with low salience; and (2) whether flows are asymmetrical or reciprocal.

SIMPLE FEUDALISTIC FIELDS

The most simple feudal field, then, is a dyadic, intermittent relationship between two autonomous units that deals with one or a few different types of activity entailing orienting (that is, informing-consulting) behavior rather than co-decision-making. As noted earlier, such patterns are notably under- or unreported when the accommodations are also informal — although extraordinary events (for example, Lassa fever) occasionally intervene to illuminate dramatically, albeit briefly, their existence. Once simple feudal configurations are more formalized, the probability that they will be written-up seems to improve somewhat. Not atypical here are those instances in which the skills of professionals such as radiologists and pathologists located in one hospital are put at the disposal of the staff in another.

The relationship between Alamosa (Colo.) Community Hospital, a 96-bed unit, and the somewhat larger 157-bed St. Francis Hospital in Colorado Springs is fairly representative of this kind of simple feudal configuration (see Reese, 1963). In 1948, Alamosa Hospital, which previously had had no staff radiologist to interpret and read x-ray films, devised a plan with a radiologist at St. Francis Hospital. Because a range of mountains and a distance of 150 miles stood between Alamosa and Colorado Springs, the original agreement called for any x-rays taken at the Alamosa Hospital in a given day to be mailed special delivery to the radiologist at the end of that day. When they arrived at St. Francis the following morning, the films were read immediately, reports were then prepared and telephoned to Alamosa.

Under this initial plan, Alamosa had an x-ray report within 24 hours. The process was speeded up even further when air mail was substituted for special delivery. Ultimately, teletype machines were installed in both hospitals. This reduced mail and phone costs and provided Alamosa Hospital with an almost immediate written report rather than merely an oral one. The original plan also called for the radiologist to make one trip a month to Alamosa Hospital. All of Alamosa's fluoroscopic work was scheduled for that day. But as the patient load increased, other men were added to the radiological staff until by 1963, a full-time radiologist was stationed by St. Francis at Alamosa Hospital. A similar arrangement between the two hospitals was made for the services of a pathologist. However, by June 1, 1963, Alamosa terminated this linkage and planned to hire its own pathologist.

We have here a picture of two health care organizations, separated by 150 miles, who have entered into an arrangement to provide diagnostic services. Hence, all bonds are dyadic and basically geared toward information exchange. In addition, they are narrow in scope. The one effort to introduce an additional task area − the pathology service − apparently has been discontinued. The original plan, at least, conceived of a more intermittent than sustained relationship, in the sense that the precise volume of interaction was not defined in the agreement but was left to fluctuate on an as needed basis. In other words, the diagnostic requirements of Alamosa Hospital, at first, almost exclusively determined whether interaction between the two units actually took place. Later on, of course, contacts became progressively more sustained. The permanent stationing of a radiologist at Alamosa Hospital probably serves as the best single indicator of the transition from an intermittent to a sustained interaction.

The fact that contacts sometimes become more sustained serves to remind us that all feudal cases cannot be easily fitted into purely simple or purely complex "boxes". For example, simpler relationships are not necessarily confined to dyadic bonds. A plurality of health care units can have similar profiles. For example, a program not unlike the one just discussed has been reported among four hospitals in Michigan that range in size from 33 to 125 beds and handle a combined total of 10,000 x-ray examinations yearly (see Williams and Rollins, 1959). These hospitals are scattered within a 125-mile area, which restricts the radiologist to one visit per week to three of the hospitals and to handling diagnostic and therapy cases in his "home" hospital during the other three days a week. However, x-ray films can be mailed to the radiologists daily for interpretation. Reports are made to the sending hospital by telephone. The hospital, in turn, is expected to transcribe each report into the medical records.

The sharing of computer sources by a plurality of health care units is of interest both to those concerned with the more effective channelling of medical and research information, and to us because it represents situations where multiple units still have relatively low-scope contacts. Such sharing goes on among both medical and psychiatric units. For example, Rockland State Hospital in New York State is the center for the Multi-State Information System (MSIS), in which seven states — Connecticut, Maine, Massachusetts, New Hampshire, New York, Rhode Island, and Vermont — are reportedly engaged in a cooperative effort to develop an automated record-keeping system involving 150,000 state mental patients. The project is partially funded by a grant from the N.I.M.H. Rockland State Hospital's 1968-1969 annual report states on page 20 that:

> The primary objectives of the Multi-State Information System are the automation of data collection and maintenance of individual psychiatric patient records for clinical, administrative, program evaluation and research purposes. A fundamental precept underlying the approach is the belief that an information system which contains an accurate picture of every patient will, in the aggregate, reflect the salient facts about the total patient population. A well designed system will, thus, serve the needs of the treating clinician as well as the needs of the public health administrator, program evaluator and researcher.

The system is reportedly based on the use of several forms that are usually designed as multiple-choice checklists, to be filled out by physicians, teachers, social workers, or others who come into contact with patients. The person filling out the form checks off only those items that are appropriate descriptions of a particular patient. Information on the forms either can be read directly by machine (optical scan sheets) or can be keypunched and stored in computer-controlled files.

Cooperating hospitals in each state either send the data by mail to the Rockland State Research Center, or the data is transmitted to the computer over telephone lines from terminals in each participating state. Using this data, the computer updates the patients' files, and then sends back to each participating unit a series of reports reflecting the information received.

Although all simple configurations are by definition narrow in scope, there can be considerable variability in this regard. For example, the bond between Alamosa and St. Francis seems to be infinitely broader in scope when one contrasts it to the relationship between Oconto City Hospital and Bellin Memorial Hospital of Green Bay — both located in north Wisconsin (see Hall, 1959). The only reported bond between these two units is that they share a "circuit riding" dietitian who shuttles between them. While in both cases the units share only one service (either x-ray diagnoses or the skills of a dietician), the two Colorado hospitals share not only personnel and information but also material (that is, x-rays). In the Wisconsin case, no material objects are transferred between the organizations. It is of interest to note that the Colorado bonds have become progressively more sustained, whereas the Wisconsin linkages apparently remain largely intermittent. We suggest that units that share only personnel (and the information they generate), but do not exchange material (for example, x-rays, ECGs, and so on) will maintain more intermittent contacts than those doing both. Certainly, comparison of the Alamosa-St. Francis link to the Oconto-Bellin bond supports the idea that the involvement of both personnel and material may push bonds further in a sustained direction. Unfortunately, the absence of systematic data precludes further explication of this hypothesis in the present monograph.

Undoubtedly, simple configurations vary also in the degree to which "bits" of co-decision-making inadvertently creep into otherwise consulting-informing relationships. However, the type of data available does not allow us to offer comparisons on such subtle differences.

The preceding examples obviously are not meant to suggest that radiological services are the paramount substance of all simple feudal configurations. Any brief review of Blumberg's monograph makes it clear that a whole array of professional, semiprofessional, and paraprofessional services is capable of being shared. Indeed, it is possible that shared services have no bearing on goal-related activities at all; that is, that they have a distinctly ancillary (non-goal) character and consequently, the content of the relationship may be of relatively low salience. However, the actual reporting of highly simple feudal bonds that deal with non-goal, low-salience activities is extremely scanty. Narrow-scope, intermittent contacts between health care units regarding ancillary tasks do not seem likely candidates for write-ups by journalists, medical adminstrators, or by social science researchers. Such arrangements for informing and consulting may be more formalized than between Yale and Columbia-Presbyterian; but the dramatic impact of a Lassa virus issue is not present when one hospital administrator occasionally helps out another. On the other hand, when low-salience contacts are more sustained — as when a hospital agrees to extend its laundry service to other units — the probability of reportage once again seems to increase. For example, the fact that Mountainside Hospital, a 361-bed unit in Montclair, New Jersey, does laundry for the 120-bed Montclair Community Hospital has not escaped reportage (Blumberg, 1966: 54).

However, it is important here to recall that we are concerned primarily with control configurations and only secondarily with the content of interorganizational relations. Hence, not all instances of shared laundry services (or shared radiological or dietitian services, for that matter) fall into the simple feudalistic category. Sometimes, a shared laundry or any simple shared service is but one part of an extremely "rich" interorganizational life. Perhaps more crucially, even if all two units have in common is a laundry, this does not necessarily mean that the one unit is providing a service for the other. In fact, there are numerous instances of laundry services being provided by outside agencies. Sometimes these are governmental and thus nonprofit; but sometimes the agency exists for profit. In any event, although the content of the relationship is the same as in Montclair, New Jersey, the control configurations may at times consist of guided or mediated patterns. For instance, in Baltimore, the Maryland Hospital Laundry Incorporated provides laundry services for six hospitals (Blumberg, 1966: 55). Any area hospital is eligible to join. Ten-year contracts with the corporation provide essentially all laundry service for that time at a price that covers the processing cost, including depreciation and dead charges. The nonprofit corporation was set up by seven Baltimore hospitals (one later withdrew). Of the $1.6 million needed for construction of the facility, the participating hospitals loaned 20 percent and banks provided 80 percent. Participating hospitals elect a board of trustees annually.

Because the most simple configurations by definition entail articulation on the basis of only one type of resource, these types of relations tend to be asymmetrical, at least in the sense that one unit is always providing the service to the others. Hence, our review of the literature provided no instance of hospitals rotating dietetic functions, radiological functions, laundry functions, and so on. However, as we shall see, the ready association of simple feudalistic configurations with asymmetrical transactions is not paralleled by a strong, similar, or obverse correlation for the case of complex feudalistic linkages.

COMPLEX FEUDALISTIC CONFIGURATIONS

A complex feudal field consists of sustained, relatively broad-scope interactions among multiple autonomous units in which some co-decision-making intrudes into the still largely consulting-informing situation. With rare exception, however, the magnitude of joint decision-making remains far below that which occurs in mediated and guided settings. (For one exception, see the Passaic case discussed later.) Perhaps the classic study of such an apparent setting is by Levine and White (1960). Although their work is most frequently cited because of its theoretical formulation — an exchange theory for interorganizational relations — it also represents one of the few empirical assessments of what seems to be a complex feudal field of 22 "health organizations" in a New England community of 200,000 inhabitants. An appreciation of their findings in fact helps us to grasp more fully why they generated the particular theoretical model they did: Levine and White conceptualize the realm of interorganizational relations largely in terms of utilitarian-pluralist presuppositions. In turn, their data suggest that their particular research site was indeed a field of largely autonomous organizations whose interactions were determined by mutual self-interest and were direct — that is, were neither mediated nor guided.

The locus of their investigation was chosen because it was fairly accessible and relatively independent of a major metropolis. In addition, the 22 health units represented a considerable and desirable diversity of types: 14 were voluntary agencies, 5 were hospitals (3 with outpatient clinics and 2 without) and 3 were "official agencies" — a health department, a welfare department, and a school. These last 3 units are not part of our definition of health care organizations (see chapter 1). The former two, in fact, lead one to feel that perhaps there may be a bit more mediation or guidance going on in the field than the authors recognize. Nonetheless, their treatment of the evidence seems to indicate that in this research setting, at least, it does not seem unwarranted to view "official agencies" as just another set of units in a fundamentally feudalistic context.

The investigators carried out intensive semistructured interviews with executive directors and supervisory personnel of each organization. Members of the several boards of trustees were given briefer interviews. In addition, Levine and White adapted an instrument developed by Irwin T. Sanders in order to locate the "most influential 'leaders' in the community" for the purpose of ascertaining the distribution of each of the boards. This served as an important indicator of organizational prestige.

Levine and White classify the "elements" exchanged by health organizations into three categories: "(1) referrals of cases, clients, or patients; (2) the giving or receiving of labor services, including the services of volunteer, clerical, and professional personnel; and (3) the sending or receiving of resources other than labor services, including funds, equipment, and information on cases and technical matters" (1960: 589). In addition, they analyze exchange not only in terms of the elements, but also occasionally in terms of the joint activities carried out by the health organizations. Joint activities occur when two organizations do not channel elements to one another, but "where elements flow from two organizations acting in unison toward a third party."

The authors categorize the 22 health organizations under study not in one but three different ways in their paper. First, they divide them into hospitals, official agencies, and voluntary organizations (all others). Hospitals are then divided into those with OPD clinics and those without; voluntary organizations are typed as corporate (those that delegate authority downward from the national or state level to the local) or federated (those that delegate authority upwards from the local level). The second way the authors classify the organizations is on the "basis of their primary health function":

1. resource organizations that provide other health units with the means to attain their goals
2. education organizations that provide information
3. prevention organizations that try to control the advent of a disease
4. treatment organizations that are geared to help overcome a disease
5. rehabilitation organizations that provide assistance in convalescing from a disease.

The last four organization types are conceived of as representing the respective steps in the control of the disease process. The final classification used by Levine and White divides organizations by whether they are direct or indirect and also on the basis of relative prestige. Direct agencies are those that provide an immediate service to the public; indirect agencies do not.

In Table 2-1 the authors rank: (1) voluntary agencies — corporate and federated, (2) hospitals — with and without clinics, and (3) official agencies in terms of their relative frequency and type of interaction. From these "exploratory" data they distill two basic findings: (1) corporate agencies interact less with other local organizations than do federated agencies; and (2) hospitals with clinics interact more than those without. Not seriously considered in their discussion is the relatively high frequency of interaction initiated by official agencies in all sectors, but especially in the realm of written and verbal communication. Does this indicate the existence of mediating or guiding tendencies not sufficiently considered by Levine and White?

Table 2-2 repeats the analyses of Table 2-1, but this time the organizations are divided into educational, resource, prevention, treatment, and rehabilitation. The authors suggest that treatment organizations generally rank highest on the interaction dimensions, while educational agencies rank lowest.

From the information in Table 2-3, Levine and White argue that organizations high in prestige lead in the number of joint activities, and prestige seems to exert some influence on the amount of verbal and written communication. Yet, it is agencies offering direct services — regardless of prestige — that lead in the number of referrals and resources received. In other words, prestige, leadership, and other organizational variables seem to affect interaction patterns within limits established by the function variable.

In essence, then, Levine's and White's pioneering work rates the relative frequency with which different types of health organizations relate to others and discusses the types of organizations they most commonly deal with and the elements they are most likely to exchange. Consequently, they take a critical step beyond the basically intraorganizational question of how factors outside an organization's boundary impinge on its performances (which had been the focus of most earlier purported interorganizational analyses). However, it is equally clear that although no longer explicitly intraorganizational in focus, they are not talking about the adjustment of an interorganizational field per se. In other words, Levine and White have shifted attention from the "individual" properties of organizations to their relational properties (how often they interact, with whom, in what ways), but the authors certainly are not characterizing the structure of the entire field — nor do they claim they are.

Although there is no systematic portrayal of the field, Levine and White do provide much more than a glimpse of what a complex feudal field is like compared to a simple one. On the dimension of intricacy alone, the mere presence of 22 units suggests a relatively complex situation. As we have just noted, the overall patterning of the relationships among the organizations has not received thoroughgoing treatment; but the analysis clearly implies that units constitute a single interacting field even if the degree of integration remains problematic.

Complementing the picture of complexity provided by the involvement of a relatively large number of units is the fact that the authors indicate that the organizations are in sustained contact and that their transactions entail a number of different kinds of resources — and therefore imply relatively broad scope. Once more, the absence of systematic characterization of the field prevents us from observing the variations in sustained interactions in different portions of the field, as well as where in the field which kinds of resources are the objects of transaction. The Levine and White piece is perhaps least helpful for our purposes when it comes to characterizing the degree of co-decision-making in a complex feudal field. Clearly, by introducing a category of joint activities they recognize that some setting, pursuing, and implementing of common goals goes on. But the questions of how much goes on, in what sectors, and in what proportion it occurs vis-a-vis informing-consulting activities are not central to their study. It is evident, however, that the authors tend to view the bulk of interorganizational articulations as not being on the level of co-decision-making (and thus on a merely informing-consulting plane). The following paragraph probably best brings out the flavor of this:

> Theoretically, then, were all the essential elements in infinite supply there would be little need for organizational interaction and for subscription to co-operation as an ideal. Under actual conditions of scarcity, however, interorganizational exchanges are essential to goal attainment. In sum, organizational goals or objectives are derived from general health values. These goals or objectives may be viewed as defining the organization's ideal need for elements — consumers, labor services, and other resources. The scarcity of elements, however, impels the organization to restrict its activity to limited specific functions. The fulfillment of these limited functions, in turn, requires access to certain kinds of elements, which an organization seeks to obtain by entering into exchanges with other organizations [Levine and White, 1960: 587].

Of course, the mere presence of a large number of units alone cannot determine the complexity of a field. Sometimes two or three units may constitute a network as complex as the one studied by Levine and White. In Passaic (N.J.), Beth Israel Hospital

(164-beds), Passaic General Hospital (320-beds) and St. Mary's Hospital (230-beds) are engaged in a program to eliminate duplication of facilities (Wagner, 1969). Regularly scheduled meetings of the administrators of the three hospitals over the past few years resulted in the Tri-Hospital plan. In 1962, with a decision by the hospitals to consolidate their home care services, the formal program was begun. At the present time, home care is based at Beth Israel Hospital. Patients are referred there by physicians at all of the participating hospitals.

The Tri-Hospital School of Radiologic Technology was Passaic's second joint effort. The school, accredited by the American Medical Association and the American College of Radiology, has its administrative headquarters at Passaic General Hospital and is financed by all three hospitals. In this school's two-year program, students are exposed to a wide range of professional services by a system of rotation through the three hospitals.

The purchase of the Tri-Hospital blood chemsitry autoanalyzer is the most recently reported joint venture of the Passaic hospitals. The autoanalyzer is kept at Passaic General, where tests are analyzed for the three hospitals.

Other results of joint planning by these three hospitals include: a poison control center, a joint mental health program, and a school of nursing, all at St. Mary's; cobalt therapy and physical therapy units at Beth Israel; and an artificial kidney unit, an open-heart surgery unit, and a diabetic-instruction center at Passaic General. In addition, St. Mary's Hospital is in the process of setting up a 26-bed psychiatric unit that will serve the three hospitals.

The three hospitals, in order to obtain further economic benefits, purchase fuel oil, oxygen, and intravenous solutions as a group. All three have contracted with one linen service, and equipment and supplies are loaned among the hospitals. Furthermore, the three blood banks have been fully coordinated.

Both of the preceding examples of complex feudal fields have involved considerable reciprocity; that is, the resource flows have not been asymmetrical or in a one-way direction. However, based on the materials we have examined, there is no overall tendency for such a correlation. Just as there are several instances of the already exemplified pattern, so there are many of the other. The linkages often found between hospitals and nursing homes provide excellent illustrations of the association between complex feudalism and asymmetry. Although the linkage is most commonly found to involve general hospitals, specialty hospitals too can play a similar role.

For example, Dammasch State Hospital a 460-bed psychiatric hospital in northwestern Oregon, has bonds with 68 nursing or old-age homes in its general area (O'Neal, 1967). In June, 1964, Dammasch State, operating on an N.I.M.H. grant aimed at improving hospital admission, release, and aftercare procedures, undertook a project to investigate, among other things, the value of making available to nursing homes and homes for the aged the services of psychiatric hospital nurses. The plan called for nurses to be involved in at least four classes of services:

1. evaluating the homes participating in the project
2. assisting in the selection of homes for individual patients
3. providing follow-up care to patients placed in the homes through court planning or upon hospital release
4. organizing the workshops presented for the personnel of community agencies

Twenty-seven homes for the aged and 41 nursing homes were involved in the project by July 1965. Evaluation by the liaison nurse, the first step for each home, reportedly provided an opportunity for two-way communication between the hospital and the private facility. From data that were collected on the physical plan, staffing, treatment program, and financial charges, it was possible to estimate the types of patients the home could manage most successfully. The goal of such analyses was to aid each home in its care of patients, while at the same time avoiding any increased demands on the personnel. In addition, suggestions were made as to techniques that would result in improvement in meeting the needs of the long-term mentally ill patient.

The liaison nurse worked with 45 patients who were released to nursing homes after hospitalization and with 21 persons who were placed directly in nursing homes by the court. At the hospital, the nurse was expected to become acquainted with the patient and to be able to assess his or her needs. She then worked with the hospital staff, the families, and, occasionally, with public welfare officials, and, with their help, she chose the residential setting in which she felt the patient would make the best adjustment. The hospital administration encouraged early placement of the prospective long-care patient.

In the six-month follow-up program, the nurse visited with the patient and the nursing-home staff, and every effort was made to resolve the patient's problems. An important aspect of these visits was the opportunity they provided for informal education of the nursing home administrators and personnel.

In addition, workshops, mainly for the personnel of nursing homes and homes for the aged, were sponsored by the research project staff. One of the conferences also included members of welfare, public health, and other public agencies. One hundred-sixteen persons attended the three-day conference, which included presentations on patient-staff relationships, on methods of treatment and medication, and on functions and services of social service, dietary, occupational and recreational therapy departments. Small-group tours of the wards, and informal discussion and question-and-answer periods followed the presentations.

However, there is no doubt that the contact between general hospitals and nursing homes is more frequent, more sustained (Dammasch's links after all were based on a government grant for a pilot project) and much broader in scope (they involve much more than the providing of services) than the contacts between specialty hospitals and nursing homes. The case of Hackensack (N.J.) Hospital is typical of the complex bonds that can be forged between a general hospital and nursing homes and illustrates the basic asymmetry of such ties (Davis, 1965). Beginning in 1962, 450-bed Hackensack developed links with 12 nursing homes in the vicinity. The hospital has:

1. aided the homes administratively (for example, it has helped them to develop standardized forms and procedures)
2. made available its training resources to nursing home personnel
3. provided professional personnel who receive training in the nursing home setting
4. provided educational services for physicians engaged in the program.

In return for this, the hospital has created options about where to locate geriatric, rehabilitation, psychiatric, and similar cases whom the hospital feels it cannot retain.

As several sociologists have noted, resource flows that are inordinately in one direction tend to generate dependence on the part of the recipient(s) and consequently power on the part of the sender. An important question for us is: At what point has the asymmetry become so "slanted" and the power of the sending unit so great that we are no longer dealing with complex feudalism but with an interorganizational empire? Certainly, the question is a difficult one to answer for a variety of reasons. First, because all units in a complex feudal field are seldom exactly equal in power, we hesitate to label all power imbalances as indicators of empires. In a sense, therefore, the difficulty is that at the moment we possess neither the theoretical nor the methodological precision to delineate the point at which "slanted" feudal bonds become empires. Also, because other concrete factors enter into the "balance of power" between two or more units, simply knowing something about the flow of resources does not allow us to make a definite determination of relative power.

We hesitate to label as empires direct linkages among health care units of differential power, and this hesitancy is reflected in the works we have reviewed — especially those in the medical and hospital administration literature. This latter tendency is probably a result of (1) administrators' unwillingness to acknowledge informal power differences when formal arrangements are looked upon as an agreement among equals; as well as (2) a general American egalitarian tendency to play down objective differentials in privilege and power. Certainly none of the articles dealing with hospital-nursing home relations ever focused on the inordinate power of the former over the latter unit(s) — although almost uniformly these bonds are marked by considerable asymmetry in the flow of resources (and thus presumably by an imbalance in power).

Another important area where complex ties are rather asymmetrical but where commentators have been loathe to attribute differential power is in the realm of medical school-Veteran Administration hospital bonds. Formally, such a relationship would seem to fall outside the boundaries of our study because medical schools are not included in our definition of health care units. But because most of the medical schools involved in V.A. links are themselves part of medical centers, these cases are in fact relevant. By 1966, 89 of 126 V.A. general hospitals were affiliated with medical schools (see Goldberg, 1966). However, there is considerable diversity in the degree to which programs have been shared or integrated. Nonetheless, in most cases the medical schools provide medical students for clinical clerkships, interns (the V.A. has few internship programs), residents, and teaching and clinical staff to the V.A. hospital. In addition, by making V.A. hospital appointees eligible for academic rank, the medical school undoubtedly improves the former's capacity to attract qualified physicians. Probably, the major benefit offered in return by the V.A. hospital to the students, housestaff, and faculty of medical schools is exposure to a variety of patients infrequently seen at a university hospital. The following statement by the chief of the medical service of the V.A. hospital, Kansas City (Mo.) describing the 18-year-old tie with the University of Kansas School of Medicine captures the essence of such a linkage rather well:

> This affiliation has worked to the mutual advantage of both institutions. The 240 medical beds of the Veterans Administration Hospital have provided additional teaching beds for the University. In addition, the medical students and residents of the University are exposed to a unique type of patient at the Veterans Administration Hospital. The great majority of our patients are medically indigent. Many of them are chronically ill with severe organic disease and are not eligible for care anywhere but at a Veterans Administration Hospital. It is a general policy of the Veterans Administration that a patient may not be discharged from the hospital with an incapacitating disease unless adequate social and economic post-hospital care is arranged. The students and residents exposed to these patients and their problems soon come to realize the full socio-economic significance of medical disease to a patient. Many of our patients are unable to obtain medical care at an early stage of their disease and reach us in an advanced stage of disease. By seeing such patients, the medical students and residents are constantly reminded of the importance of the early detection of disease. Most of the patients on the medical service of this hospital are hospitalized because of non-service-connected diseases. The diseases

seen commonly in general medical practice (pneumonia, congestive heart failure, diabetes, peptic ulcer, etc.) are seen in large numbers in our medical wards. In addition, there are always a few patients who have the rare and exotic diseases which are so stimulating to students and residents [Calkins, 1965: 113].

We have noted previously that, at the moment, it is difficult to make a precise determination of where complex feudal fields leave off and interorganizational empires begin. On the other hand, we suggest that one useful rule-of-thumb to follow is to ascertain whether a field includes a university-connected medical center. Fields containing such a complex appear to us invariably to indicate the presence of an empire. (We shall say more about this kind of configuration and why they seem clearly to be empires in chapter 4.) Consequently, it is probably a good guess that minute examination of the broader contexts within which V.A. hospital-medical school bonds exist will show that they are but one relationship in a larger empire presided over by a university medical center as the member-elite unit. In other words, although we have briefly touched on hospital-nursing home links and medical school-V.A. hospital bonds in this chapter, there is probably good, if not better, reason for placing these cases in a later chapter.

SUMMARY AND CONCLUSION

The purpose of the present chapter is to illustrate some of the major empirical manifestations of interorganizational feudalism among health care units. For primarily heuristic purposes we have divided our presentation into simple versus complex feudal fields. Simple feudalism involves intermittent, narrow-scope contacts among few units concerned exclusively in informing-consulting transactions; complex feudalism entails sustained, broad-scope bonds between a larger number of units engaged in some co-decision-making. Clearly, there are numerous concrete units that depart from these polar types. In addition, the study of interorganizational feudalism ought to consider whether goal activities, ancillary activities or both play a role in articulations;

and, hence, say something about the salience of interunit bonds. Finally, the study of interorganizational feudalism should concern itself with the relative symmetry of the relationship because the direction in which resources flow tells us something about relative power in the field and probably points to a key transition point between feudal fields and empires.

REFERENCES

ALTMAN, L. K. (1970) "New fever virus so deadly that research halts." New York Times (February 10): 1 and 25.

BLUMBERG, M. S. (1966) Shared Services for Hospitals. Chicago: American Hospital Association.

CALKINS, W. G. (1965) "Teaching affiliate: the program in medicine at the Veterans Administration Hospital." J. of the Kansas Medical Society 66 (March): 113-114.

DAVIS, L. C. (1965) "How hospital-nursing home plan works." Modern Hospital 104 (May): 111-113.

GOLDBERG, J. H. (1966) "The university-V.A. Hospital partnership." Hospital Physician (November): 50-59.

HALL, M. L. (1959) "I ride the circuit." Hospital Management 88 (August): 6-10.

LEVINE, S. and P. E. WHITE (1960) "Exchange as a conceptual framework for the study of interorganizational relationships." Administrative Sci. Q. 5 (March): 583-601.

O'NEAL, L. (1967) "Care of the mentally ill." Nursing Homes (February): 17-19.

REESE, E. A. (1963) "X-ray reports by teletype." Hospitals 37 (June): 74.

ROCKLAND State Hospital (1970) Annual Report of the Research Center, 1968-1969. Ultica, N.Y.: State Hospitals Press.

WAGNER, C. J. (1969) "Association concept promotes sharing – preserves independence." Hospitals 43 (March): 47-52.

WILLIAMS, M. S. and J. D. ROLLINS (1959) "X-ray reports by telephone." Hospitals 33 (November): 63.

TABLE 2-1

WEIGHTED RANKINGS OF ORGANIZATIONS CLASSIFIED BY ORGANIZATIONAL FORM ON FOUR INTERACTION INDICES

Interaction index	Sent by	N	Sent to					Total interaction sent
			Voluntary		Hospitals		Official	
			Corporate	Federated	Without clinics	With clinics		
Referrals	Vol. corporate	4	4.5	5	3.7	4.5	5	5
	Vol. federated	10	3	4	3.7	3	4	3
	Hosps. w/o clinics	2	4.5	3	3.7	4.5	3	4
	Hosps. w. clinics	3	1	1	1.5	2	1	1
	Official	3	2	2	1.5	1	2	2
Resources	Vol. corporate	4	5	2	1	4	5	3.5
	Vol. federated	10	4	3	3	4	4	3.5
	Hosps. w/o clinics	2	2	4.5	4.5	5	3	5
	Hosps. w. clinics	3	1	1	2	1	2	1
	Official	3	3	4.5	4.5	2	1	2
Written and verbal communication	Vol. corporate	4	5	3	2	4	5	4
	Vol. federated	10	3	1	3	3	3	2.5
	Hosps. w/o clinics	2	2	5	4.5	5	4	5
	Hosps. w. clinics	3	4	4	4.5	1	1.5	2.5
	Official	3	1	2	1	2	1.5	1
Joint activities	Vol. corporate	4	4.5	4	3	5	3.5	5
	Vol. federated	10	3	3	5	3	1	1
	Hosps. w/o clinics	2	2	5	1	2	3.5	4
	Hosps. w. clinics	3	4.5	2	2	1	5	1.5
	Official	3	1	1	4	4	2	1.5

NOTE: 1 indicates Highest Interaction; 5 indicates Lowest Interaction.   SOURCE: Levine and White, 1960: 591.

TABLE 2-2

WEIGHTED RANKINGS OF ORGANIZATIONS, CLASSIFIED BY FUNCTION ON FOUR INTERACTION INDICES

Interaction index	Received by	N	Received from					Total interaction received
			Education	Resource	Prevention	Treatment	Rehabilitation	
Referrals	Education	3	4.5	5	5	5	5	5
	Resource	5	3	4	2	4	1	3
	Prevention	5	2	1	3	2	2.5	2
	Treatment	7	1	2	1	1	2.5	1
	Rehabilitation	2	4.5	3	4	3	4	4
Resources	Education	3	4.5	5	4	5	4.5	5
	Resource	5	1.5	3	3	4	3	3.5
	Prevention	5	1.5	4	2	3	4.5	3.5
	Treatment	7	3	2	1	2	2	1
	Rehabilitation	2	4.5	1	5	1	1	2
Written and verbal communication	Education	3	4	5	4.5	5	5	5
	Resource	5	3	2	2	3	2	2.5
	Prevention	5	2	4	3	4	4	3
	Treatment	7	1	1	1	2	3	1
	Rehabilitation	2	5	3	4.5	1	1	2.5
Joint activities	Education	3	4	4	1	3	4.5	4
	Resource	5	2	1	3	4	1	3
	Prevention	5	1	2	2	2	3	1
	Treatment	7	3	3	4	1	2	2
	Rehabilitation	2	5	5	5	5	4.5	5

NOTE: 1 indicates highest interaction; 5 indicates lowest interaction.

SOURCE: Levine and White (1960) "Exchange as a conceptual framework for the Study of interorganizational relationships: Administrative Science Quarterly 5 (March): 594.

TABLE 2-3

WEIGHTED RANKINGS OF ORGANIZATIONS CLASSIFIED BY PRESTIGE OF ORGANIZATION AND BY GENERAL TYPE OF SERVICE OFFERED ON FOUR INTERACTION INDICES

Interaction index	Received by	N	High Prestige		Low Prestige		Total interaction received
			Direct service	Indirect service	Direct service	Indirect service	
Referrals	High direct	9	1	1	1	1	1
	High indirect	3	3	3.5	3	3.5	3
	Low direct	6	2	2	2	2	2
	Low indirect	4	4	3.5	4	3.5	4
Resources	High direct	9	2	2	2	2	2
	High indirect	3	3	3	3	3.5	3
	Low direct	6	1	1	1	1	1
	Low indirect	4	4	4	4	3.5	4
Written and verbal communication	High direct	9	2	2	3	1	2
	High indirect	3	3	3	1	3	3
	Low direct	6	1	1	2	2	1
	Low indirect	4	4	4	4	4	4
Joint activities	High direct	9	1	1.5	2	2	2
	High indirect	3	2	1.5	1	1	1
	Low direct	6	4	3	3	4	3
	Low indirect	4	3	4	4	3	4

NOTE: 1 indicates highest interaction; 5 indicates lowest interaction.

SOURCE: Levine and White (1960) "Exchange as a conceptual framework for the Study of interorganizational relationships." Administrative Science Quarterly 5 (March): 596.

CHAPTER 3

MEDIATED INTERORGANIZATIONAL FIELDS:
THE "COORDINATION" OF SERVICES

In chapter 1 we noted that a mediated control configuration contains two elements absent in a purely feudal setting. First and foremost, a new type of unit appears: one that funnels facilities, people, "services," information, and so on among the member organizations, but that "coordinates" without appreciably guiding. A second new feature is that the ratio of informing-consulting activities to co-deciding activities is more likely to be slanted toward co-deciding than in a feudal context. Yet, a mediated field is still strikingly different from a guided one. Its administrative unit remains largely the creature of the organizations it serves and, hence, it lacks the resources and responsibility to move decisively in the name of the field as a whole. Consequently, an overt capacity for comprehensive planning is not generally found in a mediated context. Nevertheless, among such settings there is considerable variation in the amount of joint decision-making, as well as in the degree of mediating unit autonomy. Hence, within mediated fields there is some innate push toward guidance. This chapter considers this drift toward guidance and the stresses it engenders by examining: (1) the range of co-decision-making and (2) the variations in mediating unit autonomy found in these interorganizational fields. First, however, we discuss some implications of the fact that a mediating unit is more the creature than the creator of the network it "services."

CREATURE OF THE MEMBER UNITS

The National Intern and Resident Matching Program of Evanston, Illinois, provides a good example of a typical mediating unit and of some of the factors that inhibit this kind of agency from assuming a more effective and comprehensive planning role.[1] The program was founded in 1951 as an effort to curtail the competition among hospitals for interns. Competition had been so intense that hospitals had made efforts to sign up medical students as early as their sophomore years. This led to acrimony not only among hospitals, but also between hospitals and students over broken "contracts." (To simplify our discussion, we focus here exclusively on the internship segment, although the same logic and issues apply to the later-added residency component.) The program apparently has been successful insofar as overt conflicts over students and the phenomenon of broken contracts have been largely eliminated. In 1969-70, 8,387 or between 96 and 98 percent of all seniors who expected to intern in the next year participated, as did about 734 hospital units, or almost 99 percent of those approved for internship training.

A student joins the program by signing and sending to Evanston a "Student Agreement" along with a $4.00 fee. He, in turn, is sent a directory of all participating hospitals approved by the Council on Medical Education of the American Hospital Association. The directory contains general information about each hospital and lists the various intern programs being offered. The student may apply directly to as many of these as he wishes. He then must rank them in order of preference and must file the preference list with the matching program by mid-January of the year he graduates. The participating hospitals similarly rank all their student applicants in order of desirability. A computer at Evanston finally matches each student to the highest hospital on his list that has an opening for him. The program's 1970 statistics indicate that the placing of interns remains a seller's market; 8,113 of the 8,387 participating students were placed, but more than 7,400 of the 15,567 internships offered by hospitals remained unfilled after the matching.

Certainly, the program did not create the bonds that exist among hospitals in the United States. Indeed, the reverse is closer to the truth. To reduce potential conflict, the hospitals, through the American Medical Association, created the matching program. The program, in turn, is not expected actively to transform or to penetrate the existing networks of relations among hospitals. Quite the contrary, the program mirrors the existing patterns of relationships and, at best, expedites them. Mediating (that is, nonguiding) coordinating agencies such as the matching program, appear more "antiseptic," that is, politically and administratively neutral, than they are in fact. These units — especially those whose key decisions are made by that ultimate representative of rationalization, the computer, may give the impression of operating in a realm where social power no longer plays a decisive role; but that impression is deceptive. We suggest that much of the mutual orienting behavior that goes on among hospitals in the matching program is built upon differential attributions of power and perhaps also differential exercises of power, and that this assessment goes on even if the field is very loosely integrated. That is, hospitals solicit medical students in part based on their assessment of their relative ability to control and to mobilize utilitarian and normative resources; the more "powerful" they think they are, the more likely they will be to go after the best students. Rationality dictates that weaker hospitals seek the weaker students. The computer only "sanctifies" and streamlines the intermember power processes and gives them a new chrome and plastic veneer; that is, computers and the agencies manning them do not by themselves represent very effective mechanisms for altering intermember power relations, but they do serve to reduce the manifest conflicts within them.

Thus, we argue that fields coordinated by agencies like the matching program are relatively poor risks for more extensive joint policy-making because here movement beyond the feudal context has been mainly "technological," while power remains almost entirely in the hands of the participating organizations. We further argue that two other factors, apparently characteristic of the matching program and its field, make it unlikely that co-decision-making will increase significantly. First, there is no evidence of a strong collectivity-orientation — a sense of "we" — in the feudal-base upon which the mediated field is built. This kind of orientation provides one effective foundation for increased integration and for fostering commitment to joint planning. Indeed, at this point it is difficult to determine how much of a feudal-base is present at all.

Perhaps an analogy would help to highlight the issue. When a gasoline station services cars that drive in, does the pattern formed resemble a mediated configuration? If one could determine that the aggregate of automobiles going through does not otherwise form a common "action-space," then we definitely would answer "no." On the other hand, it is difficult to imagine that these cars do not occasionally pass each other on highways and, hence, take one another into account in shifting speeds and lanes or that they may park at times in the same garage, or have owners who live on the same block or use the same drive-in movies, and so on. The matching program, like our gasoline station, funnels a resource to participants. As with the aggregate of cars, there is clearly no strong feudal-base imbedded in the mediated one. However, some of the hospitals are in interaction with one another; that is, there are numerous sociometric clusters of such units in the United States. But it is doubtful whether any of these exist by virtue of the matching program. In other words, the matching program provides a service to participating units, but this service does not create strong lateral bonds among the units. Still, we have suggested that a computerized mediating configuration seems difficult to maintain effectively unless the participating units informally interact or at least orient their behaviors to one another to some degree. Suppose all medical students applied only to the five or six most prestigious hospitals, and that all hospitals considered only graduates of elite medical schools. Under these circumstances the system would soon grind to a creaking halt. Because the system operates relatively smoothly, some kind of microscopic (among medical students) and macroscopic (among hospitals) relative appraisals must be going on. Nevertheless, mutual appraisals are hardly substitutes for strong collectivity-orientations as effective bases for expanding the zone of co-decision-making.

A second added factor limiting the matching program's capacity to expand its policy-making potential is its weak systemic power base. Moreover, it is not likely to acquire a stronger one in light of the narrow scope of the resources that pass through its hands. We hypothesize that the broader the scope of transactions a mediating unit administers, the greater the potential for co-decision-making in the field. If for no other reason, this hypothesis appears plausible because the greater the array of resources dealt with in a mediated field, the greater the manifest need for the coordination of activities dealing with the utilization and exchange of the resources. In addition, the more different kinds of resources dealt with by a mediating unit, the more likely the latter is to develop effective control of some minimal resource-base for the wielding of systemic power. Certainly, the participating hospitals will do nothing to broaden their "creature" organization's scope of resources unless such an expansion can be shown to be to their benefit.

Another aspect of the matching program's narrow scope that seems to hamper further extension of co-deciding has to do with its primary "commodity," interns. Generally speaking, the more a unit dealing in one resource can control that resource for its own purposes, the greater the advantage it has in bringing other resources under its sphere of influence. For example, John D. Rockefeller, Sr., was able to build his economic empire by first gaining control of oil refineries; and from there he was able to branch out to the oil wells themselves, to the means of transportation and so on. The matching program is particularly disadvantaged in this regard because interns are self-conscious resources whose participation is premised almost totally on self-interest and who are highly unmalleable in terms of the program's potential interests. Hence, they do not seem to provide an especially good basis for broadening interorganizational scope and consequently for expanding co-decision-making.

THE RANGE OF JOINT POLICY FORMATION

Our definition of mediated fields states that more co-deciding occurs here than in feudal settings and that there tends to be less joint policy-making than in guided configurations. Yet among the concrete cases we can label "mediated," there is considerable diversity in this regard. In some instances, the mediating unit operates largely to direct resources to the several member organizations so that they can more effectively pursue their own (individual) goals. The matching program represents this type. In other instances, the mediating agent provides, or claims to provide, sufficient coordination so that together with the units it can set and pursue policy for the entire field. A nonmedical example of the former, "looser" setting is the role played by the various television rating services (for examples, Nielson, Trendex, and so on)that provide broadcasting networks and advertisers with data about the popularity of T.V. programs. These ratings help the networks to develop their future schedule of programs and sponsors to allocate their advertising money in a way they feel will provide the most effective exposure for their products. A nonmedical illustration of the latter, more "integrated" mode of coordination is the role played by a nonbinding arbitration agency in labor-management negotiations. An arbitrator tries to facilitate agreement between parties on the precise conditions of future worker-manager interactions without being able to impose a settlement.

Comparable examples are not difficult to find in the health care literature. Agencies set up to locate vacant beds in and among hospitals and extended care facilities (ECFs) provide good illustrations of mediated fields where information is passed back and forth largely for the benefit of the individual participating units. For example, in a 1967 article the then president-elect of the San Francisco Medical Society, Henry Gibbons III (1967: 161), tells us:

> When the occupancy of San Francisco's 18 hospitals increased alarmingly close to full capacity last year, the local medical profession realized that it had to find a more efficient way to move patients out of acute hospitals. We also knew we had to prepare for the time when the cost of convalescent care would be covered by Medicare — and the nursing home bed would become a key factor in the pattern of convalescent patient flow.

Ultimately, the hospitals agreed to establish an "information center whose primary function would be to locate beds in nursing homes, convalescent hospitals, and other extended care facilities and to maintain a round-the-clock record of them" (1967: 161). On January 27, 1967, the center was opened at the headquarters building of the San Francisco Medical Society. The participating units provided a first year's operating budget of $32,000.

The center consists of a group of message recorders, a card filing system, and five telephone lines, all under the supervision of a registered nurse and a secretary. The formal operating rules of the center prescribe the following procedures: When a nursing home has a vacancy or discharges or receives a patient, it telephones the center, using a special telephone number. The caller is expected to listen for a "beep" tone, dictate the information, and then hang up. The secretary takes the data off the recorder and transfers it to a card file. A doctor's office or hospital, using another special number, telephones in a request. The secretary answers, learns the needs of the patient, and hopefully can provide complete information about available beds in ECF facilities.

Dr. Gibbons appears quite satisfied with the contributions the new information center is rendering to the health care units in the area. He states (1967: 161):

> The proof of the center's success is how well it's working. There is some difficulty here as elsewhere, of course, in finding Medicare beds. But as more nursing homes are licensed, and more are built, it's hoped that this problem will be solved. Meanwhile, doctors, hospitals, and more than 100 nursing homes are using the service and finding increasing satisfaction with it.

The Gibbons piece mentions Medicare, but probably does not do full justice to the impact this federal program has had on the interorganizational activities dealing with extended care facilities. It is wise to recall that ECFs can be certified as eligible for Medicare funds only if they have transfer agreements with general hospitals. Thus, throughout the late 1960s there was a scramble on the part of these units to develop working relationships with hospitals — or else face the specter of exclusion from new governmental benefits. For example, in early 1967, representatives of about 50 northeastern Ohio extended care facilities approached the Chronic Illness Center of Cuyahoga County and the Blue Cross of Northeast Ohio for help in establishing a liaison with area hospitals.[2] In April, 1967, the so-called "Cleveland plan" designated the Chronic Illness Center as the link between the ECFs and the more than 50 hospitals in an 11-county area. The principal benefit for the hospitals, according to Richard S. Lamden, has been that their observability of vacant ECF beds in which to place their less acute patients has increased considerably. He says (1969: 78):

> To the surprise of hospitals that had been unable to locate ECF beds, the program disclosed 259 available beds within its first week of operation. At no time during the first 16 weeks of the program were fewer than 120 beds reported available.

The formal operating procedures in Ohio differ somewhat from those drawn up in San Francisco. Each Monday morning, all participating extended care facilities are required to call the Chronic Illness Center and report the number of beds they have available. The calls are supposed to be made between 9 a.m. and noon in three time slots assigned on the basis of alphabetical order. The information is recorded by the center on a specially designed form. It is then photocopied and mailed in preaddressed envelopes, hopefully by 12:30 p.m. By Tuesday morning, hospitals participating in the program are reported to have current information in their hands on vacant ECF beds.

Every hospital is provided with a booklet containing information about each ECF. The booklet contains in outline form such data as address and phone number, simple directions for reaching the facility, bed complement, services provided, medical director's name, and other pertinent facts.

Despite these superficial differences in procedure, the San Francisco and Ohio cases have much in common. In both instances, the mediating unit channels information about available beds among health care organizations, and the latter, in turn, reallocate patients. This information is employed by the participating organizations largely to enhance their own situation; that is, it is used either to promote their eligibility for federal funds, to make known that they have vacant beds, or (in the case of hospitals) to be able to locate facilities where they can place more chronically ill patients. Thus, the information is utilized primarily for the self-interest of the participating units and not to enhance the state of the field as such — although both illustrations make clear that, implicitly at least, some decisions are being made that influence the structure and functioning of the interorganizational network viewed as an emergent entity.

On the other hand, there are many cases of mediated configurations where the coordinating agency renders, or purports to render, a much more explicit service in the pursuit of collective goals by member organizations. For instance, the Greater New York Hospital Association,[3] established in 1904, is intended to serve as "a coordinating agency for the administrative programs of all the major nonprofit hospitals, nursing homes, and municipal hospital centers in the metropolitan area" (1969: 3). Similar associations are found throughout the country. As of 1968, the Association consisted of 83 voluntary hospitals, all 21 municipal hospital centers, and 19 nonprofit chronic disease, convalescent, and nursing homes. In that year, member voluntary hospitals provided 8,668,951 patient-days of care and had 67,733 employees; the member municipal hospitals, 5,158,938 patient-days with 35,590 employees; and the homes, 1,598,417 patient-days with 4,917 employees. The Association (1969: 3) describes its mediating role as follows:

> Dedicated to serving the health and welfare needs of the community, the Association seeks to advance the interests of its member institutions by building cooperation among them, by assisting them in achieving ever-increasing levels of effective performance, by encouraging essential educational and research endeavors, and by interpreting all these functions to the general public and to allied professional, governmental, and other organizations. The Association also maintains active liaison with groups in related fields interested in improving community health and raising standards of patient care.

The governance structure of the Association clearly indicates its "creature" status. Each member organization is entitled to be represented at Association business meetings by its administrator (or his alternate) and by a duly appointed member of its governing board. They, in turn, elect the president and other officers of the Association, as well as the Board of Governors. Officers, including the president, are elected for one-year terms. Members of the Board of Governors are elected for three-year terms. These positions are all part-time. However, the Association also is staffed by full-time administrative and clerical personnel. In addition to this staff, "several hundred" executives of member organizations serve on innumerable ad hoc and standing committees. The Association (1969: 8) describes its committee system in the following terms, which claim a considerable contribution to co-decision-making:

> The Association committee structure is designed to maintain a constant awareness of developments in every aspect of hospital and nursing home functioning, and to constitute the means for informed and effective action whenever necessary. At least one representative of each member hospital is encouraged to serve on some committee. Committee findings and surveys are distributed to members whenever it appears that the information in them will be helpful.
>
> Committees of the Association meet regularly to consider and take action when indicated with respect to problems in the fields of administrative practices (accounting, purchasing, security), ambulances, auditing, blood program, codes and standards (specifically affecting patient care, construction, engineering and pharmacy), disaster planning, electronic data processing, finance, fire safety, human rights, homes, training and education, personnel, public relations and reimbursement. As new areas of hospital activity develop significant problems, additional committees are formed where necessary to study them.
>
> By thus channeling and concentrating their expertise and energies, the committee members keep themselves and the Association members fully informed as to the operations of each other's institutions, as well as with respect to all that is likely to affect the provision of hospital or home care. In this manner, too, unnecessary duplication of activities, which could become an expensive burden on the community, is avoided.

This is not to say that the Association does not report carrying on a great deal of purely information-funneling activity. For example, the full-time staff is charged with circulating films (to be used by member organizations for recruitment, training, and so on), producing periodicals (for example, Annual Report, Association Directory, Association Newsletter, Personnel Notes and so on), and publishing reports (for example, Autopsy Manual, Guide to Fire Prevention, Recommended Policies for Prenatal Clinics, Obstetrical Patients, Adoption Procedures, Security Guidelines, and so on).

Comparison of the San Francisco and Ohio cases with the

Greater New York Hospital Association heightens the plausibility of a hypothesis put forward during our discussion of the intern matching program: the broader the scope of the coordinating agency — the more different kinds of resources it funnels — the more extensive the co-decision-making that will occur in the interorganizational field. As we have stressed several times, since our cases are illustrative rather than representative, this hypothesis cannot be tested within the framework of the present study. Moreover, the existing data provide no clue about the possible independence of either of the two variables; that is, extensive co-decision-making (intended and planned) may broaden the scope of a mediating agency's activities as often as the reverse pattern occurs.

Mediating agencies, such as the Association, probably are tempted to exaggerate their role in comprehensive decision-making to some degree. This type of unit continues to exist only insofar as the member organizations regard its functioning to be in their best interests. In other words, a "good image" with the members as well as a good one with the "public" (which, presumably, will reflect on the members) is a crucial desideratum for a mediating agency. Consequently, the agency has a vested interest in presenting its public service functions in the best possible light. As a result, the statements found in official documents (for example, annual reports, brochures, and so on) are no substitute for the firsthand observation. We think that such observation would show that actual effective co-decision-making tends to be somewhat below the level of official claims.

The situation of Blue Cross is illustrative here because several works in the hospital administration literature imply an almost guiding role for it without providing definitive documentation. For example, Mark S. Blumberg reports that in some instances local Blue Cross chapters have been known to withhold payment for cases to hospitals who have failed to implement areawide planning programs. Unfortunately, he gives no specific examples (1966: 20-21). Many of the articles in the hospital journals give sketchy portraits indicating that Blue Cross "sponsored," "assisted in," or "encouraged," some collaborative practice but never with any real detail. Typical here is a 1963 article in *Hospitals* that reports on the founding of CASH (the Commission for

Administrative Services in Hospitals), a program "to assist
Southern California Hospitals in operating more economically and
effectively through improved management techniques, better
supervision, and better methods and procedures." In this item,
which ran approximately two-thirds of a three-column page, the
local Blue Cross (Hospital Services of Southern California) is
mentioned in passing only at three brief, separate points: (1) the
"Commission is composed of six members representing the
hospital council and three representatives of Blue Cross of
Southern California"; (2) "Blue Cross. . . will act as the
administrative agent of the program"; and (3) "Blue Cross of
Southern California has contributed $15,000 to aid in establishing
the program and help defray first-year expenses" — estimated at
$100,000. Needless to say, the precise nature of Blue Cross
involvement is far from clear in this article (*Hospitals*, 1963: 206).

Fortunately, one of the few studies that examines the relative
efficacy of a mediating unit to co-decide in a health-related
interorganizational field has focused on Blue Cross. Edward M.
Kaitz's *Price Policy and Cost Behavior in the Hospital Industry*
(1968) assesses the ability of Blue Cross to control hospital costs.
The evaluation of Blue Cross's effectiveness as a health
coordinator has more than passing academic interest because it is
the single largest provider of third-party health payments in the
United States. Specifically the focus of Kaitz's study is:

> an analysis of the financial decision-making process within the hospital
> industry and the effect of the third-party payment system upon this
> process: In the "third-party payment system," a third party (an
> insurance company or Blue Cross, for example) pays the hospital and
> medical expenses for the patient. The system thus involves: Party 1,
> who receives the services; Party 2, the hospital or other provider of the
> service; and Party 3, the organization that pays Party 2 for the services
> provided to Party 1 by Party 2. Specifically, this study has sought to
> establish the relationship between the financial and accounting
> techniques used by the cost-based, third-party payment systems and the
> price-determination, cost-control, and capital-budgeting decisions
> within the individual hospital [1968: v].

The origins of Blue Cross (which Kaitz treats in Appendix A,
pp. 123-134) must be grasped in order to appreciate his

conclusions fully. The first plan was devised by Baylor University Hospital in Houston, Texas. Originally, the plan was for school teachers because the hospital discovered that this occupation was heavily represented among its accounts receivable. Local business organizations subsequently joined. In the early 1930s, the plan was copied in several states; the first among these were California, New Jersey, and Minnesota. The Great Depression provided much of the impetus for these plans. Indicative of the plight of hospitals at that time is the fact that more than 700 U.S. hospitals closed during the period because of lack of operating capital. By 1972, there were 80 regional Blue Cross associations in the United States with more than 75 million subscribers.

Despite their financially depressed situation, local hospitals provided the major portion of initial funds for the original Blue Cross plans. Kaitz notes a study by Robert D. Eilers (1963) of 39 hospital service (Blue Cross) associations that found that 22 received their initial funds exclusively from the hospitals, five from both hospitals and other private sources, and six from local foundations. Further, as early as 1933, the American Hospital Association, acting as the representative of hospital interests, began to spell out guidelines for organizations wishing to enter the health-insurance industry. The Association still administers the nationwide certification program of Blue Cross; no Blue Cross chapter can be formed without its approval. Further, the A.H.A. specifically requires that at least one-third of the Blue Cross governing board be drawn from the administration and trustees of contracting hospitals. Reinforcing the leverage hospitals have within Blue Cross is the enabling legislation in 18 states that requires that the boards of directors of the local chapters contain hospital representation; some even require that a majority of the governing body be representatives of the hospitals (for example, Massachusetts). The prevalence of this legislative pattern is not difficult to understand because Blue Cross enabling acts were pushed through the state legislatures with considerable assistance from hospitals, local hospital associations, and the medical community in general. In sum: Blue Cross was largely created by the hospitals of America to provide a third-party guarantor for payments, and hospitals still maintain critical influence in its formal governance structure.

In light of its origins and development, it is not surprising that Kaitz concludes that Blue Cross has failed to provide effective coordination in the regulation of hospital costs. He says (1968: 88):

> The most decisive conclusion that can be drawn . . . is that the hospital industry has not yet developed any normative standards for judging or evaluating its managerial performance. From the evidence developed by this study, it can be concluded that the hospital industry lacks an adequate notion of administrative efficiency. Prices and costs are evaluated on a relative, not absolute, basis; the industry is not concerned with its level of prices and costs just so long as the prices are within the range of those in similar or nearby hospitals. Resources are allocated to new buildings, new equipment, and new personnel with virtually no attention paid to the costs of these programs or to the benefits that will be produced for the consumer by these costs. Prices rise along with costs with no premium placed upon institutional efficiency.

In other words, the members of local hospital networks coordinate their activities to the degree that an acceptable range of costs and prices is maintained. However, there are no inducements in such a system for managerial rationality and operating efficiency nor for commensurate pressures to reduce and control costs and prices (as in the price-oriented business sector); Kaitz holds that an "underlying cause" of this failure to coordinate activities to curtail increasing costs has been Blue Cross's cost-based payment system. Blue Cross, he believes, operates to remove a significant portion of the "business risk" in running hospitals "while failing to provide either an incentive for efficient production of medical care or a penalty for inefficient production" (1968: v).[4] In the last analysis, Kaitz agrees, "Blue Cross does not regulate the hospital industry. The hospital industry is, in fact, self-regulating" (1968: 92).

The case of Blue Cross supports our earlier suggestion that, while some mediated fields have tendencies toward co-decision-making (for example, establishing an acceptable range of prices and costs), the "creature" status of the coordinating unit severely limits the prospects for more comprehensive planning (for example, efficiently controlling costs and prices). The case of Blue

Cross, at first glance, also seems to contain negative evidence regarding our proposition linking high scope with greater co-decision-making. Blue Cross, after all, deals in only one principal resource, money; yet it is involved in more joint planning than, let us say, the matching program. However, the type of resource dealt with is crucial. Money is different from students, sheets, syringes, or cobalt machines; it is a generalized medium of exchange. Hence, the constraints that narrow scope impose on more particular media are not applicable to money because money can buy all of these items and serves as the unified measure of value for all of them as well.

THE RANGE OF AUTONOMY

If greater mediating unit autonomy indeed enhances co-decision-making, a fuller understanding of the determinants of autonomy is especially useful for those interested in expanding comprehensive planning. We suggest that there are at least four factors that are important here: ecological autonomy, independent staffing, attribution of responsibility for co-deciding, and control of an independent resource-base. Of course, when all four factors are present, we have a guided and not merely a mediated field. On the other hand, the absence of all of them indicates a feudal rather than a mediated setting. The presence of the first two — ecological autonomy and independent staffing — is especially critical for allowing a unit to escape being solely an "administrative facade" for a parent organization. Whether or not a mediating unit is "real" is often difficult to determine. Sometimes an outsider may think that such a "facade" indicates the existence of an autonomous mediating unit, when actually there is only a "front" for a member organization of a feudal field, or, perhaps more likely, for an elite unit of an interorganizational empire. The pre-World War II Comintern represents a more macrosociological instance of this. Purportedly, a unit intended to coordinate the activities of Communist parties throughout the world, the Comintern, in fact, was almost totally controlled by the Soviet Union and functioned as a vehicle through which the latter guided the activities of foreign communists.

Ecological autonomy and independent staffing of mediating units make their fields something more than exclusively feudal. The acquisition of a resource-base and the attribution of some responsibility for planning bring them closer to corporation-guided fields. Yet, elements of these latter also can be present to varying degrees in some mediated fields. In these, their incongruent mix is likely to expand co-decision-making, but may generate strains in the field as well.

We consider first ecological autonomy and independent staffing and how they contribute to the social autonomy of the mediating agency from its feudal-base. Then, we move to an examination of the disparity between resource-control and decision-responsibility and how this may generate "crises" in mediated fields.

ECOLOGICAL AUTONOMY AND INDEPENDENT STAFFING: BEYOND FEUDALISM

The acquisition of a distinctive "physical plant" enhances the probability that a potential mediating unit can develop a degree of autonomy; that is, it is something more than a "branch" of the organization housing it. We do not argue that "ecological space" is inevitably coextensive with "control space." However, the correlation is sufficiently nonproblematic that it is the alleged absence of a positive correlation that must be viewed with suspicion in any particular instance.

Coordinating activities carried on with computers, when they are given distinctive administrative labels, often hint at the existence of an autonomous mediating agency when in fact there is none. This is especially true when the activity is housed by a parent organization. A good example of the dilemmas a researcher can encounter in trying to discern whether an autonomous mediating unit is present can be found in the following article from *Hospitals* (1966: 126):

Computer Fills Bed Requests
in Experimental N.Y. System

An experimental computerized pediatric bed assignment system went into operation in New York City during March and within two weeks had weathered its first crisis.

The system, known as EMBERS (Emergency Bed Request System), links nine hospitals to a computer center located at the State University of New York Downstate Medical Center. Its objectives are to prevent delays in hospitalization of infants and children and to distribute patients among cooperating hospitals so that pediatric facilities are neither overcrowded nor underutilized. According to Jonathan T. Lanman, M.D., chairman of the department of pediatrics at the university medical center and chief of pediatrics at Kings County Hospital Center, one of the participating hospitals, pediatric wards at Kings County have often been seriously overcrowded, while other hospitals in the area have had only 50 to 60 per cent of their pediatric beds filled.

To overcome the problem, a system was designed connecting each of the nine hospitals by telephone lines to the computer center. Each time a pediatric patient is admitted or discharged, information is transmitted from a terminal in the hospital to a computer which stores exact patient census information in its "memory bank." When a patient appears at a hospital that has reached 90 per cent of pediatric bed capacity, that hospital makes a "bed request" so that the patient may be referred to another hospital. Within 10 seconds, the computer matches the patient's address with the nearest hospital that has an available bed, advises the overcrowded hospital, and simultaneously advises the second hospital. When the patient appears at the receiving hospital, the hospital informs the computer so that its data is kept current. The computer then supplies the receiving hospital with an up-to-date recapitulation of its patient census.

The system encountered its first problem just 10 days after its installation when a pneumonia patient who had arrived at overcrowded Kings County Hospital was dispatched to the Jewish Hospital of Brooklyn — itself filled to capacity — instead of to the Brooklyn Hospital where a pediatric bed was available. According to a spokesman at the Downstate Medical Center, the error was traced to "the human element," a misreading of the computer's instructions by an intern at Kings County.

Other hospitals participating in the trial program are the Maimonides Hospital of Brooklyn, Coney Island Hospital, Methodist Hospital of Brooklyn, Brooklyn-Cumberland Medical Center, the Long Island College Hospital, Greenpoint Hospital, and the Bedford Stuyvesant Health Center.[5]

There is no doubt that the EMBERS system was (and still is) providing a kind of "coordinating" service for the participating units; that is, it functions as a mechanism for funneling data on bed occupancy among pediatric facilities as well as allocating the patients to these facilities. No one can quibble about whether the IBM 360-40 computer represents a technological means of mediation. However, the more crucial question for our purposes concerns sociological mediation rather than technological.

In this particular instance, further inquiries on our part determined that the EMBERS system has not evolved into an autonomous sociological entity. The computer is owned by Downstate. The EMBERS program, it was reported to us, is "practically automatic." Moreover, the one staff member who is formally responsible for its operation is a full-time employee of Downstate. The only expenses incurred by the other participating units is for the telephone lines and the rental of the terminals on their premises. In other words, EMBERS appears to be one ecologically based coordinating activity that is an integral part of the "host" organization. As one member of the Downstate administration, who is involved in data processing, told us: "We consider EMBERS as a community service we render."

The EMBERS example points out that the failure of activities to become minimally autonomous of the parent organization results from more than the inability to acquire ecological autonomy. The failure of EMBERS to develop a distinctive staff seems to play an important part, too. In other words, whether or not an agency has employees or staff members of its own is likely to be another major mechanism for evolving beyond feudalism. The reader will note that the "looser" fields like the one coordinated by the San Francisco information center and under the "Cleveland plan," as well as more "integrated" ones "presided" over by Greater New York Hospital Association and Blue Cross, are all marked by this criterion. They all have their own staff paid out of their own budgets. On the other hand, the EMBERS program at Downstate Medical Center does not qualify: its staff is on the Downstate payroll. The case of THMEP is informative here.

In February 1963, St. Mary's, a 280-bed, church-affiliated hospital; the Pima County General Hospital, a 160-bed hospital for indigents; the Tucson Medical Center, a 450-bed voluntary hospital; and the St. Elizabeth of Hungary (Out-patient) Clinic jointly inaugurated the Tucson Hospital Medical Education Program (THMEP), whose stated purpose was "to establish a strong unified program with fully approved internships and residencies in all major specialities; additionally, it was hoped that better qualified graduates would be attracted" (1965: Ramsay and Durbin, 993). During the first two years of operation, libraries at all three hospitals were improved; auditorium and classroom space have been expanded "where needed"; and it is reported that "the available service beds at the private hospitals have been increased for the use of county and non-county-eligible service patients" (1965: Ramsay and Durbin, 995).

In addition, the Tucson Hospitals Medical Education Program attempted to standardize the graduate programs at the three hospitals and the clinic; requirements for eligibility for teaching-staff members were enumerated; and combined THMEP appointments were made. According to a report in the *Journal of Medical Education* (Ramsay and Durbin, 1965: 993-997), regular departmental meetings are now firmly established, including mortality and morbidity reviews. In addition, regular clinical pathological conferences involving the three hospitals were reportedly initiated. THMEP also undertook a medical school graduate recruitment program. In 1965, there were 16 interns and 33 residents in the unified program, compared to 16 and 14 respectively in two separate programs that antedated THMEP.

The critical question in the present context is: To what degree has Tucson Hospital's Medical Education Program "transcended" the merely feudalistic bonds among three hospitals and a clinic? There are several good reasons why an observer might decide that THMEP has no real autonomy. For instance, under the 1963 agreement, the three hospitals retain their own chiefs of services and program directors, and St. Elizabeth's also retains its program directors. Still, some doubt about such a decision arises in light of the fact that there is a coordinating committee — the joint advisory board — which is delegated final administrative responsibility for THMEP. On the other hand, this board and its executive and educational committees are drawn from the staffs of the participating organizations. Thus, the critical question becomes how "real" the board and its committees in fact are: Can they be treated as functioning entities in their own right, or are they merely legalistic labels affixed to direct communications among the four member units?

Primary research would doubtless provide the answer to this question without too much difficulty. However, the journal article on THMEP does not. Nonetheless, the article does offer a critical fact that firms up our view that this program has a strong capacity for autonomy and, hence, could become more than a "branch" in a feudal field. It points out that a full-time director of medical education was appointed who was an employee of THMEP and not of any one of the individual organizations it coordinates. Let us reiterate that this factor did not by itself lead us to place THMEP in the mediated category. However, this additional factor, along with such evidence as the existence of a coordinating board, makes such a classification the most plausible one in the absence of primary research.

Ecological autonomy and the ability to recruit its own staff makes a mediating unit more "real," that is, less an administrative device of one or more member organizations. However, in themselves these factors do not promote extensive co-decision-making. When a mediating unit acquires control over some resources, or when it is attributed some responsibility for planning — when it drifts toward a guiding role — the capacity for co-deciding expands somewhat.

RESOURCES AND RESPONSIBILITY: THE DRIFT TOWARD GUIDANCE

While a unit with an unequivocal guiding function has both resources and attributed responsibility resolutely in its hands, there are numerous empirical instances when these two factors are not found together. Broadly speaking, these instances may be considered manifestations of mediated control configurations. Departures from the guiding prototype may take one of three logical directions. First, of course, a coordinating unit may have neither attributed responsibility nor control of the requisite resources — in which case, it resembles the prototypical mediating agency. The second case is one in which a coordinating unit has some responsibility but not the resources. The third pattern is when the reverse is true, that is, the agency controls resources necessary for the wielding of systemic power, but it does not have formal responsibility attributed to it for setting, pursuing, and implementing policy for the field.

Typical of a relatively "pure" mediating agency is the Greater New York Blood Program, which was created in 1968 out of the uniting of the blood programs of the American Red Cross in Greater New York and the Community Blood Council of Greater New York, Inc.[6] The latter agency, the CBC, itself founded only in 1965, has taken on the administrative responsibility for the merged program. The GNYBP claims to provide approximately 260 hospitals in the metropolitan area with available blood during emergencies or periods of unusually high demand. It is reported that all participating hospitals need to do is to telephone the program to get information about available supplies at other hospitals. The program has arrangements with 45 hospitals to report daily on how much surplus blood, by type, they can make available to the blood inventory. Through such a routine monitoring, the program says it can anticipate "blood crises." In addition, the GNYBP expects that participating hospitals occasionally may overstock, and it has assumed the obligation of saving unused blood by making it available to other agencies.

However, the GNYBP not only facilitates the rotation of blood among hospitals by informing them about what is available and where, but in addition, it maintains its own inventory gained largely through blood donation campaigns. The GNYBP (CBC/GNYBP, 1968-69: 6-7) describes other related activities as follows:

> There are now workable systems developing between the GNYBP and the 16 upstate hospitals, three new blood bank affiliates and 17 substations participating in the Blue Cross Program. The GNYBP has two full-time representatives, assigned to serve Participating Organizations in that program, who have improved their methods of blood exchange to the end that there is better use of blood, given by many more donors; and there is the added comfort to PO's in having their paperwork done by the GNYBP.
>
> A full-time supervisor of Blue Cross records is now in charge of three facets of that program, involving 70 per cent of GNYBP blood donors and all Blue Cross member hospitals. Blue Cross subscribers are covered for blood by agreeing to give it. Hospitals providing them with blood must check for eligibility with the GNYBP before releasing credit for it.

And out-of-state people entitled to N.Y. Blue Cross coverage usually receive it through a reciprocity clearing house system involving affirmation of their eligibility by the GNYBP. These by no means minor details are part of the Community Blood Program. If bringing them into line took longer than anyone anticipated, that's yesterday's newspaper. . . the situation is now in hand.

Thus, the Greater New York Blood Program provides one of the most unambiguous instances of a mediated field that we have come across. This agency has little or no attributed responsibility to wield systemic power over the network of blood-user agencies but, rather, it is a "creature" of the member organizations, charged primarily with a "traffic regulation" task. Neither does it have exclusive nor even effective control of the prime requisite resource (that is, blood), although it does maintain some supplies of its own. On the other hand, the GNYBP's sanguine assessment of the efficacy of the blood distributive process is not shared by other observers. Richard Titmuss (1971) has meticulously dissected the failures of America's "free enterprise" distributive system in contrast to Great Britain's under the National Health Service. Compared to Britain, the American scene is a patchwork of local, voluntary, and commercial systems that provide highly unreliable data about the donation and allocation of blood. More important, the American system is characterized by higher rates of spoilage of blood, far higher incidence of serum hepatitis, more frequent shortage crises, and a growing commercial exploitation of the need for human blood. In America, blood is usually bought; in Britain, it is freely donated. In America, blood is most often taken from the lowest socioeconomic strata and disproportionately used by those on the upper socioeconomic levels, whereas in Britain donations and utilization more closely approximate the actual proportion of various classes in the population (although some residual bias in favor of the upper classes remains).

In fairness, we must note that Titmuss gives the New York program better grades than most of the rest of the country, especially as regards wastage (1971: 63-65). However, the overriding significance of his study in terms of our considerations is that the guided British blood distribution system is far more efficient, effective, and humane than the crazy-quilt American system. Even the better American programs, coordinated by

nonprofit mediating agencies (for example, in New York) are no
match for the British system. We conclude, along with Titmuss,
that this is explained partly by the inability of local mediating
agencies effectively to penetrate and to transform an inefficient
distributive system increasingly dominated by the utilitarian moral
code of the marketplace.

Agencies that are attributed some responsibility for wielding
systemic power but have no effective control of the requisite
resources coordinate fields that are largely mediated but have
some tendency toward guidance. Typical here are the roles that
interagency councils and committees commonly play. These
entities allow the coordinated organizations to deal collectively
with third parties in their common environment (for example, the
federal government). Hence, councils and committees serve both
as "organizational weapons" to advance the members' interests as
well as "lightning rods" for environmental pressures otherwise
aimed at the participating organizations. However, such entities
often do not control the resources usually required to control
their members and to manipulate their environments (for example,
funds, equipment, professional manpower). Moreover, while they
have some formal systemic power obligations, councils and
committees remins the creatures of their members, whose own
personnel comprise the boards of directors and the staffs of most
of the key committees.

Basil J. F. Mott, who sees such councils and committees as the
most frequent mode of coordination in the health field,
nonetheless regards them as only marginally successful:

> A coordinating council is therefore a relatively ineffective
> mechanism for achieving managed coordination. Any formal goals can
> be carried out only to the extent that the coordinated organizations
> find it mutually advantageous to do so. This largely means avoiding
> controversial questions, which often are the most important questions.
> A coordinating council is however likely to achieve a valuable degree of
> unmanaged coordination.
>
> Although it is exceedingly difficult, if not impossible, to show, the
> interaction among the coordinated organizations probably results in
> desirable adjustments among the member agencies in their outlook,
> objectives, and methods of operations. A council also can be a valuable
> mechanism for indirectly managing competition among the member

organizations by helping them discover the true extent to which they have competing interests, and thus avoid needlessly injuring one another outside of the council. Moreover, by helping the coordinated organizations deal more effectively with their task environments, and by helping them exploit opportunities for cooperating among their programs, a council is an instrumentality by which the members are better able to maintain themselves as viable organizations. This outcome probably contributes to more effective performance of agency goals, whatever they may be [1970: 10].[7]

Extremely good examples of this type of coordinating agency are to be found among some regional planning and health facilities councils. The Health and Hospital Planning Council of Southern New York is often held up as an exemplar in this realm.[8] While this agency in fact mediates a field composed of the health care units in the New York metropolitan area, formally the member organizations are not these more primary units but, for the most part, other agencies charged with mediating and guiding subsectors of the field. In 1969, the Council had 25 members:

Associated Hospital Service
 of New York
Association of Private
 Hospitals, Inc.
Catholic Charities, Diocese
 of Rockville Centre
Commerce and Industry Association
 of New York
Community Council of
 Greater New York
The Coordinating Council of
 the First District Branch
 of the Medical Society of
 the State of New York
Federation of Jewish Philanthropies
 of New York
Federation of Protestant
 Welfare Agencies, Inc.
The Greater New York Fund
Greater New York Hospital
 Association

Catholic Charities, Archdiocese
 of New York
Catholic Charities, Diocese
 of Brooklyn
Metropolitan New York Nursing
 Home Association, Inc.
Nassau-Suffolk Hospital
 Council, Inc.
The New York Academy of
 Medicine
New York City Central Labor
 Council AFL-CIO
Public Health Association of
 New York City
State Communities Aid
 Association
Teamster Joint Council No. 16
United Hospital Fund of New
 York
Westchester County AFL-CIO
 Central Labor Body

The Hospital Association of
Southeastern New York
Long Island Federation of
Labor AFL-CIO

The Westchester County
Association Inc.
Westchester County Hospital
Association

The Council, founded in 1937, is one of seven such agencies operating in different regions of New York State. It is a private agency and reportedly plays an important advisory role for a broad spectrum of medical planning and coordination in its area. For example, in response to a request from the New York City Department of Hospitals for recommendations regarding the replacement of "obsolete" municipal facilities in the Bronx, the Council, in 1967, proposed: (1) the construction of a new 950-bed hospital to replace the 307-bed Lincoln Hospital to be affiliated with the Albert Einstein College of Medicine; (2) the replacement of Fordham Hospital south of its present location by a 400-bed site near 180th Street and Third Avenue, more convenient to rapid north-south transportation; (3) the construction of approximately 375 general care beds at the Montefiore Hospital and Medical Center complex; and (4) the building of a neighborhood ambulatory care center near the present Morrisania Hospital. Critics of the Council have charged that decisions such as these are biased in favor of the large university-linked medical centers such as the "Einstein-Montefiore" empire (see chapter 4).

However, the Council has played more than an "advisory," that is to say, purely mediating role. It does not merely offer information and policy recommendations to agencies that request it. Rather, although a private entity, it has some political muscle delegated to it by the state; that is, it has some nascent guidance responsibility. Probably the Council's most publicized task has been its review of applications for approval of construction of medical care facilities. This activity is mandated by the Metcalf-McClosky Act, which became effective in 1966. Under these acts, the decisions of the Council are not advisory but, for all intents and purposes, binding. Briefly, the legislation requires that the Council review and provide recommendations to the appropriate state agency on all proposals dealing with the creation or expansion of health care facilities in its area. It describes its criteria for decision-making in the following terms:

In conducting these reviews the Council concerns itself with public need and other matters, such as competence of the sponsors and adequacy of financing. In addition, on those applications involving construction, the Council's architectural staff reviews plans for functional adequacy and conformity with code requirements [Mott, 1968: 24].

Between July 1 1967 and June 30, 1968, the Council made formal recommendations on 133 new applications. Table 3-1 summarizes its actions in detail. Overall, it approved 123 of the 133 applications.

Nonetheless, the Council does not have the potential for comprehensive planning possessed by a guiding "corporation." Although it dispenses advice and information, and even though it exercises a kind of negative guidance insofar as it is attributed veto power over construction, it does not have control over the resources necessary for the efficacious wielding of systemic power. The fact that it accepts practically all of the construction proposals submitted (for example, 123 of 133), further suggests that effective decision-making occurs before formal proposals generally reach the Council. Where those decisions are made (inside or outside the Council) has yet to be determined, although the Council claims to discourage informally applications which meet "no discernable public need" (Mott, 1968: 24-25). In addition, one informant, a former staff member, has told us that the Council is experiencing a kind of "identity crisis" because of the increased direct governmental involvement in health care planning. The Council, he reports, is not at all sure of its future role in a domain progressively more dominated by federal, state, and municipal comprehensive planning agencies. In the late 1960s the Council lost its battle to become the official comprehensive planning unit for health in New York City. However, he feels that the Council will survive because of the backup it receives from the powerful and influential voluntary hospitals in the city and because of its long experience and reputed expertise in collecting and analyzing health data.

Despite this optimism, the future role of essentially private agencies like the Council in the field of medical planning remains in doubt. Governmental agencies have far clearer mandates to make decisions, and they have control of perhaps the ultimate resource; that is to say, money. Therefore, they have both more responsibility and greater resources with which to guide. In contrast, the Council to a large degree is still controlled by the agencies it serves, and its muscle depends on other units' capacities to command resources (that is, the state, powerful voluntary hospitals and so on). Thus, it falls short of being a guiding unit while, nevertheless, being attributed some guiding responsibilities. We hypothesize that ultimately it will either have to scale down its ambitions — and hence, resemble more the "ideal type" of mediating unit — or it will have to gain control of a stable resource-base and become a guiding agency; otherwise, it may lose all of its planning prerogatives to emerging governmental or "public" units.

Underlying this hypothesis is the assumption that the optimally effective way of obtaining desired outcomes involving a plurality of actors requires some differential attribution of this responsibility as well as some differential control of necessary resources. In this light, agencies such as the Health and Hospital Planning Council of Southern New York are in a quandary because they are charged with making decisions without control of a reliable resource-base for implementing them. Organizational fields with coordinating units of this type, in other words, are faced periodically with "crises of competence" of varying intensities. A crisis of competence, as we use the term, suggests a dissatisfaction among the member units with the inability of a coordinating agency to obtain a goal whose pursuit they do not question. Much of the criticism of the Council by groups like Health-PAC (see chapter 4) is concerned with its alleged lack of competence.

Units that control the requisite resources but that have minimal attribution of responsibility also face difficulties; however, these are of a different sort. Whereas agencies like the Council are endowed with a relatively high degree of legitimacy for what they are trying to do, the other type of agency must periodically mobilize support among the member units to wield some degree of power for the network as a whole; power that it clearly has the resource-capabilities to follow through on. The preceding instance of incongruence between responsibility and resource-control was called a crisis of competence; the present one represents a "crisis of legitimacy." We suggest that fields faced with crises of legitimacy that are short of open rupture require an excessive expenditure of resources to keep them going. This seems to be the case because the coordinating agencies are not granted appreciable "zones of indifference" within which members can be counted on to comply with commands.[9] Rather, the zone is small and relatively tenuous, thus requiring the agency to expend resources repeatedly in order to guarantee the acquiescence of participating units. Resources spent in constraining, inducing, or persuading members (in gaining their compliance) are not available for mobilization in pursuit of a collective goal. Clearly, all units with any tendency toward guidance must be able to do both; that is, they must have the capacity to overcome resistance of others and the ability to realize collective goals. However, when resources are excessively deflected to the former enterprise, the latter pursuit is inevitably weakened. Legitimacy or a zone of indifference forestalls the inevitability of this pattern but, when it is weak or narrow, resources must be mobilized to meet potential resistance to a variety of incremental decisions.

In the realm of medical organizations, of course, this resistance generally does not entail the pervasive active or passive alienation one sometimes sees in political life. Indeed, the resistance is likely to center on a coordinating agency's presumption to a guiding role (and its efforts to solidify such a position) rather than on its overall "right to exist." As a matter of fact, insofar as such agencies play a key role in the raising and allocating of funds, they are endowed with considerable legitimacy by member units. Robert Morris' study (1963a: 248-259 and 1963b: 462-472) of six Jewish welfare federations is highly illustrative of such a situation.

Six cities were selected for "retrospective study of attempts to alter the patterns of institutional service in the direction of cooperation, coordination or integration" (Morris, 1963a: 249). In studying St. Louis, Toronto, Cincinnati, San Francisco, Philadelphia, and Detroit, Morris focused on the efforts of the local Jewish welfare federation in each city to promote new links between a general hospital and an extended care facility (either a home for the aged, a chronic diseases hospital, or a nursing home). The investigation sought to isolate the factors "which resulted in a new pattern of association, or which failed to achieve this objective" (Morris, 1963a: 249). Morris, therefore, compared successes with failures in the realm of joint planning. A success was defined as: "Alteration of a specified working relationship between two institutions, established as a goal by a community planning organization, adopted by the affected agencies, and operationally effective within ten years of the initial planning. . . . Failure was defined as the inability to agree on a specific plan, lack of agency acceptance, or termination of the plan within ten years" (Morris, 1963a: 249).

Morris (1963a: 253-254) summarizes the plans for hospital-ECF linkages and their related success as follows:

St. Louis — A complete corporate merger of a general hospital, a chronic disease sanitorium, a rehabilitation center, and a medical social service bureau. In addition, the new medical center and an independent home for the aged evolved a plan for medical care in which the hospital staff assumed responsibility for medical care in the home, while the latter retained administrative fiscal, and policy autonomy. This represents a complete integration and complete success of the planning objectives.

Toronto — A plan to independently rebuild both a hospital and a home for the aged, the latter to add a large unit for care of the chronically ill. Plans to integrate medical and nursing care between the hospital and the chronic disease unit were successfully carried out. In effect, one medical staff serves two institutions, but the fiscal policy and nonprofessional administrations remain independent of each other. There is also a high degree of cooperation between the home for the aged and the hospital. A successful planning effort.

Philadelphia — Two simultaneous planning efforts were carried out since efforts to combine both in one scheme were not possible. A nursing home, once administered by a general hospital, was legally separated from the hospital and launched upon an independent career, but medical, nursing, and other professional services (except for social services) continued to be provided by the hospital. In time, the separate nursing home was to become a modern rehabilitation service. Concurrently, a home for the aged independently developed its own medical program. Plans to integrate its medical service with that of the hospital failed. A partially successful planning.

Cincinnati — The construction of a new and independent chronic disease center for active nursing and rehabilitation. This was loosely associated with the adjoining general hospital, but medical care was not fully integrated as planned originally. The new institution depended upon close cooperation by the hospital and two homes for the aged, but only limited cooperation resulted for several years. Attempts to merge two homes for the aged to improve infirmary care failed. An incomplete planning attempt. Later a plan for medical cooperation between the hospital and one of the homes for the aged was developed. The results are not yet known.

San Francisco — A plan to erect a rehabilitation hospital independent of, but associated with a general hospital. The unit was built, but association between the hospitals was never completed. Relationships between these two and a home for the aged were not developed until the failure of the original plan, and the final closing down of the rehabilitation unit. Before the plan finally failed, the rehabilitation hospital and a nursing home were merged and patients of both lodged in one building. An unsuccessful planning effort.

Detroit — A Federation committee met over a period of several years to coordinate medical and health programs of the Sinai Hospital and Home for the Aged. Several plans were projected ranging from a "cooperative medical program between home and hospital" to a "hospital-administered program of medical service at the home including research, teaching, and direct service to residents." No agreement was reached over several years' time.

Morris feels that six factors account for these differential patterns of success and failure:

1. simultaneous crises in member unit operations
2. the existence of "substantial" extraorganizational, associational webs that bind together the members of different boards of trustees
3. the availability of an effective "planning structure"
4. community leaders who can bridge competing organizational interests
5. the ability to gain access to reliable data ("expert studies and consultations")
6. the skillful manipulations of utilitarian and normative resources by a local federation (the "discriminating use of incentives")

Morris argues that the first two factors are best viewed as preconditions for success, while the latter four are elements that determine success during the ongoing process of planning. For the purposes of illustrating the tensions in an interorganizational field when the coordinating unit controls resources but is not allocated comparable responsibility, we believe Morris' points (1), (3), and (6) are especially important (although we will not deal with them in that order).

His treatment of the third factor, the existence of a planning structure, reminds us that on a manifest level, high resource-low responsibility coordinating units have basic similarities to all other mediating agencies. He sees a federation primarily as a mechanism that "provides a meeting ground for the various groups and organizations concerned with any (voluntary) community policy decisions" (Morris 1963b: 462). This is true both or the successful and the unsuccessful cases. What distinguishes the two classes is that in the two "fully successful" settings, the federations brought together all groups actively engaged in planning for the chronically ill; in the two cases of "relative failure," the federations had a history of dealing with only certain subcliques and, hence, efforts to involve the entire field failed "presumably because the basis for confidence had not been developed" (Morris, 1963b: 462). Hence, the federations studied by Morris, regardless of level of success, are very similar to the coordinating councils (for example, the Health and Hospital Planning Council of Southern New York) and all other mediating agencies discussed in this chapter because all are to some degree the creatures of their member organizations.

Nevertheless, there is an important difference in high resource-low responsibility agencies that is highlighted by Morris' sixth point: — the discriminating use of incentives. Jewish welfare federations are highly effective in their fundraising activities. This gives them control over utilitarian resources not matched by the coordinating councils discussed above. The six-city study found that the selective utilization of utilitarian resources had an appreciable impact on successful interorganizational planning. Morris argues that his data indicate that successful coordination "can be influenced, if not completely determined, by a discriminating use of incentives on the part of the planning groups" (1963b: 468-469). The most frequent and most successful incentives were financial and took the form of federation-sponsored building fund campaigns. In other words, unlike the Health and Hospital Planning Council, at least some of the Jewish federations control resources sufficiently to overcome the potential resistance of member units.

Moreover, the resources are not exclusively utilitarian. Morris reports that in some instances, leaders of less prestigious organizations were added to the boards of the hospitals to win their support. Hence, successful federations apparently also have some capacity to manipulate normative resources. There also are indications that they control resources of a mixed utilitarian-normative quality. For example, in some cases funds were provided for prestige-conferring new programs, such as home care plans or rehabilitation programs or for more professional nursing staffs in nursing homes.

Nonetheless, the capacity to manipulate utilitarian and normative incentives to overcome member unit resistance is a mixed blessing. It gives a coordinating agency a flexibility it would not enjoy in a purely mediated field; nevertheless, it presents a more costly mode of obtaining acquiescence than guiding corporations tend to employ. Because a guiding unit presumably is attributed a legitimate right to set, pursue, and implement goals, its commands are more readily unquestioningly obeyed. Morris' successful federations apparently had to spend a great deal more time persuading, cajoling, and buying-off the potential opposition. The member units did not feel any obligation to conform to policy automatically. This takes its toll of federation resources, for if its resources must be used as incentives, then they tend to be deflected from planning and implementation. In turn, we suggest that under such circumstances, comprehensive, long-range decision-making looks highly utopian because the success of each particular piece of policy is so problematic and requires winning over anew several relatively autonomous member units through incentives.

Hence, we come finally to Morris' very first point, crises in member unit operations. He tells us that, in the last analysis, unless the boards of trustees of the involved units are convinced that the planned collaboration is in the best interests of their organizations, they will resist. Moreover, they have the capacity to resist pressures successfully because in all cases the federation agency provides only a small portion of the unit's budget. The federation plays a major role only in capital construction. Morris (1963a: 256) continues:

More significant, certain factors militate against the withholding of funds by central agencies. The welfare federations are voluntary associations in which authority is widely dispersed among members. Antagonistic acts against one agency member can easily be countered by withdrawal from the association, without necessarily destroying the seceder. In other words, the central financial bodies are limited in the freedom of action.

Therefore, not only does the absence of legitimacy make the need to manipulate resources more necessary, but at the same time it places constraints on its use for social control (incentive) purposes.

SUMMARY AND CONCLUSIONS

In this chapter we have been concerned with understanding the dynamics of mediated fields. We stated that some mediated fields are very loosely coordinated and involve little or no joint policy-making; others are marked by high coordination and extensive co-decision-making. We offered several hypotheses to account for the variation: The central proposition that pervades this chapter (indeed, this entire monograph) is that the capacity for comprehensive co-decision-making tends to increase in the degree to which the field contains an autonomous, vertically differentiated coordinating unit. In addition, we suggested that a strong collectivity-orientation among the member organizations as well as broad scope enhance co-decision-making.

We also looked at some of the factors that promote the autonomy of the coordinating agency. We said that technological mediation need not imply sociological mediation. However, we argued that ecological autonomy and independent staffing lead to the development of a real mediating agency as distinct from a mere branch of a member unit in a feudal or an imperial field.

The autonomy of mediating units is enhanced further by the magnitude of the responsibility for wielding systemic power that is attributed to them and by the resources they control. Mediating units do not meet these criteria as well as do guiding units; some of the former are attributed varying amounts of responsibility or endowed with some of the necessary resources but never both to a significant degree. Consequently, we have argued that mediated fields with tendencies toward guidance are faced either with periodic crises of competence (not enough resources to do the job) or of legitimacy (not enough "right" to do the job).

This chapter, more than the preceding one, focused on control configurations at the expense of the content of interorganizational relations. Although we said something about scope, the issues of resource-types, salience, and symmetry have not been touched upon systematically. Given our central concern with joint policy formation, this neglect is not only benign but to some degree positively desirable. Nonetheless, it seems useful to say something briefly about each of these other dimensions before concluding the chapter — especially because mediated fields are intermediate points between feudalism and guidance.

First, the literature on mediated fields that we have reviewed speaks much more of money as an interorganizational resource than is true in our feudal cases. Because our study sample is not presumed to be representative, this point may not in itself be noteworthy, except if we recall that money is a generalized medium of exchange that can greatly facilitate interorganizational transactions in a manner similar to the ability of a money economy to more readily facilitate economic rationality than a barter economy. Thus, if we view mediated fields as more guided than feudal fields and less guided than guided ones, we expect that a generalized medium is likely to play a greater and greater role in interorganizational processes the more one desires effective coordination among member units.

Second, regarding salience of the resources involved in mediated fields, the literature provided us with no clues as to the relative magnitude of involvement of goal-related and ancillary resources. However, if the sharing or exchange of an ancillary resource was discussed in our sample, the item tended to be one that has great budgetary significance for the member units. That is, it dealt with an administrative item that cost a lot (for example, a computer). Nonetheless, the tendency may represent another instance of the reporting bias we have touched on several times before.

Finally, in the realm of symmetry an important development occurs. The introduction of a coordinating unit irrevocably undermines the likelihood of straightforward reciprocal exchanges as they occur in a feudal field. Although our material provides no detailed information in this regard, it seems almost self-evident that as coordinating units acquire more responsibility and resources for systemic power, the flow of resources and commands will take a progressively more downward slant — and hence, they will be more asymmetrical.

NOTES

1. Our discussion of the matching program is based heavily on the 1971 edition of their annual brochure, *The Student and the Matching Program.*

2. Our discussion of this program is based on an August 16, 1967 report in *Hospitals,* as well as Richard S. Lamden's (1969: 78 et seq.) piece in the same journal.

3. Our discussion of the New York Hospital Association is based on its 1969 brochure simply titled "The Greater New York Hospital Association."

4. Support for this negative appraisal of Blue Cross is found in "High Cost of Hospitalization," *Hearings Before the Subcommittee on Antitrust and Monopoly of the Committee on the Judiciary, United States Senate,* 91st Congress, Second Session, Pursuant to S. Res. 334, Par 2 "Blue Cross." January 26, 27, and 28, 1971. For a comprehensive treatment of the role of health insurance in the U.S. health system, see Somers and Somers (1961).

5. Reprinted by permission from *Hospitals,* Journal of the American Hospital Association, Vol. 40, June 1966, p. 126.

6. Our treatment of the Greater New York Blood Program is based largely on information in the continued 1968-69 annual report of CBC and the CNYBP.

7. See also Mott, *Anatomy of a Coordinating Council* (1968), which examines the operations of a coordinating agency dealing mainly with rehabilitation. This agency's coordination activities were focused primarily on other units within the governmental structure of New York State.

8. Our subsequent discussion of the Health and Hospital Planning Council of Southern New York is based largely on its 1967-68 annual report.

9. For a discussion of the convergence of the Weberian concept of "legitimacy" and Barnard's "zone of indifference," see Hopkins (1961).

REFERENCES

BLUMBERG, M. S. (1966) Shared Services for Hospitals. Chicago: American Hospital Association.

CBC AND GNYBP (1968-69) Annual Report — Community Blood Council of Greater New York, Inc., combined with Year One Report — The Greater New York Blood Program.

GIBBONS, H. III (1967) "Faster way to find a nursing home bed." Medical Economics 44 (June): 161.

GREATER NEW YORK HOSPITAL ASSOCIATION (1969) "The Greater New York Hospital Association." New York

HEALTH AND HOSPITAL PLANNING COUNCIL OF SOUTHERN NEW YORK, INC. (1968) Thirtieth Annual Report, 1967-1968. New York.

HOPKINS, T. K. (1961) "Bureaucratic authority: the convergence of Weber and Barnard," pp. 82-98 in Amitai Etzioni (ed.) Complex Organizations: A Sociological Reader. New York: Holt, Rhinehart & Winston.

HOSPITALS (1963) "Southern California hospital group starts program to improve administration." Volume 37 (April): 206.

――― (1966) "Computer fills bed requests in experimental New York system." Volume 40 (June): 126.

――― (1967) "Ohio Blue Cross initiates pilot ECF information plan." Volume 41 (August): 23.

KAITZ, E. M. (1968) Pricing Policy and Cost Behavior in the Hospital Industry. New York: Praeger.

LAMDEN, R. S. (1969) "Cooperation between hospitals and E.F.C.'s solves bed location problem." Hospitals 43 (June): 78-80.

MORRIS, R. (1963a) "Basic factors in planning for the coordination of health services, part I." Amer. J. of Public Health 53 (February): 248-259.

――― (1963b) "Basic factors in planning for the coordination of health services, Part II." Amer. J. of Public Health 53 (March): 462-472.

MOTT, B. J. F. (1968) Anatomy of a Coordinating Council. Pittsburgh: Univ. of Pittsburgh Press.

――― (1970) "Coordination and inter-organizational relations in health," pp. 55-69 in Paul E. White and George J. Vlasak (eds.) Inter-Organizational Research in Health: Proceedings of the Conference on Research on Inter-Organizational Relationships in Health. Washington, D.C.: U.S. Department of Health, Education and Welfare.

NATIONAL INTERN AND RESIDENT MATCHING PROGRAM (1971) "The Student and the Matching Program." Evanston, Ill.

RAMSAY, E. G. and R. L. DURBIN (1965) "Integration of training programs in Tucson." J. of Medical Education 40 (October): 993-997.

SOMERS, H. M. and A. R. SOMERS (1961) Doctors, Patients, and Health Insurance. Washington, D.C.: Brookings Institute.

SUBCOMMITTEE ON ANTITRUST AND MONOPOLY OF THE COMMITTEE ON THE JUDICIARY (1971) Hearings before the Subcommittee on Antitrust and Monopoly of the Committee on the Judiciary, United States Senate, Ninety-First Congress, Second Session: High Cost of Hospitalization. Washington, D.C.: U.S. Government Printing Office.

TITMUSS, R. M. (1971) The Gift Relationship: From Human Blood to Social Policy. New York: Pantheon Books.

TABLE 3-1

APPLICATIONS FOR ESTABLISHMENT OF CONSTRUCTION OF MEDICAL CARE FACILITIES PROCESSED[a] BY THE COUNCIL UNDER ARTICLES 28 AND 28-A OF THE PUBLIC HEALTH LAW AND SECTION 35 OF THE SOCIAL WELFARE LAW, BY REGION AND TYPE OF PRODUCT FOR THE 12-MONTH PERIOD, JULY 1, 1967 THROUGH JUNE 30, 1968

Application	Total	Approved	Long-term Disapproved	Long-term care beds
Total 12 Counties[b]	133	123	10	7,393
New York City Total	88	82	6	6,361
Voluntary hospitals	35	34	1	—
Voluntary long-term care	21	21	0	4,399[c]
Proprietary hospitals	7	3	4	—
Proprietary long-term care	10	10	0	1,962
Municipal hospitals	3	3	0	—
Municipal long-term care	0	0	0	—
Neighborhood Health Centers	6	6	0	—
Other	6	5	1	—
Northern Metropolitan Total	45	41	4	1,032
Voluntary hospitals	18	18	0	—
Voluntary long-term care	5	4	1	230[d]
Proprietary hospitals	1	1	0	—
Proprietary long-term care	18	15	3	766
Local government hospitals	1	1	0	—
Local government long-term	2	2	0	36
Other	0	0	0	—

a Formal letters sent to appropriate governmental agency(s) after Board(s) decisions.
b New York City: Bronx, Kings, New York, Queens, Richmond; Northern Metropolitan: Dutchess, Orange, Putnam, Rockland, Sullivan, Ulster, Westchester.
c Including 4,244 beds in 13 28-A Projects.
d Including 234 beds in 2 28-A Projects.

SOURCE: Health and Hospitals Planning Council of Southern New York, Inc., 1967-68: 25.

CHAPTER 4

INTERORGANIZATIONAL EMPIRES:
GUIDANCE BY A MEMBER-ELITE

Of late, the term "empire" has been heard increasingly in discussions of the health sector. Unfortunately, it is employed more often as a political weapon than as a tool for incisive analysis; that is, the term has been endowed with strong ideological overtones that obscure the scientific utility of drawing parallels between political empires and some health systems. Specifically, the notion of empires in the medical realm has been popularized by the Health Policy Advisory Center (Health-PAC) of New York, a group committed to both a relentless critique of what it perceives as the liberal medical establishment as well as to a radical transformation of American health priorities. For Health-PAC and its supporters, the major roadblocks standing in the way of more effective, efficient, and responsive health service delivery systems are no longer the traditionalistic forces epitomized by the American Medical Association; rather, they are the "medical empires" dominated by major teaching centers that "display an internal dynamic of their own, compelling them to expand through more and more affiliations, more and more buildings . . . because they have to, just in order to maintain their status and prestige" (Health-PAC, 1970: 34).

In this chapter, we suggest that the Health-PAC indictment of the medical empires contains many compelling insights into the liabilities of current health delivery systems. Yet, its partisanship tends to soften the impact of the critique as well as to overlook the potentially positive aspects of medical empires, especially in comparison to feudal and mediated fields. There is no doubt that this group sees empires as dominated by unredeemable villains and it uses that concept solely for this connotative value rather than for any precise denotative significance.

The Health-PAC usage must be understood within the broader New Left perspective that views the United States as an internal as well as an external imperialistic power. The holders of this view contend that the existing power-elite sustains itself not only through the exploitation of overseas economic "colonies" but also through an internal "colonialism" (by exploiting the Blacks, the Puerto Ricans, the workers, and so on). The medical empires that Health-PAC attacks are lumped with the colonialist "exploiters" and "oppressors." This perspective suggests that the alleged imperialism of the American system manifests itself as clearly in our treatment of the ill as it does in the rice paddies of Southeast Asia; and, moreover, that these two forms of imperialism are part of a single more encompassing exploitative system.[1] Although Health-PAC's documents rarely make this position explicit, the view permeates their weltanschauung. Occasionally, the position is made overt but only in passing. For instance, in the process of analyzing the operations of the Columbia-Presbyterian Medical Center empire, *The American Health Empire* bitterly compares Dean Houston Merritt's hasty flight to treat Portugal's dictator Salazar for a stroke with the assertion that "most Harlem stroke victims are considered scientifically uninteresting at Presbyterian. . ." (Health-PAC, 1970: 56). The impact of their statement is to associate in the mind of the reader the medical deprivation of Blacks at home with the catering to right-wing dictators abroad without offering any adequate demonstration for such a linkage.

In other words, while the Health Policy Advisory Center uses the term "empire" as a political weapon, we begin by using it in a more neutral manner derived from comparative political analysis. The treatment of empires in chapter 1 provides our starting point here. An empire is a multiunit field where substantial co-deciding occurs, as well as where one of the member units (or some subset of the members): (1) is attributed a specialized responsibility for effecting policy, and (2) has sufficient control of resources to build a systemic power base. An empire resembles a feudal field insofar as the participating units are roughly of the same type (for example, territorial, sociopolitical units often with an ethnic base, in the case of political empires; medical centers, hospitals, and clinics, in the case of medical empires), but the two types differ because a guiding unit is absent under feudalism. An empire resembles a corporation-dominated field in this latter respect but these two settings differ because the corporation is an administrative unit that is to some degree vertically differentiated from the interacting member units. Great Britain's former role in the Empire is an example of a member-elite's guidance of an imperial field, whereas the federal government of the United States plays more of a corporate role vis-a-vis the solidary groups and the local and state governmental units that make up American society.

Our use of the concept of empire is explicitly structuralist in outlook. (Our treatment of political empires relies most heavily on the works of Eisenstadt, 1963 and Etzioni, 1965.) That is, we designate what we mean by empire in terms of a specified set of social structural attributes. We do not build into our definition the potentially positive and negative consequences of imperial fields (as some authors do when they tell us that historical empires are less efficient than modern nation-states). Presumably, the association between a set of structural characteristics and their consequences remains a problem for proposition-building and empirical investigation and cannot be asserted merely by definition. Indeed, a better understanding of the relative efficacy of medical empires is one of this chapter's prime concerns.

In addition, our use of the term "empire" is primarily analytical. Our discussion profits greatly from a reading of S. N. Eisenstadt's *The Political System of Empires* (1963). However, the central focus of that work is on "historical bureaucratic empires," and, consequently, Eisenstadt skillfully weaves back and forth between using the term "empire" analytically (transhistorically) and historically (as a type between "feudal systems" and "modern societies"). His double emphasis gives his treatment of historical bureaucratic empires a subtlety and flexibility it would not have otherwise. Nevertheless, because we are not concerned primarily with the evolution of political or medical systems, our usage is

fundamentally ahistorical; that is, we do not view medical empires
as mere transition points in some inevitable movement from feudal
and mediated fields up to corporate ones. (For a background on
the main modern empires, see Fieldhouse, 1966.) As a matter of
fact, the future organization of health services in America seems,
at the moment, to be highly unpredictable. Indeed, the goal of
health policy researchers is to help shape the course U.S. health
services will take rather than simply to issue prohetic statements.

MEDICAL EMPIRES AND THE AFFILIATION PLAN

Health-PAC views New York City as the "Empire City" not
because of its nickname, but rather because of the concentration
of medical empires it contains. Whereas many major American
cities have one or two empires (for example, Johns Hopkins in
Baltimore, the University of Southern California in Los Angeles),
New York City is "dominated" by seven medical empires "which
together control more than three-quarters of the city's hospital
beds, more than half its health professional resources, and the
lion's share of public money for biomedical and sociomedical
research and development" (Health-PAC, 1970a). In a word, New
York is the imperial center par excellence and, hence, it affords us
a strategic site for examining the emergence of empires as well as
some of their functions and dysfunctions. Yet, while we rely on
New York City data for our key examples, the propositions put
forward here are intended to be applicable to all medical empires
and not just to those in one city.[2]

In studying the relations among medical organizations in
imperial fields, one particular set of bonds is of special interest:
the links forged by New York's so-called Affiliation Plan that tied
the foundering city-owned municipal hospitals to voluntary
hospitals and to medical centers. We suggest that the bonds
between medical centers and municipal hospitals are critical for
our purposes because they are the most "imperial" sectors of
empires: that is, they represent the most unambiguous instances of
control of subordinate units by a superordinate (elite) member
unit. In the course of this chapter we provide evidence that
justifies our special attention to affiliations. We begin with a brief

description of the New York health system and a background sketch of the Affiliation Plan.

The present era of health services in New York began in the early 1960s with the development of the Affiliation Plan to improve the crisis-torn municipal hospitals.[3] These hospitals are nonprofit organizations owned by the city. About one-quarter of all hospital beds in the five boroughs are in these hospitals. In addition to the municipal system, there are four other types of hospitals in the city. First, there are voluntary hospitals — nonprofit, private organizations that control approximately 39 percent of the bed capacity. Included within this category are units of widely differing quality: all the way from internationally renowned university-associated medical centers to rather undistinguished entities that consistently fail to match any of their vacancies in the intern and resident matching program. Second, there are the proprietary hospitals — private units run for profit — that account for about 7 percent of the city's bed space. Third, there are the Veterans' Administration hospitals operated by the federal government. These control almost 8 percent of the beds. Finally, there is the state hospital system, which has about one-fifth of all the beds in the city. Compared to the voluntary and municipal systems, New York State's system is heavily weighted toward the care of long-term patients.[4]

However, it would be a mistake to assume that affiliations exploded de novo on the New York scene in the seventh decade of the twentieth century. Indeed, Bellevue Hospital has had a variety of links with medical schools dating back as early as the eighteenth century. Dr. Ray E. Trussell, who served as Commissioner of Hospitals between March 1961 and July 1965, and who was perhaps the prime mover behind the Affiliation Plan recalls:

> Back in the late 1950's the municipal hospital system was a two-phase system — six hospitals staffed by medical schools that were getting along reasonably well, medically doing quite well — and sixteen hospitals that were in varying stages of deterioration [1967: 211].

The six hospitals that had some sort of affiliation in 1960 were: Bellevue, with long-standing links with Columbia, Cornell, and New York University medical schools; Delafield, a special cancer hospital, which was affiliated with Columbia; Metropolitan, which was affiliated with New York Medical College; Ewing, another cancer hospital, which was affiliated with Memorial Hospital for Cancer and Allied Diseases, and, hence, indirectly, with New York Hospital and Cornell Medical Center; Bronx Municipal Hospital Center, which was linked to the Albert Einstein College of Medicine of Yeshiva University; and Kings County Hospital Center, which was affiliated with the Downstate Medical Center of the State University of New York. (Since that time, Ewing has become an integral part of the Memorial complex.) The first four of these hospitals were located in Manhattan; the other two in the Bronx and Brooklyn, respectively.

Hence, the Affiliation Plan of the 1960s represented a broadening of activities that had been carried forward on a smaller, more piecemeal basis for some time. The older arrangement prescribed a rather clear-cut and simple exchange between municipal participants and teaching centers. The university provided house staff, clinical instructors, and medical students under the supervision of clinical staff in return for access to patients of teaching (and secondarily, research) interest. The teaching hospitals bore the financial responsibility for this staffing. The benefit to the city was "reputedly high quality municipal service subsidized by private educational institutions" (Ostow, 1971: 98). In a word, these earlier affiliations more closely resembled the feudal bonds discussed in chapter 2. Under the new plan, the fields affected increasingly began to display the unmistakeable marks of member-elite guidance.

What social forces contributed to the massive expansion of affiliations in the 1960s and hence to their imperialization? Most commentators find much of the explanation in parallel crises in the public (municipal) and private (voluntary) hospital systems. Of the two, the crisis in the municipal system was by far the more acute and more visible.

As far as the city-controlled hospitals are concerned, the history of the twentieth century has been a chronicle of long-term erosion in quality. Evidence of the decline became especially apparent in the decade or so following the end of World War II. A chronic problem had become acute, and the crisis was and still is multidimensional. Municipal hospitals are plagued by skyrocketing costs, limited budgets, major staffing deficiencies, inadequate plant construction and maintenance, and failure to keep abreast of the latest medical technological innovations. All of these converge to raise serious doubts about these hospitals' capacity to deliver adequate health services to a population made up, to an increasing degree, of the indigent and "medically indigent."

While each factor is of critical importance for understanding the deteriorating state of the municipal hospitals, the "keystone" of the crisis is probably the failure to maintain an adequate medical staff. The staffing issue should not necessarily be attributed a special causal priority. Rather, the staffing problem is central because most of the others impinge on it in some way, or flow from it. Thus, inadequate funding and a dilapidated physical plant discourage the potential participation of qualified physicians. In addition, the same demographic shifts that make the population proportionately more indigent, that is, the flight of the white middle class to the suburbs also promote a shift of physicians from the central city to the suburbs. Consequently, municipal hospitals faced with dwindling private practice in ghetto areas suffered a significant attrition in physicians offering their services, which, in turn, forced them to rely more and more on house staff (interns and residents). However, failure to keep up with new medical technology (with its necessary increase in medical specialization and post-graduate medical training) made city hospitals unattractive to American-trained medical graduates. Hence, by 1960, both Harlem Hospital and Gouverneur Hospital were staffed largely by physicians trained overseas who had failed to pass the newly required examinations of the Education Council for Foreign Medical Graduates. Whether either organization could survive was openly debated. Gouverneur lost its accreditation and most of Harlem's house staff was disqualified. The situation at other municipal hospitals was only slightly less acute (for example, certain residency programs at Greenpoint Hospital were eliminated).

The crisis in the voluntary hospitals was relatively less dramatic. Miriam Ostow (1971: 107) describes the incentives to participate in the program by various hospitals:

The strongest and most heavily committed are Einstein, Mount Sinai,

Montefiore, Maimonides, and Beth Israel, aggressive institutions, committed to the medical school teaching-research-centered model of health service leadership and organization, underendowed in terms of their expanding educational and research programs and staff. With the growth of insurance, affiliation offered them a substantial increase of service (teaching) beds and ambulatory patients to supplement their shrinking supply, and additional funds with which to obtain quality staff in an expensive market. To the weaker institutions, for example, Misericordia and Mary Immaculate, it offered the possibility of financial strengthening and professional upgrading to the level of teaching hospitals rather than permanent retreat to the ranks of mediocre community hospitals and the disaccreditation of existing residencies. Middle-rank teaching hospitals, such as Brooklyn Jewish and Brooklyn, also anticipated financial bolstering and improved status. The blue chips of the medical school universe, with substantial funds of their own or from the federal government without encumbrances, and having an exclusionary view of public responsibility, either refused to participate (Cornell-New York Hospital) or undertook limited programs (Columbia-Presbyterian Hospital).

In sum, most voluntary hospitals were caught in the same squeeze of spiralling costs as their municipal counterparts. Hospital administrators claimed that the reimbursements of Blue Cross and other insurance plans failed to keep pace with expenses. In addition, they complained about the city's inadequate level of reimbursement for indigent cases. Although not so hardpressed as the municipal hospitals, the voluntary hospitals also faced a decrease in capital funds for plant and equipment. Consequently, all but the most heavily endowed medical centers (Columbia and Cornell) looked to the Affiliation Plan as a vital source of financial respite.

Affiliation also was viewed as the font of one additional resource − patients. Burlage has reported that "with the rise of more insurance-covered, semi-private and private room patients, medical schools and teaching hospitals faced a shortage of ward patients for expanding research and teaching programs" (1967: 35). Access to municipal hospital patients was expected to relieve this plight.

At the core of the Affiliation Plan, then, lay two central tenets: (1) as many municipal hospitals as possible should be affiliated with medical schools or with voluntary hospitals having "strong" teaching programs; and (2) the financing of the voluntary hospitals should be placed on a sounder basis with affiliation serving as the principal mechanism for compensation by the city. On a more specific level, Burlage (1967: 69-70) suggests that the "medical-political coalition" supporting affiliation had the following "explicit and implicit" agenda for the city-run hospitals:

1. Find higher quality voluntary institutions, medical schools and major teaching hospitals, if possible, to provide more independent and innovative leadership in the different municipal hospitals (that is, end the control of the unaffiliated hospitals by private volunteer-dominated medical boards);

2. Construct and relate municipal hospitals around voluntary teaching hospital and medical center cores;

3. End the civil service administrative and staffing rigidities of the municipal system by transferring as much personnel authority and control to the voluntary agencies as possible;

4. Emphasize at first the financial support of their basic shifts in agency, control, and location, even if it means postponing needed auxiliary staffing and minor supply expenditures — use the leverage of affiliation demands to get at least major equipment purchase and better paid medical staffing;

5. Provide full-time, specialist-qualified chiefs of services and better trained and more innovative administrators for all the hospitals.

However, actual implementation gave the program a distinctly "ad hoc character," in the words of Miriam Ostow (1971: 106). Or, in Commissioner Trussell's own terms, the program was one of "worst things first" or "operation bailout" (see Burlage, 1967: 98). This incremental pattern of implementation is understandable in light of the extensive opposition generated by the original recommendations. By starting with situations that were officially labelled "crises," Trussell sought to fragment resistance. Sayre and Kaufman (1960), among others, have reported that the capacity to dramatize "impending crises" traditionally has been an effective mechanism used by city policy-makers to neutralize opposition to new programs or to legitimate demands for increased appropriations for existing programs. In effect, what Trussell and his supporters had visualized as a single comprehensive policy, became, under the exigencies of New York City politics, a patchwork of distinctive programs. Only in the face of relentless political onslaughts in the late 1960s (capped by an intensive fiscal audit by City Comptroller Mario Procaccino in 1966) was greater uniformity introduced into reviewed affiliation contracts.

The original contracts varied greatly in the services covered and consequently in the magnitude of reimbursement to the affiliate (the voluntary hospital). For instance, inpatient services at Gouverneur were closed and affiliation here consisted of Beth Israel Hospital assuming responsibility for ambulatory services. Other affiliations ranged from complete responsibility by the affiliate for all professional and auxiliary services (medical records, medical library, social service and speech and hearing) as in the case of Montefiore and Morrisania to limited interdepartmental relationships as between Harlem Hospital and Columbia.

Despite these initial variations, by 1965 all but one of the previously unaffiliated municipal hospitals had been linked to voluntary hospitals (Sydenham being the exception). Also, all of the first-round contracts had certain common features. Ostow points to five specific similarities:

1. all affiliates were responsible for providing municipal hospitals with professional (medical) services
2. each contract called for the affiliates to provide full-time chiefs for the services they covered
3. each affiliate undertook to provide house staff to its affiliated hospitals
4. the city retained at least nominal responsibility for the administration of the municipal hospitals, for the upkeep of their physical plants as well as for the provision of supplies and supportive personnel
5. reimbursement to all affiliates was on a cost-plus overhead (10 percent) basis (see Ostow, 1971: 105)

Beginning in 1967, contracts became more uniform and explicit and overall fiscal responsibility was given to an Office of Affiliations of the Department of Hospitals (now the Affiliation Administration of the Health and Hospitals Corporation). Those changes largely resulted from the charges of loose management and accounting procedures levelled by the opponents of affiliation. Ostow (1971: 110) describes the activities of the new office in the following way:

In a series of directives this office introduced limitations and regulations governing such matters as timekeeping, purchase, payroll and standards. Contracts were similarly redrawn for greater specificity and uniformity, and a unit value of equating services was devised as a basis for budgetary computation. Job transfers over a wide range of aides and non-technical categories from city to affiliate payrolls were frozen as of early 1967. The direction. . . was to fix firmly the inherent dualism of the system: professional services deriving from the voluntary sector with its distinctive standards and interests, and management devolving upon the city with a separate set of constraints and commitments.

It is wise to caution against exaggerating the nature of this "dualism." In the realm of management especially, it should be noted that voluntary hospitals always have played some role. The Executive Assistant of the Affiliation Administration told us on April 21, 1971:

> The administrative arrangements for the affiliations vary significantly from hospital to hospital. This is also related in part to whether the affiliate is a voluntary hospital or a medical school. Generally there is a "liaison administrator" whose office is on the premises of the corporate hospital who is employed by the affiliate to administer the contract. In most cases this individual functions in large part as an integral member of the corporate hospital's administrative staff. In addition, there may be other affiliation personnel who have administrative responsibility for certain specific areas such as labs, emergency room, etc. (private communication).

Hence, all affiliates wield some administrative as well as professional power within the affiliated hospitals, although there is no doubt that the city has made some effort since 1967 to maintain its prerogatives in the administrative domain.

As of July 1, 1970, 16 city-owned hospitals with inpatient services had affiliation contracts.[5] The face value of all these contracts is close to $162 million per annum. All but four of the hospitals had more than one contract. The most frequent type of contract is for "general" services; only Coler, Goldwater, and Kings County did not have this type. "General" services include medical care professional services (physicians, technicians, some paramedical personnel) for the usual hospital departments such as

Medicine, Surgery, X-Ray, Laboratory and so on. The second most frequent contract type is for psychiatric services. Eleven of the 16 hospitals have affiliates here. Table 4-1 lists the 16 municipal hospitals that have inpatient services, with whom they are affiliated, the type of contract and the face value of each contract.

A closer examination of Table 4-1 provides some indicators that point to two clusters rather than a single one, under the umbrella of affiliation: the university medical center pattern and the voluntary hospital pattern. In terms of the number of affiliates involved in each cluster, the distribution looks about equal: there are seven voluntary hospitals and there are six university medical centers (if we treat Einstein and Montefiore as one entity). However, the university medical centers are tied to 11 different municipal hospitals whereas the figure for the voluntary hospitals is five. Moreover, five of the six university medical centers have three or more contracts (Columbia 4, N.Y.U. 3, Einstein-Montefiore 5, Downstate 4, New York Medical College 3), while none of the voluntaries has more than two, and four have only one. Indeed, three of the voluntary hospitals share responsibility for one hospital (Queens) and no other; in contrast, none of the university medical centers currently "doubles up" in this way. Rather, four of the six have affiliation contracts with more than one municipal hospital. Perhaps the best single statistic with which to summarize the differences between the two patterns is the flow of payments from the city: the face value of all university medical center contracts is $118,913,942, whereas the voluntary hospitals' total is $42,938,224. Thus, the average university medical center receives $19,818,990 and the average voluntary hospital's affiliation income is $6,134,032. Even if one controls for number of contracts, the preeminent status of university medical centers remains: the average university-linked contract is worth $5,661,569, the average voluntary hospital contract is $4,293,882; that is, the average university contract is $1,368,747 or 31.9 percent higher.

The one interpretation that cannot be applied to these differentials is that university medical centers are being disproportionately rewarded for the same level of service. It is generally agreed that rules governing reimbursement are standardized and monitored. Rather, any "nonconspiratorial" view of the New York medical system must acknowledge that these data illuminate the fact that the university centers are more deeply immersed in the affiliation process. The greater value of the average contract points to the relatively greater penetration into the operations of the municipal hospitals. Montefiore, for instance, is so deeply involved in Morrisania that the contract also calls for the provision of nursing services. Moreover, not only do the university centers tend to be more involved in the typical program, but they also provide more programs to more hospitals.

In sum, those interested in the dynamics of medical empires need not survey the entire spectrum of affiliation relationships. The voluntary-municipal linkages generally are marked by less intensive, less controlling dyadic bonds, while university-municipal affiliations are more intensive, more controlling, and more comprehensive. Further, without primary research it would be unwarranted to claim that all of the voluntary municipal linkages even fit under the rubric of empires. Indeed, there is much about these units that might suggest a feudal setting. Consequently, for those interested in medical empires, the fields dominated by university medical centers are the primary focus of attention.

SEVEN MEDICAL EMPIRES

According to Health-PAC, the New York City medical scene is characterized by seven such empires. With the sole exception of the Cornell University Medical College domain, all of the empires have as their backbone affiliation-derived linkages. Harlem and Delafield are bound to Columbia. Coler and Metropolitan help form the nucleus of the New York Medical College empire. Goldwater, and especially Bellevue, stand at the core of the New York University's empire. Morrisania, Lincoln, and Bronx Municipal are at the hub of the Einstein-Montefiore realm. The massive Kings County Medical Center is the mainstay of the Downstate Medical College empire. Health-PAC puts forward an eighth empire: the Catholic Medical Center empire. But they add that this "is a concept, not an actual institution" (Health-PAC *Bulletin,* 1968b: centerfold). Here the Center apparently means that the last empire is more of an administrative blueprint than an empirical reality.

In the November/December 1968 issue of their *Bulletin,* Health-PAC lists the eight actual and potential empires and their "colonial" outposts as follows:

A. Columbia University-College of Physicians & Surgeons Empire
   1. Presbyterian Hospital
   2. New York State Psychiatric Institute
   3. Francis Delafield Hospital
   4. Harlem Hospital Center
   5. St. Luke's Hospital
      5a. Riverside Neighborhood Health Center [In addition to the listed functioning neighborhood health centers, more than 40 are projected by 1973 in the City budget, most of which will be part of the major medical center empires.]
   6. Roosevelt Hospital
   7. Manhattan Eye, Ear & Throat Hospital
   8. Brookdale Hospital Center (Brooklyn)
      8a. Brownsville Neighborhood Health Center

B. New York Medical College Empire
   9. Flower Fifth Avenue Hospital
   10. Metropolitan Hospital
   11. Bird S. Coler Hospital & Home
   12. St. Vincent's Hospital (Staten Island)
   13. Flushing Hospital (Queens)
   14. Interfaith Hospital (Queens)
   15. Jamaica Hospital (Queens)
   16. Wyckoff Heights Hospital — Main Division (Brooklyn)
   17. Lutheran Medical Center (Brooklyn)

C. Mount Sinai Medical College Empire
   18. Beth Israel Hospital
   19. Gouverneur Ambulatory Care Unit   .
   20. Elmhurst Hospital (Queens)

D. Cornell Medical College Empire
   21. Hospital for Special Surgery
   22. Memorial Hospital
   23. New York Hospital
   24. James Ewing Hospital

E. New York University College of Medicine Empire
   25. Bellevue Hospital
   26. Veterans Administration Hospital
   27. St. Vincent's Hospital
   28. Goldwater Hospital

F. Yeshiva University-Albert Einstein College of Medicine Empire
   29. Montefiore Hospital
      29a. Neighborhood Medical Care Demonstration [Health Center]
   30. Veterans Administration Hospital
   31. Morrisania Hospital
   32. Lincoln Hospital
   33. Bronx Municipal Hospital Center
   34. Bronx State Hospital & Kennedy Mental Retardation Center
      34a. Throgs Neck Community Mental Health Center

G. Catholic Medical Center Empire
   [The Catholic Medical Center is a concept, not an actual institution, which will eventually include a medical school. Capital construction on the six Catholic hospitals listed below will exceed $60 million.]
   35. St. John's Hospital (Queens)
   36. Mary Immaculate Hospital
      36a. Neighborhood Health Center
   37. Queens Hospital Center (partial affiliation with Mary Immaculate)
   38. St. Joseph's Hospital
   39. St. Mary's Hospital
      39a. Neighborhood Health Center
   40. Holy Family Hospital
   41. Providence Hospital (under construction)

H. State University of New York-Downstate Medical College Empire
   42. Long Island Jewish Hospital (Queens)
   43. Greenpoint Hospital (affiliation with Brooklyn Jewish)
      44a. Long Island College Hospital (Prospect Heights)
      44b. Red Hook Neighborhood Health Center
   45. Cumberland Hospital (through affiliation with Brooklyn Hospital)
   46. Brooklyn Hospital
   47. Methodist Hospital
   48. Veterans Administration Hospital
   49. Coney Island Hospital (through affiliation with Maimonides Hospital)
   50. Maimonides Hospital

51. Jewish Hospital of Brooklyn
52. Brooklyn State Hospital
53. Jewish Chronic Disease Hospital
54. Kings County Hospital Center

Clear-cut though it seems, this classification raises several problems. We know why municipal hospitals are part of empires; but we are not informed by what criteria the other units are categorized under imperial centers. Health-PAC never systematically spells out the grounds for imputing the existence of these other bonds. Intentionally or not, this leaves the impression that all units are controlled by an imperial center in the same manner and to the same degree as are the municipal hospitals. For example, can we assume that St. Luke's is linked to Columbia in the same way as Harlem or that Beth Israel is bound to Mt. Sinai in a way similar to Elmhurst? Of course, anyone with any familiarity with the New York health scene knows that this is not the case. For example, a relatively prestigious hospital like St. Luke's inevitably has very different links to Columbia than does Harlem; after all, in 1971, the former, on its own, matched two of its four intern-residency programs completely and overall, matched 17 of its 28 slots, while Harlem in its preaffiliation days could not match at all. Further, a May 14, 1971 article in the *New York Times* suggests that units like St. Luke's, as well as Roosevelt, are not nearly so subordinated to Columbia as is Harlem. The former two units clearly have resources that Columbia needs and must "trade off" for. The *Times* article reports that henceforth St. Luke's and Roosevelt will be fully affiliated with Columbia University. Before the new agreement, the two hospitals had limited linkages: Columbia medical students could receive part of their training at St. Luke's and Roosevelt; and some physicians from these hospitals had Columbia academic appointments. As a result of the new agreement, all new medical staff members will have appointments both from the individual hospital and from Columbia. All new staff members will be on the Columbia faculty and old staff members not on the faculty are to have their status reviewed. Columbia will be permitted, according to the report, to use the "specialized facilities" at each hospital and to develop research programs there.

As far as Beth Israel is concerned, Health-PAC itself variously treats it as a colony of Mt. Sinai Medical School and as an empire in its own right. (See, for example, its October 1970 *Bulletin* in which Beth Israel is designated as the "second medical empire on the lower east side" following N.Y.U.) In any event, the Beth Israel Medical Center directed by Dr. Trussell, the father of Affiliation, hardly can be viewed as merely a passive subordinated unit of Mt. Sinai.

Moreover, Health-PAC is not always consistent about how far the boundaries of medical empires extend. For example, in another publication the realm of Einstein-Montefiore is expanded beyond the above enumeration. Note the following statements (Health-PAC, 1970a: 66) that add three hospitals to the list of "colonies":

> Considered "eminent domain" for Einstein-Montefiore are the two other sizeable hospitals in the Borough, 570-bed Bronx-Lebanon in the west Bronx (also part of the Federation of Jewish Philanthropies), and 330-bed Misericordia in the northeast (a Catholic institution, currently the private affiliating hospital for 400-bed Fordham City Hospital in the west central Bronx). Dr. Cherkasky [director of Montefiore and chairman of Einstein's Department of Preventive Medicine and Community Health] has physicians whom he considers his own people (part-time faculty in Einstein's Department of Community Health) in key program development spots at these two voluntary hospitals. Various approaches are being made by empire promoters toward a Montefiore merger with Bronx-Lebanon and toward a Misericordia-Fordham affiliation with Einstein-Montefiore.

The principal positive value of the quotation is that it does provide us with a clue about the nature of nonmunicipal imperial bonds. It suggests that university appointments are crucial aspects which link other units to empires (compare the case of Roosevelt and St. Luke's vis-a-vis Columbia). However, even if the above quote from Health-PAC's *The American Health Empire* does provide indirect data about the bonds within empires, it nevertheless reminds us that the boundaries of empires have not been reliably circumscribed. The quotation causes us to wonder whether Health-PAC draws the boundaries of empires to serve the political needs of the moment.

A final difficulty with Health-PAC's presentation is that it conveys the image that control configurations are generally as uniform *among* imperial fields as they are *within* any given one. We already have argued that the imputation of internal homogeneity is highly questionable. Similarly, we suggest that Health-PAC has not seriously explored the obvious diversity among empires. For example, in most of their *Bulletins* they refer to the "Einstein-Montefiore" empire, while in the list cited above they speak of the "Yeshiva University-Albert Einstein College of Medicine" empire, and apparently relegate Montefiore to the status of colony. There is no question that elsewhere Health-PAC demonstrates that Montefiore is not a colony. Indeed, the Einstein-Montefiore complex is probably a duopolistic empire presided over by two member-elites, that is, the field has two guiding centers and not one. (We suggest that the bonds between Mt. Sinai and Beth Israel also may be indicative of a duopolistic empire.)

Given Health-PAC's central concerns, failure to be aware of the monopolistic-duopolistic distinction probably is not critical. Nonetheless, it might help in some matters. For example, in contrasting Einstein-Montefiore's "outward bound" style with the "patrician" approach of Columbia, Health-PAC makes much of the former's "aggressive," "Jewish," "liberal," attributes, but says nothing of duopolistic control (Health-PAC, 1970: 66-67). Thus, although they have written more than anyone else about the topic, their publications shed little light on the possible implications of monopolistic versus duopolistic empires for decision-making in a medical field. Neither do they elaborate on the nature of the collaborative practices among the two elite units beyond the fact that Montefiore staff members have Einstein appointments and that they share certain unspecified programs. (For some clue as to the nature of what is obviously a complex association, see the January 6, 1969 article of the *New York Times*, which reports the "merger" of the 375-bed Hospital of the Albert Einstein School of Medicine and the 600-bed Montefiore Hospital. See, too, the announcement in the February 1, 1969 issue of *Hospitals*, p. 22).

In brief, Health-PAC has introduced the concept of empires to the study of health fields and it has demonstrated its general utility by circumscribing the seven medical empires in the city with some degree of accuracy; but it has brought to bear on the issue neither conceptual clarity nor empirical precision. Consequently, its diagnosis of the New York health scene, while often illuminating, never can be accepted at face value. Further, its policy suggestions must be understood and weighed in light of these deficiencies.

SOME FUNCTIONS OF EMPIRES

Because no adequate scientific characterization of medical empires exists, how can we best assess their ability to deliver health services? The strategy we use here is to focus primarily on those aspects of empires about which data have been published, that is, the affiliation contracts, and examine some of their positive and negative consequences. This concentration, although made necessary by the dearth of other data, also makes theoretical sense. Because we are concerned with imperial relationships (member-elite guidance) the university medical center-municipal hospital bond comes close to providing the type-case. As we implied earlier, these are the most likely to be unambiguously imperial (for example, Columbia-Harlem), whereas other bonds in the overall field have a much stronger feudal tinge (for example, Columbia-St. Luke's, Mt. Sinai-Beth Israel). In other words, the university links to municipal hospitals display the most member-elite guidance, but this guidance probably is more diluted in relations with other participating units. As a consequence, affiliation-induced bonds are the most imperialistic sectors of an empire, and the field in general probably tends to be somewhat less dominated by its member-elite.

Empires, by definition, are interorganizational fields where there is more specialized systemic power and, hence, more co-deciding than in a feudal field. What are some of the positive consequences of such arrangements? The study of political empires suggests that fields controlled by member-elites represent settings where system-level resources are used more efficiently and effectively than in more feudal contexts. Transposed to the medical realm this proposition suggests that the building of medical empires improves the scope and quality of services delivered to the public while cutting back on the inefficient duplication of resources within the field. The study of affiliations offers an especially critical instance for testing this proposition because these contracts created formal interorganizational bonds where, generally, there had been none before. Thus, the researcher has the rare opportunity to treat empire-bonds in ways similar to a test-variable in a "before-after" experiment.

The only detailed study of affiliations to date has been Robb K. Burlage's *New York City's Municipal Hospitals: A Policy Review* (1967). This informative monograph has two disadvantages: (1) Health-PAC ideologizing (Burlage is one of the Advisory Center's founding fathers); and (2) the fact that it is slightly dated (it was published in 1967, just before the second wave of more uniform contracts were implemented). Burlage's work nonetheless offers the would-be researcher a compendium of statistics and references. Thus, while his interpretations and conclusions cannot always be uncritically swallowed, Burlage's study and data must be consulted by anyone who seriously wishes to understand the New York health scene and the nature of medical empires in general.

Indeed, Burlage devotes an entire section (pp. 204-244) to a review of the "achievements" of affiliation, which provides us with some tentative indicators of the functions of medical empires. True, much of his review is of the "well, yes . . . but . . ." variety; still, he offers data upon which independent assessments can be based. Burlage organized his list of tainted successes under seven headings:

1. more doctors
2. expanded physician training approval
3. more house staff
4. more modern equipment
5. new construction and renovation
6. more emphasis on research
7. more patients and more services, particularly in clinics.

Items (1) through (3) point to the major reason that the Affiliation Plan was drawn in the first place: to overcome the staffing and educational deficiencies at the municipal hospitals. Burlage generally concedes that affiliation has had some success in this regard. City hospitals tended to improve their positions in the intern and residency matching program, which suggests an increase in both the quantity and quality of house staff. Burlage does offer a few "yes, buts"; but these caveats have to do largely with the fact that relatively weak voluntary hospitals have not been as successful in acquiring and deploying better quality, American-trained house staff as have the university empire centers. As Burlage himself admits in his book, these weak voluntary hospitals were included in the original Affiliation Plan in order to win broader-based political support for the program. But despite these qualifications, it is apparent that full-fledged medical empires attract more qualified house staff into the system and allocate them to units previously manned by persons of inferior professional quality. Further, affiliation has brought more highly trained, Board-eligible and Board-certified medical specialists into municipal hospitals as full-time and part-time attending staff. As a result, the number of approved internship and residency training programs at city-owned hospitals has increased since affiliation.

Regarding equipment, Burlage (1967: 217) concedes:

From the beginning of the expanded affiliations program, a major emphasis was on improving facilities and major equipment with high scientific standards under the direction of the affiliating institutions. Some real improvements were made at each institution in this regard.

As far as construction and renovation are concerned, Burlage (1967: 219) tells us:

A major program of municipal hospital construction stretching throughout the 1960's and already projected into the 1970's, was re-directed and in some cases increased under the affiliation arrangements. In some cases new municipal hospital construction was re-located on voluntary hospital grounds or adjacent land. . . Changes in other previous construction plans resulted. . . . Widespread renovation, painting and expanded maintenance were applied much more generally than before.

Burlage goes on to review the expansion of teaching and research programs at municipal hospitals as a consequence of affiliation. The principal impetus in the teaching sector came from the addition of full-time, salaried chiefs-of-service who held academic appointments at the affiliate.

Speaking of research, he says (1967: 221):

The most striking programmatic difference under the affiliations was the intensive new emphasis on bio-medical and clinical research. There was a transformation of space and equipment to facilitate a whole range of special research projects, which were allegedly attracting better trained physicians into the hospital. . . City hospitals continued to provide the location for new medical breakthroughs under new and old affiliations.

Here Burlage's "yes . . . but" strategy is especially interesting because, like his Health-PAC allies, he tends to view the advocates of teaching and research as the enemy of humane health care. Hence, after noting research advances and the "alleged" implications for staff quality, he (1967: 221) offers the following parenthetical remarks, which neatly summarize a central theme of Health-PAC:

But too often the patient constituency for such specialized breakthroughs was not being well provided with the needed basic general medical and preventive services. In some ways, these patients were becoming more and more eligible for the world's most excellent medical care for the exceptional cases and subject to the most unavailable, inadequate, or negligent medical care for the ordinary case and particularly for preventive services.

The American Health Empire (Health-PAC, 1970a: 47-48) states the case against research — and teaching — more baldly:

The asserted ability of the major teaching hospitals to provide quality care has been apparent only for certain specialized and interesting treatment and diagnostic procedures. The empires' control has usually. been antagonistic to the achievement of medical quality in social terms, i.e., comprehensive, low-cost patient-centered services. . . [I]n many cases, the narrow research, teaching and profit priorities of the private empires have actually led to worsened conditions in the public hospitals, greater fragmentation, dehumanization, and neglect of basic health services. Through the affiliation program, medical empires gained greater power of selection over their patient intake, dumping uninteresting and nonpaying patients on their affiliated public hospitals. In turn, the empire-controlled affiliation staffs at the city hospitals are also more interested in maintaining an interesting mix of patients than in providing public health services, and they dump the least interesting patients on to the city's dumps of last resort — Bellevue, Kings County, Harlem Hospital, etc. If the patient dies in transit while being dumped — as scores are known to have done — that is not considered the fault of the institution which rejected him. In municipal hospitals affiliated with private empires, patients have undergone dangerous and unnecessary diagnostic procedures, chemotherapy and surgery, not in the interests of treatment, but in the interests of research.

What is advocated, in other words, is a kind of zero-sum concept of organizational goals. Inherent in this approach is the position that insofar as an organization (or group of organizations) ceases having only a single goal (patient care) and acquires multiple goals (adds teaching and research), the salience of the original goal and how effectively it is pursued is inevitable diluted; that is, teaching and research systematically undermine patient care. The zero-sum approach neglects the fact that, although different goals are always competitors for limited resources, they also may be mutually supportive. No one, for instance, can deny that the best overall patient care is provided by precisely those hospitals that most heavily engage in research and teaching.

Probably the most critical point to be made here is that we should not view the resources available to an organization as an inevitably fixed quantity. Indeed, a benefit of promoting multiple goals is that they may expand the potential pool of resources (for example, research and teaching attracts more staff, more money, and better equipment to hospitals) as well as increase the capacity to mobilize effectively these resources (for example, better trained, research-oriented doctors can more effectively utilize the latest medical technology).

What is called for, then, is a degree of tolerance of ambiguity by the social analyst: granted, the unbridled pursuit of research and teaching may erode treatment goals, but we must not argue hastily for the total abandonment of these activities. In the final analysis, what the proper mix of the three goals ought to be is not so much for the policy researcher to decide by himself. His more proper role is to ascertain what the costs of different mixes are (both in terms of human and nonhuman inputs), what their various outputs

COORDINATING HEALTH CARE
Explorations in Interorganizational Relations

Volume 17, Sage Library of Social Research

POLICY RESEARCH SERIES

Sponsored by the Center for Policy Research, Inc., (New York)

Series Editor: Amitai Etzioni

Policy research is concerned with developing solutions to societal problems by taking into account both effects and costs on a long- and short-term basis. Unlike "applied" research, policy research is broader and more encompassing—as well as being less abstract than basic research, and more willing to recommend changes and specific courses of action. Policy research also offers alternative lines of approach to the conception and solution of fundamental problems, and to the advancement of major social programs.

Coordinating
Health Care

Explorations in
Interorganizational Relations

Edward W. Lehman

Foreword by AMITAI ETZIONI

Volume 17
SAGE LIBRARY OF
SOCIAL RESEARCH

 **SAGE PUBLICATIONS**   Beverly Hills   London

For information address:

SAGE PUBLICATIONS, INC.
275 South Beverly Drive
Beverly Hills, California 90212

SAGE PUBLICATIONS LTD
St George's House/44 Hatton Garden
London EC1 8ER

International Standard Book Number: 0-8039-0512-2 (p)
0-8039-0442-8 (c)
Library of Congress Catalog Card Number: 75-691

First Printing

FOR BUNNIE

CONTENTS

are likely to be and then to communicate to the society and all interested groups the implications of alternative strategies. Which strategy is more desirable is, however, in the end, a decision based primarily on value premises and only secondarily derived from "facts."

The final "achievement" of affiliation that Burlage cites is "more patients, more services, particularly in clinics," and increased numbers of outpatient and emergency room visits in newly affiliated city hospitals despite the fact that the citywide population remained relatively static. In some cases, he acknowledges the increases as being "dramatic": Gouverneur's outpatient visits increased from 56,009 in 1961 to 155,378 in 1965; and Greenpoint from 110,862 to 170,666 during a comparable period. Burlage (1967: 224) goes on to say:

> The number of clinic specialties and sessions at these municipal hospitals was greatly expanded, including, for example, new comprehensive child care, narcotics treatment, and speech and hearing programs. There also have been rising occupancy percentages of inpatients at some newly affiliated hospitals.

In sum, a self-admitted critic of affiliation and of medical empires offers some substantiation of our hypothesis on the relative benefits of imperial fields. Affiliation apparently has arrested the steep erosion in the delivery of health care services within many municipal hospitals and actually provided some improvement in others. Moreover, it has brought in some new, higher quality resources (both human and nonhuman) and has deployed them in a way that minimizes duplication. Yet, to focus only on functions of empires presents an extremely one-sided picture. In the next section, we consider some of the negative consequences (dysfunctions) of empires. It is worth noting here that some factors have both positive and negative implications. Thus, while it is true that empires prevent duplication by allocating resources more effectively, it is also important to recognize that this distributive system is extremely slanted; that is, resources are dispersed quite unequally.

DYSFUNCTIONS OF EMPIRES

When the functions of "historical bureaucratic empires" are discussed by political sociologists, their statements generally are couched in comparative terms and the bases of the comparison are systems that are even less differentiated and less modernized. When the dysfunctions of political empires are examined, the base of comparison is likely to shift to modern or postmodern nation-states. In a sense, we are told that empires have been more successful than the tribal or feudal systems that preceded them but that they are not nearly so efficacious as the contemporary nation-state. Our own treatment of the dysfunctions of medical empires will be analogous to this mode of evaluation. We have said that medical empires deliver services and allocate resources better than systems in which there is less specialization in systemic power. Now we argue that to assign systemic power to one or more member-elites tends to generate certain constraints on the potential effectiveness of a medical system. Further, we suggest that the impediments to ever increasing effectiveness generated within medical empires are strikingly similar to the limitations faced by historical bureaucratic empires. However, we again caution the reader that the comparison of political and medical realms is based on an analogy and only that. Probably the most important dissimilarity to have in mind prior to launching into our discussion is that political empires are historical types usually appropriate to periods between feudalism and the rise of the nation-state, whereas medical empires are contemporaneous with feudal, mediated, and corporate fields.

The basic dilemmas faced by political empires may be summarized as follows. In premodern empires, imperial policy tends to be superimposed on local systems that remain rather feudal or tribal in character. An important factor, although by no means the only one, which accounts for this lack of transformation within nonelite members of empires is the geographic distance between the metropolitan center and the colonial outposts and the concomitant absence of a technology to compensate for the difficulties in communication and control generated by distance. Consequently, even though guidance occurs within empires, the capacity of the imperial center to control and to guide effectively is severely hampered.

This impaired capacity for control and guidance is not merely a product of communication gaps. Rather, it also stems from the low differentiation of supramembership administrative activities within empires. This means that, compared to the participants in the modern nation-state, the subjects of empires (both individual actors and collectivities) rarely have political roles sharply differentiated from other societal roles (that is, mainly in local communities). Moreover, local traditional ascriptive units and their elites generally carry out what political functions there are and serve as the principal units of political participation. Hence, empires are marked neither by interest groups that cross-cut the formal, member-unit boundaries, nor by extensively developed political and administrative organizations that are structurally autonomous from the member units (including the member-elite).

The persistence of local elites and its correlative — the absence of empirewide elites — diminishes the ability of imperial centers to build strong supramembership identification among other members. Consequently, the commitment that leaders in local communities have to imperial goals and policies is, at best, problematic. Empires often do not effectively control the territories nominally under their sway. Perhaps more critically, the inability to create systemwide elites blocks any possibility of penetrating local structures and reorganizing them along lines more suitable for imperial interests. Indeed, local resistance to imperial domination is sufficiently strong that empires tend to rely more heavily on coercive power than most contemporary nation-states. Because coercion and constraint are likely to promote alienation, imperial control, while territorially extensive, rarely goes very "deep," that is, the scope of political activity and participation is rather narrow.

The absence of a strong supramembership bureaucracy means that the elites at the imperial center are likely to view system issues in terms of their own narrow self-interests; that is, what was good for the Roman Empire was viewed in terms of what was good for Rome. As a result, resources are allocated in a highly unequal manner with the colonial outposts suffering at the expense of the imperial center. Moreover, the center remains highly unresponsive to other units. There is no institutionalized distribution of rights among the ruled. The institutionalized political competition associated with modern democratic society is almost totally absent. Consequently, the whole notion that rulers might in some way be formally accountable to the ruled (which flows from the acknowledgment of the latter's political rights) is practically nonexistent. These factors further narrow the scope of political activity and participation. Can we draw any hypotheses about the dysfunctions of medical empires from the discussion of the strains inherent in political empires?

We suggest that the following problems, originally discovered for political empires, are also present in medical systems dominated by member-elites: *(1) The capacity for effective control and guidance in medical empires remains relatively low, in part because of the low differentiation of units specializing in supramembership administrative activities. (2) The internal organization of the member units is not significantly altered by virtue of empire bonds. (3) The strategic interest groups remain essentially local (clustered in or around member units) and they resist control by the elite unit. (4) The allocation of resources is highly unequal and slanted in favor of the member-elite. (5) There are no institutionalized rules, or only weak ones, on participation by nonelites in decision-making; further there is little institutionalization of rules governing elite unit accountability to other members of the system.*

The relatively low control and guidance capacities of empires are hard to observe directly. Certainly, administrative facades for guidance exist (for example, the Health and Hospital Planning Council), but administrative facades frequently are empty shells or, at best, mediating agencies coordinating activities among empires. Within empires, administration is synonomous with the internal administrative apparatus of the member-elites; that is, an empire is not a corporation. Consequently, control is inferred more readily from an examination of what empires have and have not done since their consolidation following implementation of the Affiliation Plan. That is, we can ask whether affiliation to a university medical center has altered drastically the operation of the municipal hospitals or whether things have changed only marginally. In the section on positive consequences, the incremental accomplishments of empires were reviewed. The data were drawn from Burlage's study and, to some degree, they were drawn out of context. The principal thrust of his lengthy monograph is the charge that affiliation has changed the overall situation of the municipal hospitals very little. Miriam Ostow, who may have less of a political axe to grind, comes to the same conclusion in her short paper on affiliations. She tells us (1971: 116-117):

> Municipal hospitals are committed to provide medical services to the poor; the objectives of the voluntary sector, specifically its most exemplary subset, the teaching hospitals, are explicitly multifunctional — patient care, clinical instruction, and research constitute an interlocking triad which informs both policy and standards. In contracting with the teaching hospitals for service *implicitly* at their level of quality, the city gave little hard thought to the cost and functional implications of such an alliance. The innovative relationship in the fluid hospital system did not simply fill a void; it developed a momentum of its own with unanticipated consequences for both networks. The claim of the voluntary institutions upon the city financing was extended beyond historic tax abatement and per diem reimbursement for care of indigent patients to payment for the application of their standards of professional service in the operation of the municipal hospitals. With the outreach of this new standard it became increasingly evident with the passage of time that the infusion of physician manpower alone into the municipal system would not suffice to insure quality care. . . What was the nature of the city's plan to upgrade its hospitals? Essentially, the affiliation contracts constitute a system of inputs linked to a conceptualized but undefined output, "quality care." Given the unresolved problems of quality and output measurement inherent in the production of medical services and the affiliation system's passivity even in the areas of program review and overview what could eventuate? Despite avowed improvement, grave systemic deficiencies persist — deficiencies that are discernible to any observer and that have been repeatedly documented by investigation. With increasing expenditure of public funds, there has been a reversion to the classic strategy to meet public criticism and the exposure of deficiencies with the imposition of administrative restrictions and an at least partial return to the *status quo ante* of tight fiscal control.

Curiously, use of the label "imperialism" obscures the fact that empires suffer not so much from overcontrol as from ineffective guidance. Ostow's statement points to this and Burlage concurs when he says: "Many municipal hospitals were caught in dual administrative patterns with neither private nor public authority to coordinate the hospital's operations" (1967: 268). Regardless of ideological position, most observers of the affiliation scene are in agreement that the university medical centers have not intervened decisively enough to transform the municipal system. They tend to look to the public sector to provide adequate guidance for the overall field albeit the observers advocate different policies. The Piel Commission report of 1967 visualized such a remedy with its recommendation that a public corporation be responsible for a single system of health care in the city (*Community Health Services for New York City,* 1969). However, when the Health and Hospitals Corporation actually was established in 1970, the voluntary hospitals were able to have themselves excluded from any direct guidance by the Corporation, thus leaving the latter in control of the same municipal hospitals formally under the jurisdiction of the city's department of Hospitals. (The Health and Hospital Corporation will be discussed further in the next chapter. See also *Community Health Services for New York City* − 1969.)

The lack of effective guidance within and among New York medical empires alerts us to another critical dissimilarity between medical and political domains. Medical empires are encased or "nested" in larger systems that impinge heavily on their operations. Obviously, political empires also are affected by external exigencies. However, the medical empires are woven together largely by a web of local, state, and federal health regulations and agencies as well as with units in the private sector such as Blue Cross. These agencies have the potential to serve as guiding corporations for networks of empires in ways units exterior to political empires generally do not. Hence, much more of the variance in policy-relevant behavior within medical empires is accounted for by these external forces than within political empires.

We do not imply here that the government (or the insurance industry or anyone else) has begun to provide truly effective guidance to the overall health care field. Indeed, both Burlage and Ostow have made clear that, at least as far as the guiding of affiliations is concerned, governmental intervention has been disappointing.

The second dysfunction of medical empires we put forward is that the internal organization of the member units is not appreciably altered by empire bonds. In a sense, we just have been speaking about this issue because the absence of significant change was used as a major index of low-guidance capacity. Burlage presents the argument for this in extremis when he holds that the major professed goals were not fulfilled. He state (1967: 267-70):

> *The integration of public "charity" and private "paying" hospital care through application of more private hospital medical resources to the municipal hospitals was, in fact, not achieved. The attraction of the high quality of medical resources in the major voluntary teaching hospital centers and medical schools* occurred only in a piecemeal and secondary way... *Elimination of the rigidities of the public sector* of health services — restricted salaries, bureaucratic bottle-necks, agency conflicts — was not achieved... *Ending of the generally dreadful conditions in municipal hospitals* because of inadequate maintenance, auxiliary staffing, and routine supply ... was not achieved in most cases because expenditures and administrative efforts were not concentrated on these "supplementary" areas until too late... *Elimination of what had often been narrow medical and social orientation among the private practitioner — dominated medical boards* of the previously unaffiliated municipal hospitals was achieved in many cases only by replacing them ... with full-time and part-time medical specialists without any ability to organize the general hospital... *Increase of expenditure by the City for the improvement of care for the medically needy* was diluted greatly by the looseness, ineffectuality, and indirectness in actual services-payoffs... *Claims of less costly as well as more effective physician recruiting* ... were often vitiated by the overwhelming increases in salaries, fees, and fringe benefits required to fill positions under affiliations... *The strategic assertion that emphasis on core-hospital physician staffing as the first priority* would lead to improvement of auxiliary staffing over a length of time did not prove to be true after five years... *The strategic projection that emphasis on improving medical programming in the hospital inpatient and specialized clinic setting first* ... would lead to more improvement of health services in the general community ... did not prove true after five years.

The third dysfunction ascribed to medical empires is that their failure to develop viable empirewide interest groups produces a high potential for local resistance to centralized decision-making. The resisting local units need not hold formal elite positions within a given hospital or even be hospital personnel; often they are community-based interest groups demanding more "community control" and denouncing the "exploitation" by the imperial center. During the early stages of the Affiliation Plan, resistance tended to come from local medical elites (medical boards of municipal hospitals and local practitioners) who felt threatened by the influence of the voluntary hospitals, their administrators, their clinical and teaching staffs, and their house staffs. Opposition was especially strong at Elmhurst, Fordham, and Harlem. However, these conservative forces ultimately lost the battle over affiliation.

More recently, the opposition has come from community interest groups whose orientations are not conservative but militant in nature. While many municipal hospitals linked to empires have experienced some controversy over community control, none has had as many episodes or more dramatic ones than Lincoln Hospital. Lincoln is a 360-bed unit in the South Bronx affiliated with Albert Einstein. It is located in a run-down, high crime area populated largely by Puerto Ricans and Blacks. The intensity of the community response probably is caused by the magnitude of the medical problems faced by the neighborhood, plus the fact that Einstein initially actively encouraged community participation only to find that it could not be controlled once mobilized.

During 1970 alone, there were four separate instances in and around hospital property of multiple arrests of community activists protesting alleged injustices. The major crises during that year had five separate focal points.[6] Early in the year, the local interest groups fought for and finally succeeded in obtaining the appointment of a Puerto Rican doctor as hospital administrator. Later protests focused on demands for the establishment of a preventive medicine program, an attack on the department of obstetrics and gynecology over an allegedly "genocidal" abortion program and efforts to oust the chief psychiatrist. However, the most publicized crisis of the year occurred in pediatrics where local groups, including a consumer group called "Think Lincoln" and the Young Lords, in tandem with the "Pediatrics Collective," spearheaded by the newly recruited activist house staff, managed to bring about the resignation of the department chief in favor of a Puerto Rican doctor. This crisis became a major political event in New York during which charges and countercharges of racism and anti-Semitism were acrimoniously exchanged.

The pediatrics crisis is important because it highlights a potentially new coalition emerging between community groups and more politically active young physicians. The pattern is of interest here because it points out that local, nonconservative resistance also can develop within the hospital among the staff. Einstein obviously accelerated the process when in 1969 it deliberately recruited interns for Lincoln especially for their political commitment. However, the internal resistance is not necessarily restricted to house staff. In 1969, Lincoln was the scene of an earlier "rebellion," which led to the resignation of Dr. Harris Peck, the director of Lincoln's Mental Health Service. At the center of this action were the so-called indigenous paraprofessionals, that is, nonprofessional mental health workers recruited from the community. Also involved in the action were social workers and psychologists from the program.[7] However, in all the Lincoln crises that we have cited, staff opposition to empire control tended to remain hospital-centered, that is, the staff does not seem to have organized effectively on an across-hospital basis. Thus, when house staff have taken antiempire positions they have ordinarily done so as a local interest group although they originally came from outside the community. (Of course, there are some groups that represent interns' and residents' interests on a more systemwide basis. The Committee of Interns and Residents − C.I.R. − which claims to represent more than 1,500 house staff at municipal hospitals and at a few voluntary hospitals is such a group. However, it seems to be functioning primarily as a kind of trade union. For a detailed discussion of the "new breed of doctors," with a special emphasis on C.I.R., see Health − PAC Bulletin, 1968b.)

It is wise to remember that the intensity and magnitude of the conflict at Lincoln probably is accounted for in part because Einstein initially encouraged community participation and political activism by the house staff. This could lead some to argue that the local resistance in medical empires is substantially different from that in political empires because the former actually created and nurtured its future opposition. However, we suggest that this also often occurs in political situations. The political imperial center may give indigenous elites numerous privileges but these cannot guarantee their loyalty during times of turmoil because their orientations may remain primarily local in nature. Moreover, political motives enter into the mobilization of local elites both in the political and medical sectors. Political empires need local support to obtain resources and acquiescence. The same is true of medical empires; but, in addition, higher level units — that is to say, the federal government — often require community mobilization as a prerequisite for funding.

The fourth dysfunction of medical empires is the unequal allocation of resources among members so that their dispersal is slanted in favor of the imperial center. A major determinant of this inequality is the tendency by the imperial center to see its own interests and the interests of the entire system as almost totally synonymous. This is true both of political empires and of medical empires. The plan to put a new Morrisania Hospital on the premises of Montefiore in the northeast Bronx demonstrates the empire mentality. Such relocation would have made the logistics of affiliation easier for Montefiore. Yet, if the plan had been implemented, no facility would have replaced Morrisania in the socially and economically depressed southeast corner of the borough. Intensive community pressure ultimately led to a program for building the new Morrisania close to the old one.

However, factors unique to the American health care system further compound the tendencies toward inequality in medical empires. Chief among these is the fact, previously mentioned, that medical empires are not self-contained entities but are "nested" in larger systems where local, state, and federal agencies have the potential for considerable penetration. Especially salient here is the fact that medical empires increasingly are financed by federal funds to promote research, training, and "demonstration projects." These monies play a crucial role in the health field. Health care units are not like industrial organizations; that is, they do not have the capacity to overcome their own financial insolvency, especially in light of the spiraling cost of medical care. Increasingly, hospitals and other units have looked to government grants to relieve their financial plight. However, not all units are equally successful fund raisers in this regard. Federal monies tend to be put into medical empires through the imperial center because it alone has the staff and resources to develop acceptable programs, as well as the reputation to assure the granting agency that the funds will be appropriately used. The flow of grants to the imperial center not only gives it financial leverage over other member units, but grants bring expensive equipment into the system (for example, hyperbaric chambers) and these tend to be located on elite-unit premises. Moreover, even when funds are for programs at member units (for example, a community mental health center at Lincoln) they are likely to be channelled through the imperial center because it provides the key professional and administrative staff.

Of course, those who charge that the member-elite unit gains a disproportionate share of the field's resources do not limit their attacks to the area of government grants. Burlage lists ten "direct benefits" that voluntary hospitals, especially university medical centers, derive from affiliation. All of these are resources (in the broad sense of the term) over which they have increased their control. The list includes:

1. increased working capital, especially capital funds
2. augmented educational and research revenues
3. greater selective access to clinical cases often leading to the expansion of approved residency programs
4. more citywide control over patient admissions
5. increased space for private paying patients
6. greater prestige
7. a broader base for professional and subprofessional employment
8. access to new equipment
9. expansion of research programs
10. increased control over the "regional planning process"

We cannot ascertain from Burlage's listing the degree to which the differential allocation of resources represents more rational distribution that avoids duplication (for example, one cobalt machine per empire after all is sufficient) versus the degree to which it is the outgrowth of exploitation. Inevitably, the effective division of labor means that some units will have things that other units do not have. However, at the moment we possess no sociological calculus that allows us to determine when inequality is the result of differential needs and when it is the outgrowth of differential power and privilege. Nevertheless, it seems hard to justify in purely functional terms the existing concentration of resources in the hands of the imperial center. In fairness, on the other hand, it must be said that the gap that currently exists between university medical centers and municipal hospitals predates the solidification of empires under affiliation. Indeed, affiliation has increased the absolute flow of resources to the municipal hospitals. But in the last analysis, it does not appear to have succeeded in reducing the relative differentials between affiliate and affiliated hospitals.

The final dysfunction of medical empires considered here is that they are marked by the absence of anything approaching a democratic political process. The existing constituencies have not been effectively brought into the decision-making process. Efforts in this regard have been sporadic and have frequently resulted in turmoil (for example, at Lincoln). Other potential constituencies — especially those which might cross-cut local administrative boundaries — remain largely unmobilized, for example, insurance subscribers, paraprofessionals, house staff. Thus there are few institutionalized rules in empires that prescribe access by nonelites to those making decisions that affect them. Moreover, there is no mechanism for accountability; that is, there are few rules that require that the elite legitimate to subordinate units what they are doing. Consequently, medical empires tend to be very weak in their capacity to build supramembership identifications and to generate normative bonds. In addition, this may result in "crises of legitimacy" in empires similar to those found in some mediated fields (see chapter 3).

Of course, there is an accountability in medical empires, but it is not the accountability to constituencies that political analysts ordinarily speak about. Rather, to varying degrees, medical empires are accountable to agencies in the larger system in which they are "nested." For example, the introduction of more standardized affiliation contracts in 1967 has made affiliates far more accountable to the city government (and now to the Health and Hospitals Corporation) especially in the realm of budgets.

However, no one is quite certain how effective these mechanisms for accountability are beyond the tightening of fiscal control. Certainly, successful guidance by the city, which flows in part from effective accountability, does not exist in the health sector.

Here again, we must caution about being too simple-minded about the analogy between political and medical systems. There is a general understanding of what participation and accountability mean in the political sector as well as a relative consensus among those committed to the ideal of democratic policy on why participation and accountability are good things. What do these terms signify when they are applied to the health sector? Should patients vote for medical directors? What indeed are the basic units of representation? Should medical policy only be implemented with the consent of the governed? These issues are too broad for the present chapter. However, we will return to them in our concluding chapter when the policy implications of our analyses are discussed.

OTHER EMPIRES

As we stated earlier, New York was selected because it was a strategic research site, rich in documentation about the operation of medical empires. However, New York City is not the only locus of medical empires in the United States. We suggest that wherever there is a health network that contains a university medical center, the language of medical empires is likely to increase our understanding of what is going on. Nonetheless, only in New York has there been a comprehensive effort to study these empires, to chart their boundaries, and to point out their consequences (the positive, the negative, or both).

A possible exception to this rule is found in *The Politics of Mental Health* by Robert H. Connery and his associates. The book contains case studies of the political factors that shape the organization of community mental health programs in Houston, Seattle, New Orleans, Syracuse, Boston, and Minneapolis – St. Paul. In none of these case studies are medical empires in themselves explored. Rather, the analyses focus on mental health empires or only those aspects of medical empires that bear on

mental health. The Houston State Psychiatric Institute is typical
of the kind of empire found in this study. We are told:

> [T]he Houston State Psychiatric Institute (and Baylor Medical School's
> Department of Psychiatry; the two are virtually synony-
> mous) . . . provides the psychiatric staff for the county Psychiatric
> Diagnostic Center and . . . for the psychiatric services available at the
> city-county charity hospital. HSPI furnishes consultants for the county
> school superintendent's program of psychological services for school
> districts, and for the various school districts that provide services
> beyond what the county superintendent offers. While relevant to their
> function, most private social agencies buy a few hours of psychiatric
> consultation each month, and HSPI is the chief provider. It has
> developed a training program in cooperation with the Child Guidance
> Center and is similarly engaged with the Junior League Out-Patient
> Clinic and Texas Children's Hospital. The outpatient clinic for alco-
> holics at Methodist Hospital is staffed and serviced by HSPI. Institute
> personnel are involved in the management of two small local
> foundations in the mental health field. The list could be extended
> further, but the point is surely clear: the Houston State Psychiatric
> Institute comes close to omnipotence. Involvement is not necessarily
> policy leadership. The institute is undoubtedly handicapped in trying to
> play any kind of leadership role by its status as administrative unit of
> state agency, particularly when the state office has at times been less
> than enthusiastic about community involvement. It is no doubt limited
> as well by the fact that it is a relatively new institution, still occupied
> with a host of internal administrative and organizational problems.
> And, of course, there is the intractability of the community and its
> institutions. One cannot honestly state that the Psychiatric Institute has
> been a highly successful leader in mental health, although it does
> overshadow all others (Connery, 1968: 130-131).

As an analysis of a health empire, the discussion is not nearly so
thorough as what has been written about New York medical
empires. (Of course, this is largely because Connery and his
colleagues were not primarily concerned with the same issue of
imperialism as Burlage, Health-PAC, Ostow, et al.) Nevertheless,
some of the things we said about empires in our treatment are
affirmed in this excerpt. Notably, HSPI, like other medical
empires, guides but does not guide effectively. Much of its
behavior can be understood only in terms of the larger system

within which it is nested. Furthermore, its colonies do not seem to have any deep commitments to the empire. The passage also suggests some stirrings of community resistance — although it is not clear whether the passage is speaking of the community at large or of pockets of local interest groups clustered around particular mental health facilities.

Despite its different focus, the vast majority of empires touched on in *The Politics of Mental Health* is associated with universities. However, because much of the hospital administration literature is concerned with operating efficiency rather than control configurations, it is difficult to detect reports on other interorganizational bonds that might point to possible medical empires. The literature on satellites, multiple-unit hospitals, and mergers undoubtedly contains cases of empires. However, it is difficult, if not impossible, to substantiate that there is indeed a member-elite unit that presides over the field. In any event, although not uncommon, these certainly are not the major instances of empires either in terms of frequency or in terms of the delivery of health services in the United States.

SUMMARY AND CONCLUSIONS

In this chapter we have considered guidance of health care fields by member-elites. Because of their visibility and significance for the national health scene, New York's medical empires were selected for intensive examination. At the core of six of these seven empires are affiliation contracts that link university medical centers to decaying municipal hospitals. The affiliations constitute the most imperial sector of empires. An examination of these bonds suggests that they have both positive and negative effects on the delivery of health services. Positively, they have arrested or slowed the deterioration process by bringing in new resources and allocating them more effectively. On the other hand, empires have failed to make anything more than surface incremental changes, they have failed to mobilize the support of their constituencies, they have benefited mainly the empire builders, and hence, while they have guided, it has been with only limited effectiveness.

Little has been said in this chapter about the content of

interorganizational relations. It is difficult from the literature to make definitive statements about this aspect of our paradigm as it applies to empires. We gain the impression, however, that empires are focused mainly on goal-related activities and that money as a generalized medium of exchange is at least as critical as in mediated fields. The scope of transactions seems to be broad with many different types of goal-relevant resources exchanged. Finally, as we have implied in our treatment of inequality, the imperial center controls the lion's share of resources so that exchanges seem to be more asymmetrical than in feudal or mediated fields.

We have noted also at several points that empires are not autonomous entities but are nested in larger control configurations. We now move to consider these configurations.

NOTES

1. See the May 1971 issue of the Health-PAC Bulletin, "America in Vietnam: Democracy for Dead People," which intertwines a discussion of U.S. debacles in Southeast Asia with a critique of the American health system — notably the V.A. hospitals.

2. The boundaries of New York's health empires are never static but always shifting. Moreover, the affiliation contracts that are the core of most empires (see below) also are periodically realigned. Hence, the portrait of empires presented in this chapter reflects largely the period from 1968 to 1971. Although there have been subsequent changes, these is no way affect our basic propositions. The reader should recall that our main focus is theoretical rather than historical.

3. Our subsequent discussion of the Affiliation Plan, its implication for medical empires, as well as its functions and dysfunctions rests primarily on these sources: Burlage (1967), Health-PAC (1970) and Ostow (1971).

4. These data are drawn from Hiestand (1971: especially 12).

5. The linkage between Gouverneur and Beth Israel is no longer formally an affiliation. Their ties are now part of a program in Ghetto Medicine supervised by the New York City Health Services Administration.

6. Our brief description of the five crises at Lincoln are based on reports in the *New York Times*. See the following 1970 issues of the *Times:* January 31; February 2 and 3; March 4, 5, 6, and 7; June 28; July 8, 15, 16, 29 and 30; August 4, 6, 26, 27, 28, 29, 30 and 31; September 1, 2, 3, 4, 8, 17, and 18; October 16; November 11, 17, 18, 19, 20, 21, 23, 24, and 29; December 4, 8, 11, 14, and 22.

7. For a discussion of Lincoln's mental health crisis, see the following 1969 issues of the *Times:* March 5, 6, 7, 8, 9, 19, 21 and 25; and August 9.

REFERENCES

BURLAGE, R. (1967) New York City's Municipal Hospitals: A Policy Review. Washington, D.C.: Institute for Policy Studies.

CONNERY, R. H. (1968) The Politics of Mental Health. New York: Columbia Univ. Press.

EISENSTADT, S. N. (1963) The Political Systems of Empires. New York: Free Press.

ETZIONI, A. (1965) Political Unification. New York: Holt, Rinehart & Winston.

FIELDHOUSE, D. K. (1966) The Colonial Empires: A Comparative Survey from the Eighteenth Century. London: Weidenfeld & Nicolson.

HEALTH Policy Advisory Center [Health-PAC] (1968a) "Interns and Residents: City Hospital Neglect Challenged." Bulletin 3 (August): 1-12.

——— (1968b) "Medical empires: who controls?" Bulletin 6 (November/December):1-8.

——— (1970a) The American Health Empire: Power, Profits, and Politics. New York: Random House.

——— (1970b) "Empire roundup: caught in the squeeze." Bulletin 24 (October): 1-14.

——— (1971) America in Vietnam: democracy for dead people." Bulletin 31 (May): 1-19.

HIESTAND, D. L. (1971) "Pluralism in health services," pp. 10-31 in Eli Ginzberg (ed.) Urban Health Services: The Case of New York. New York: Columbia Univ. Press.

HOSPITALS (1969) "Consolidation Announced by Two New York Hospitals." Volume 43 (February): 118.

NEW YORK TIMES (1969) January 6, March 5, 6, 7, 8, 19, 21 and 25, August 9.

——— (1970) January 31, February 2 and 3, March 4, 5, 6, and 7, June 28, July 8, 15, 16, 29 and 30, August 4, 6, 26, 27, 28, 29, 30 and 31, September 1, 2, 3, 4, 8, 17 and 18, October 16, November 11, 17, 18, 19, 20, 21, 23, 24, and 29, December 4, 8, 11, 14 and 22.

——— (1971) May 14.

OSTOW, M. (1971) "Affiliation contracts," pp. 96-119 in Eli Ginzberg (ed.) Urban Health Services: The Case of New York. New York: Columbia Univ. Press.

PIEL, G. (1969) Community Health Services for New York City: Report and Staff Studies of the Commission on the Delivery of Personal Health. New York: Praeger.

SAYRE, W. S. and H. KAUFMAN (1960) Governing New York City: Politics in Metropolis. New York: Russell Sage.

TRUSSELL, R. E. (1967) "Current effort in the municipal hospitals." Bulletin of the New York Academy of Medicine 24. (March): 211-218.

TABLE 4-1

TYPES AND FACE-VALUES OF HOSPITAL AFFILIATION CONTRACTS IN NEW YORK CITY AS OF JULY 1, 1970

Hospital	Affiliate	Service	Face Value
Bellevue	N.Y.U.	General	$7739719
Bellevue	N.Y.U.	Psychiatry	5347279
Bronx	Einstein	General	15481338
Bronx	Einstein	Psychiatry	2905000
Coler	N.Y. Med. Col.	Chronic	4370000
Coney Is.	Maimonides	General	7446200
Coney Is.	Maimonides	Psychiatry	1061000
Cumberland	Brooklyn	General	6893000
Cumberland	Brooklyn	Psychiatry	558769
Delafield	Columbia	General	1987875
Elmhurst	Mt. Sinai	General	13059293
Elmhurst	Mt. Sinai	Psychiatry	1569000
Fordham	Misericordia	General	6338700
Goldwater	N.Y.U.	Chronic	4090000
Greenpoint	Bklyn Jewish	General	5227866
Greenpoint	Bklyn Jewish	Psychiatry	299899
Harlem	Columbia	General	16592572
Harlem	Columbia	Psychiatry	2378491
Harlem	Columbia	Alcoholic	143220
Kings County	Downstate	Radiology	2411365
Kings County	Downstate	Ped/OPD	1738700
Kings County	Downstate	Child Psy.	1395000
Kings County	Downstate	Alcoholic	603272
Lincoln	Einstein	General	9145818
Lincoln	Einstein	Psychiatry	997600
Metropolitan	N.Y. Med. Col.	General	14343100
Metropolitan	N.Y. Med. Col.	Psychiatry	2640000
Morrisania	Montefiore	General + Nurs.	9995300
Morrisania	Montefiore	Psychiatry	*
Queens	Long Is. Jewish	General	12587550
Queens	Mary Immac.	General	947338
Queens	Hillside	Psych. & Alcoh.	1577902
Total			$161852166

* Not yet implemented.

SOURCE: Data provided by the New York City Health and Hospital Corporation.

CHAPTER 5

CORPORATION-GUIDED FIELDS:
CONTROL FROM ABOVE

In analyzing and comparing different control configurations, we generally have adopted a nonevolutionary stance. That is, we have treated feudal, mediated, and imperial patterns largely as contemporaneous phenomena; the simpler types are not viewed merely as stepping-stones toward an inevitable development of more complex ones. Similarly, these three patterns are not solely recent developments; rather, forms of all (including empires) have been prevalent for quite some time. However, any treatment of the final type, the medical corporations, must view it as eminently contemporary, because its most significant empirical manifestations are deliberate responses to the current crisis in the delivery of health services. This is not to suggest that there were no medical corporations until recently (for example, municipal departments of health have been around for a long time; the Kaiser-Permanente system — discussed later — has existed since World War II). Nonetheless, in the past decade or so there has been a major push in the public as well as the private sectors toward increased corporate guidance.

This trend is based on the assumption that the delivery of health services will improve when multiple health care units coordinate their activities under the aegis of a superordinate agency that will administer all of them. On a deeper level, the rise of those whom Robert Alford has called "corporate rationalizers" is associated with a growing belief that the "sickness" of the American health system can be cured largely by stressing such themes as cost-consciousness, administrative rationality, managerial efficiency, and so on. (See Alford, 1972.) The corporate rationalist perspective implicitly assumes that health delivery systems will improve once efficient administrative superstructures are developed and, hence, that the delivery problem is most effectively tackled from the top down, that is, by first rationalizing the bureaucratic shell in which networks of health care units are nested.

This emphasis has exposed medical corporations and their advocates to charges that they are callous, that they "don't really change anything," and so on. In fairness, the corporate rationalist perspective has been implemented so recently that it is impossible to judge whether indirect reform-from-above will lead utlimately to a major transformation in how illness is defined, diagnosed, and treated. Nevertheless, the criticisms pinpoint the key issue upon which the success or failure of corporate rationalism ultimately rests: Is the satisfactory delivery of health services subject to the same criteria of success as the manufacture of goods? Moreover, they alert the observer to the fact that medical corporations are vulnerable to the same charge as medical empires. that is to say, that they are predominately concerned with "downward" control and that they largely stifle demands that flow "upward" from the community, from consumers, from staff, and so on.

MERGERS: AN ELEMENTARY FORM

All of the corporations we discuss in this chapter face these difficulties, albeit in varying intensities. They are found even among hospital mergers, although not all mergers are, strictly speaking, instances of corporate fields. As we noted in the preceding chapter, mergers frequently have many of the characteristics of interorganizational empires. However, some mergers also often resemble corporations in the sense that the functional units remain intact after consolidation (that is, most hospitals retain their own physical plants, which are now called divisions, branches, and so on) while the significant element that is added is a new administrative overlayer that is responsible for all the member units and not bound to any single one. Insofar as a particular merged entity qualifies for the label "corporation," it probably represents a relatively elementary manifestation of this type. This is likely to be the case because mergers occupy the "grey zone" that is at the interface of intraorganizational fields, empires, and corporations. It is especially worth noting that mergers, formally speaking at least, are efforts to convert interorganizational fields into intraorganizational ones in the name of cost-consciousness, managerial efficiency, and so on. (For a theory of hospital mergers, see Starkweather, 1970.)

Hospital mergers, then, if they lead to medical corporations at all, are likely to produce rather circumscribed fields that appear quite minuscule, ecologically and sociologically, compared to some of the corporation networks we consider later in this chapter (for example, the Kaiser-Permanente Plan, the Health and Hospitals Corporation of New York, Regional Medical Programs). Despite these differences, however, mergers seem motivated by the same corporate rationalist orientation as other corporate patterns; hence, they exhibit some of the same dynamics. The case of the Wilmington Medical Center is instructive here.

Dr. Ernest C. Shortliffe (1968: 109), the first director of the medical center, describes the factors promoting its formation in the following terms:

Between the period from 1959 through 1963, in Wilmington among the boards of directors of three equal-sized community general hospitals, there was a preoccupation with rising operating and capital costs and with the deterioration of medical education as measured in terms of quantity and quality of intern and resident applicants, as well as the quality of ongoing medical education for the members of the three medical staffs. Efforts were made through a mechanism of cooperation not only to resolve some of these problems but to examine their implications and possible new and somewhat startling methods of reorganization. These efforts at voluntary cooperation, in the opinion of the three hospital boards involved as well as the medical leaders of the community, were not highly successful.

The hospitals involved were Delaware Hospital, with a 378 bed-capacity, Memorial Hospital, with a capacity of 360, and

Wilmington General Hospital, with 317 beds; all were private, nonproft units. In response to their lack of success in voluntary cooperation, the three hospitals in 1963 agreed to create a Joint Hospital Management Committee (made up of representatives of the three boards as well as two prominent physicians) to examine all possible means of coordinating their programs. After approximately ten months of deliberations, the Joint Committee made a unanimous recommendation to the three boards for the total corporate merger of the hospitals and for the retention of a full-time executive director to prepare a detailed proposal for merger. The three boards accepted this recommendation. The Proposal for Merger was completed in May 1965, voted upon by the three medical staffs, and subsequently approved by the three boards of directors. The three units were officially merged on November 1, 1965, as the Wilmington Medical Center. In line with the corporate rationalist orientation that seems to underlie many mergers, the creation of a new administrative overlayer (the consolidation of administrative operations) took precedence over efforts at significant alteration within units engaged in the direct delivery of health services. At the time of merger, former administrators within the individual hospitals assumed staff functions (for example, director of fiscal affairs, director of supportive services, director of special services, director of planning service, and so on.) under the executive director. The assistant directors became the administrators of the three ecologically distinct divisions of the medical center and they too were expected to report directly to the executive director. The latter, in turn, reported to a combined board of directors drawn from the trustees, who were unified at the time of merger. The medical staffs, however, were given a full year to establish unification. To this end, an Interim Medical Advisory Board was created to develop a set of by-laws for a single clinical system.

Some unification of clinical services has taken place since administrative consolidation. On October 3, 1966, the three medical staffs were formally merged; three sets of clinical departments were replaced by a single set with only one set of departmental directors. However, merger does not seem to have been uniform from department to department. "The primary services affected," said Dr. Shortliffe in 1968, "were obstetrics and gynecology, pediatrics, medicine, and general surgery" (1968: 110). He (1968: 110-111) elaborates these transformations as follows:

(a) *Obstetrics and Gynecology.* — This service was totally eliminated in one of the three divisions, and agreement was reached to concentrate obstetrics and gynecology in the remaining two divisions or hospitals of the Wilmington Medical center. At the same time it was agreed that all ward service and teaching services be concentrated in one of the two divisions involved. This represented essentially a consolidation of an obstetrical service involving over 5,500 births per year and a gyneocological service involving approximately 3,500 gynecological procedures per year.

(b) *Pediatrics.* — The Department of Pediatrics was consolidated in one of the three divisions even though the particular division chosen was not the division in which the primary obstetrical and gynecological teaching program was consolidated. This gave us a pediatric unit of approximately 100 beds plus the usual newborn facilities.

(c) *Department of Medicine.* — The primary teaching service in the Department of Medicine at the ward level was consolidated into one of the three divisions. In addition, a private teaching service was established not only in the division but in a second division of the remaining two.

(d) *General Surgery.* — The ward teaching program in general surgery has been consolidated in one of the three divisions to the greatest possible extent. Positive efforts are being made to consolidate the internship and residency program in general surgery in that division.

This quotation makes it clear that changes have occurred in the delivery of health services; but we cannot deduce from it precisely what these changes entail nor their magnitude. In a third-year assessment of the merger, published the same month as Shortliffe's piece, Dr. Norman L. Cannon draws a portrait of uneven accomplishments (1968: 55-59). Dr. Cannon uses the "list of benefits to be expected" in the merger proposal of the Joint Hospital Management Committee as his yardstick. The following are his seven criteria and our summary of his evaluation of success:

1. Coordinated planning and authority in the development of clinical programs and the facilities to support them.

We are told that many projects are "already in the works."

2. Coordinated operational authority leading to a more effective use of existing resources.

Here Cannon notes some improvements (for example, consolidation of some clinical departments), but also areas where no improvements are cited (for example, library services, data processing in clinical care and research).

3. Coordinated educational authority with one medical staff and higher educational standards.

"The educational accomplishments," say Cannon, "are uneven. . . The center currently is not using its full bed capacity for a fully coordinated teaching resource" (1968: 55-56).

4. The reduction of lost time by physicians as they devote their energies to the affairs of one medical staff instead of three.

Uneven accomplishments are noted because "it takes much more involvement and work to create and launch centerwide programs during the initial phase of mergers. . ." (Cannon, 1968: 56).

5. The consolidated effectiveness of a major medical center in the resolution of the problems associated with the care of indigent patients.

Medicare and Medicaid, according to Cannon, solved most of this problem.

6. Coordinated control over the total bed capacity through a central admitting office will decrease waiting lists and increase flexibility in the utilization of beds presently occupied at less-than-optimum rates.

In this regard, Cannon tells us: "Though strongly urged, this recommendation is not easily implemented. Coordination of existing offices has been developing gradually. A qualified administrative person has been selected to head up a centerwide admitting office" (1968: 56).

7. Coordinated development of a higher caliber clinical research appropriate to the resources of a 1000-bed complex.

"Much is possible in this area," Cannon says.

Aside from these seven points, both the Shortliffe and the Cannon articles make it evident that an overarching goal of the merger was to form a medical center with sufficient power and prestige to acquire affiliation with a medical school and to develop intern and residency programs. Three years after merger, the Wilmington Medical Center had not yet accomplished this goal. However, it had entered into a dialogue with the University of Delaware and Jefferson Medical School.

· In sum, the Wilmington data suggest that mergers entail almost immediate creation of a corporate supra-agency to coordinate all the member units. However, besides the formation of new administrative layers, other changes are slower in coming and are far more problematic. (For similar findings on a three-hospital merger in Phoenix, Arizona, see Stuart, 1970.)

Mergers, such as the one in Wilmington, Delaware, tend to represent corporations that involve relatively few health care units and cover comparatively small geographical regions. This is not true of all medical corporations in the private sector. Hospital chains, for instance, commonly encompass more units and a far wider area.

HOSPITAL CHAINS

Hospital chains, although privately owned, are of two distinct types: nonprofit chains and proprietry or for-profit chains. The Kaiser-Permanente Plan probably offers the most celebrated example of a nonprofit chain (although, as we shall see, it has a profit component). However, because of its special importance (it is often touted as the ideal model for the solution of America's health crisis) it will be treated in a separate section of this chapter. There are numerous nonprofit chains in the United States, many of them quite old. Generally, for-profit chains are Johnny-come-latelies compared to these. In fact, according to a special report of the American Hospital Association (Neely, et al., 1970) the latter date back only to 1960, but it was not until mid-1967 that significant numbers of for-profit chains were translated from concepts to realities.

NONPROFIT CHAINS

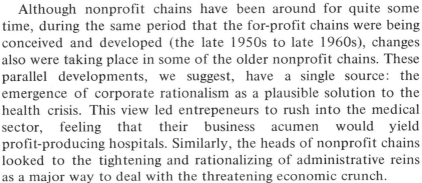

Although nonprofit chains have been around for quite some time, during the same period that the for-profit chains were being conceived and developed (the late 1950s to late 1960s), changes also were taking place in some of the older nonprofit chains. These parallel developments, we suggest, have a single source: the emergence of corporate rationalism as a plausible solution to the health crisis. This view led entrepeneurs to rush into the medical sector, feeling that their business acumen would yield profit-producing hospitals. Similarly, the heads of nonprofit chains looked to the tightening and rationalizing of administrative reins as a major way to deal with the threatening economic crunch.

Networks run by units within the Roman Catholic Church (by bishops of particular dioceses or by religious orders) are good illustrations of older, nonprofit chains. They, too, in one way or another, have begun to rely on a corporate rationalist approach. For instance, the 11 hospitals operated by the Third Order of St. Francis in Illinois, Iowa, and Michigan, with headquarters in Peoria, began augmenting corporate control as early as 1957. The hospitals ranged in bed size from 76 to 210. In 1957, a study of the capital expenditure budgets of the 11 projected costs of about $15 million. A committee composed of laymen recommended that the Motherhouse Governing Board in Peoria appoint a General Lay Financial Advisory Board to further coordination among the units and especially to pass on all future loan applications. This board, in turn, recommended the employment of a general administrator and staff "to advise the Motherhouse on methods and procedures to effect more efficient and economical hospital operation from a central office location" (Adams, 1963: 135). Centralized offices of overall administration and accounting were formed in 1958; engineering was formed in 1960; nursery service coordination has since been added.

Publications by the director of purchases (Adams, 1963, 1968) and the controller (Huff, 1964) have described the operations of their divisions (central purchasing and accounting) in promoting more effective corporate control. The director of purchases, especially, makes clear that the activities of his unit involve corporate control rather than mediated control (discussed in chapter 3). He says (Adams, 1963: 135):

> The Central Purchasing Division since 1960 would, at first glance, seem to be an emulation of the cooperative buying group but a close look would disclose two major differences. Since the Order wholly owns and operates the 11 hospitals, their participation in the consolidated buying effort is not optional or contractual but directed by policies promulgated by the Mother General and the Governing Board.

Under this obligatory centralized purchasing plan, all supplies and equipment must be directed through the central purchasing division with the exception of perishables (fresh meat, vegetable, fruit, and so on), pharmaceuticals (prescription ingredients), "minor services" (typewriter repairs, and so on), and emergency purchases. Hospital administrators are responsible for local purchases of these exceptions and no purchasing personnel have been retained outside of the central office. As regards actual buying practices, we are told:

> While agreeing with the concept that the department head should have a definite voice in the determination of the quality level of his/her supplies and equipment, C.P.D. maintains that the responsibility for selection of the vendor to supply these needs rests only with the purchasing department. Therefore, it is required that department heads express their needs by specifications that do not restrict vender selection and that in compiling these specifications, no vendor favoritism be expressed by work or implication. This has been most helpful in promoting good vendor relationships, since it has resulted in an open-door policy, giving all legitimate vendors an opportunity to compete for the business [Adams, 1963: 136].

Centralized accounting under one controller predates the corporate control of purchasing by almost two years (Huff, 1964: 81 et seq.). It soon became apparent that efficient centralized bookkeeping would require the installation of a data processing department, originally staffed by a supervisor and one key punch operator. As of 1964, after the purchase of a computer, the staff consisted of a systems coordinator, a programmer, a machine supervisor, two machine operators, and three key punchers.

Centralized payroll. was the first application installed on the machines in 1961. All payroll checks for the 11 hospitals are drawn from one bank account. Each hospital is furnished with duplicate copies of the payroll register to allow their department heads to keep track of the current status of their budgets. The utilization of data processing equipment also has made feasible the preparation of a combined general ledger (consisting of information on the current operating fund, the building expansion fund and the plant fund) and financial reports, as well as the consolidation of accounts payable and accounts receivable. In a 1968 article, the director of purchases indicates that the data processing equipment also has been used to rationalize further both group purchasing and inventory control (Adams, 1968: 65-68).

Not all medical corporations controlled by religious orders have followed the corporate rationalist impulse as far as the sisters in Peoria. For example, the St. Claire Province of the Franciscan Sisters of the Poor, with headquarters in Cincinnati, also has rationalized the control over its hospitals starting in 1960, but the degree of corporate consolidation apparently has not been so great as that by the Peoria group (Borczon, 1965: 89-91). Nine hospitals are under the jurisdiction of this province. They are located in eight different cities across five mid-Western states. In 1965, these hospitals contained 1,955 general acute beds, 249 extended care beds, and 195 bassinets. Until 1960, each of the hospitals was separately incorporated and had its own board of trustees formally appointed by the mother provincial (head of the religious community within St. Claire Province). These boards, according to Robert S. Borczon (in 1965 the administrative coordinator of all nine hospitals), in effect served as governing boards and were responsible for hospital policy formation and all appointments to the medical staff (1965: 87). The local superior also was the hospital administrator and the president of the board. (According to the pre-1960 Rule of the order, a local superior was appointed by the mother provincial with the approval of the provincial council and confirmed by the order's superior in Rome, that is, the mother general and her council.) Borczon (1965: 87) informs us that only in such "extraordinary matters" as alterations or additions to the physical plant of hospitals were policy decisions made by the mother provincial and the mother superior. Otherwise, he says, each of the boards of trustees functioned as "a separate and distinct entity."

In 1960, when the American community was formed as a separate entity from the European branch (that is, in effect it became a distinct religious order), centralization in the coordination of the nine hospitals was increased. All nine were given a single board of trustees consisting of the mother provincial as president, the assistant provincial as vice-president, the provincial bursar as treasurer, the provincial secretary as corporate secretary, and the three provincial counselors as trustees. Each hospital now has a separate local governing board, distinct from the board of trustees, which consists of the hospital administrator, and at least two assistants appointed by the mother provincial (the president of the board of trustees). According to Borczon, (1965: 88) the role of the local boards is:

> to aid in the management and control of the property and ordinary funds of the hospitals. The primary function of the local governing board is to provide advice and counsel to the hospital administrator. However, all matters of major importance must be referred to the board of trustees.

The hospital administrator is appointed by the mother provincial. Borczon (1965: 87) describes the rights and obligations of the office of administrator as follows:

> Each administrator is empowered to act as the authorized representative of the board and is held responsible for the administration of her hospital in all activities and departments, subject only to policies and directives of the board. The definition of the role and responsibilities of each administrator are contained in the letter of appointment:
>
> 1. She must submit to the board of trustees for approval a plan of organization; all policies governing medical, nursing, financial and legal services; a long range plan for the hospital; an annual budget for income, expenses and capital improvements; a position control plan for all hospital personnel; all contracts with medical specialists; a schedule of rates and charges for the services

rendered by the hospital, and regular reports showing professional services and financial experience of the hospital.

2. She recommends the appointment of physicians to the medical staff.
3. She supervises and controls the selection and employment of hospital personnel.
4. She supervises and controls plant services and maintenance of physical properties.
5. She selects members for the advisory board.
6. She is directly responsible to the president of the board of trustees.

In 1962, the office of administrative coordinator for hospital affairs was created and filled by a layman. This office, according to Borczon "is primarily responsible for providing advice and counsel to the board of trustees concerning the coordination of hospital affairs" (1965: 88). He (1965: 88) lists the following factors as considerations that led the trustees to create this office:

Even though the board for each hospital is composed of the same persons, the hospitals were independent and autonomous. Financial and managerial policies bore little resemblance to each other. Group contracts for the purchase of materials, supplies, capital equipment and insurance were discussed but not implemented. Commingling of funds for investment and capital financing purposes was not even discussed. Basic pricing policies and discount allowance policies varied from institution to institution, even when two were located in close geographical proximity. Employment practices including programs for pre-employment testing, physical examinations, training and employee health services varied from institution to institution. Employee benefit and welfare programs such as group life, hospitalization, and retirement plans were in force in some hospitals and nonexistent in others. Advisory boards were functional in some hospitals and dormant in others.

Unlike our Peoria example, the sisters in Cincinnati established guidelines that are intended to encourage optimal local autonomy in the face of corporate control. Coordinator of Hospital Affairs Borczon (1965: 88-89) describes his role as follows:

The office of the administrative coordinator is being developed as an agency to assist planning and control of policy. Its primary function is assistance to the board of trustees in formulating over-all objectives, while at the same time acting as the governing body in the appraisal of local performance relative to the established objectives and policies. Its secondary functions are being established by the application of the following assumptions:

1. All hospital work and related functions are the responsibility of the local hospitals if they can be accomplished as effectively and economically as at the provincial level, without adversely affecting other parts of the province.

2. If a decision affects more than one hospital, the authority to make such a decision is vested in the board and cannot rest with the respective administrators.

3. If a decision affects a succeeding hospital administrator, it must have approval of the board to provide a greater measure of continuity and stability to local operations.

Another of the functions of this office is the provision of counselling or consulting services to managerial personnel at the local hospitals, upon request. . . .

The office of the administrative coordinator provides such staff services as scheduling meetings, drafting agendas, recording minutes, and distributing information. This office serves as the secretariat to the hospital coordinating council and its committees and is responsible for the administrative functions of the structure and for the conduct of all projects and programs of the council and its committees.

The coordinating council and the committee system were created soon after the office of administrative coordinator and seem to represent efforts at promoting collaborative practices without the corporate consolidation that occurred in Peoria. The coordinating council is the direct agent of the trustees and is responsible for overseeing the activities of all operational committees. Its membership is made up of one administrative representative from each hospital. Appointments are made by the board of trustees for an indefinite duration. In 1965, there were seven committees: planning and development, accounting, insurance, nursing education, purchasing, personnel, and nursing service. The committees are expected to operate as "investigative, developmental and advisory groups" in their respective areas. Borczon reports that the appointments are made by the trustees with an effort to have each hospital represented on each committee.

During the first 18 months of operation, a number of positive accomplishments are claimed for this system. Among them are: a uniform chart of accounts and a uniform monthly financial and statistical report; budgetary policies; purchasing policies; standardization of business office forms; personnel policies for faculty in the schools of nursing; guides for termination and dismissal of employees; preemployment tests; comparative financial and statistical analyses; travel reimbursement policies; a retirement plan; a basic risk program for insurance coverage; pooling of purchases, and standard personnel forms.

In sum, most of the functions consolidated in any administrative overlayer by the nuns in Peoria remained, to some degree, in the hands of the local units in the St. Claire Province. The formal character of the coordinating council and the seven committees might lead one to believe that the latter field is more mediating than guiding. Nevertheless, it is important to remember that the system of administrative coordination, coordinating council and committees, however mediating or advisory it may look in blueprint, is embedded in the larger system of the hierachically organized religious order. Hence, the overall character of the control probably is corporate in nature. Borczon inadvertently describes the essence of this control in the process of offering a disclaimer for the fears that the new system will lead to "loss of autonomy and control, absentee and uniform decision making, imprudent directives, etc." (1965: 90). While arguing that lay functionaries will not erode the autonomy of the hospitals, he (1965: 90) tells us much about the ultimate control exercised by the sisters:

> However, these fears are not totally justified in Catholic hospitals. The ultimate controlling body will always be composed of the sisters. So long as a system is developed in which the ultimate governing body (board of trustees) is in actual control of hospital operations, then the hospitals will be operated under the philosophy and objectives of the particular religious congregation, regardless of who actually administers the units or who recommends policies to the board. In addition, it has never been said that sisters cannot be staff members of the central office group or that a sister cannot head the central office.

FOR-PROFIT CHAINS

A major difference between the hospital chains run by the religious orders and for-profit chains is that the former look to corporate rationalism to help them promote operating efficiency for its own sake, while the latter hope that corporate rationalism increases profits and stock appreciation. Technically, the term "for-profit chain" refers to the ownership of multiple hospitals by public stock corporations; that is, by companies that have completed or are in the process of completing a full registration of securities with the Security and Exchange Commission (SEC), and whose primary business, or whose subsidiary's business, is owning and operating health care facilities (Neely, et al., 1970: 2).

By 1970, there were 42 such public stock companies engaged in purchasing, building, leasing, or contracting to manage for-profit hospitals. "Most of the activity to this point," according to the A.H.A. study of for-profit chains, "has involved the acquisition of, and in some cases leasing or contracting to manage, existing facilities, including a limited number of psychiatric and osteopathic institutions" (Neely et al., 1970: 34). These companies control 214 hospitals with about 21,000 beds (1970: 34-35). For-profit chains include 157 community (nonfederal, short-term, and other special) hospitals – or about 3 percent of all community hospitals. Non-profit hospitals still dominate the community field with 87 percent; about 10 percent of community hospitals are for-profit but independent of any chain (Ferber, 1971: 50).

Two of the corporations – American Medicorp, Inc., of Bala Cynwyd, Pennsylvania, and Hospital Corporation of America of Nashville, Tennessee – control one-quarter of the chain hospitals and one-third of the beds. American Medicorp has 31 hospitals with 3,800 beds and Hospital Corporation of America controls 23 with 2,500 beds. However, domination is far from complete, because four other companies control over 1,000 beds and more than half have 200 beds or more. "Moreover," the A.H.A. study says, "almost all of the companies . . . have announced plans to agressively seek to acquire and, in some cases, construct additional for-profit hospitals" (Neely et al., 1970: 35). If all construction planned for 1970 goes through, the existing 42 chains will expand from 214 hospitals with just under 21,000 beds to 343 hospitals with 42,300 beds (Neely et al., 1970: 64).

The majority of the acquisitions to date have taken place in Florida, Alabama, Tennessee, Texas, and California. These five states account for 75 percent of the existing beds controlled by the 42 companies. This concentration generally reflects the distribution of for-profit institutions in the United States. However, overall activities are widely distributed: 29 states in all regions, except for New England but including Puerto Rico, and Great Britain have been affected (Neely et al., 1970: 36). Two companies are operating in ten or more states, while five others are active in five states or more. Of the 42 companies, half have operations extending into at least two states. California has 23 different chains owning, operating, or building facilities within its borders; Texas and Florida each have 12; there are five in Tennessee, and four each in Alabama and Pennsylvania (Neely et al., 1970: 36).

Market penetration has been particularly high in certain states. The chains have acquired more than 60 percent of the for-profit beds in Pennsylvania, Alabama, Tennessee, California, and Washington; more than 70 percent in New Jersey; over 80 percent in Arizona and Nevada; and over 90 percent in Florida. Measured in terms of effect on the total number of community hospital beds in these states, the chains now control more than 10 percent of that group in four states – Alabama, Texas, Nevada, and California. The penetration exceeds 5 percent in Tennessee (Neely et al., 1970: 36).

There is considerable opposition to for-profit chains from the voluntary sector. In 29 of the 50 states, chains have not yet been established (see Neely et al., 1970: 67-70). However, in only one state is there a specific legal prohibition on the establishment and operation of chain-operated, for-profit hospitals. In New York, amendments to the Social Welfare Law were adopted, effective April 1967, which specifically prohibit the operation of a hospital by a stock corporation. The amendment reads:

> Only natural persons may hereafter establish or operate hospitals for profit, except such hospitals as are in operation on the date this section, as hereby amended, takes effect. The business of operating or

conducting such a hospital shall not be a business for which a stock corporation may be organized to engage in.

Certificates of incorporation for the purpose of establishing or maintaining a hospital, infirmary, dispensary, clinic, home for the aged, convalescent care facility, or maternity center are issued by the state Board of Social Welfare. This agency also monitors the solicitation of funds for charitable purposes. The state board is vested with the authority to do what is necessary to protect the public interest against unreasonable exploitation by persons or organizations operating designated enterprises (such as hospitals, child care centers, and clinics).

A more frequently used mechanism to control the expansion of for-profit chains is to put them under the supervision of the recently created areawide planning agencies established by Congress in 1966 (and discussed later). According to the A.H.A. study of chains:

> There are approximately fifteen proprietary hospitals operating in Massachusetts under the "original license rule," which requires proof of need for the hospital facilities for which a license has been sought. This permit procedure includes all hospitals not previously licensed, or an existing licensed hospital for which there is to be a change in ownership or location. The latter requirement would appear to place a heavy burden on a corporation seeking to acquire an existing facility. Further, the state's Rate Review Commission is now adopting stringent rules governing certification of need with respect to new facilities and services. These rules are to be enforced through rate-setting decisions.
>
> Health care planning laws have recently been introduced for adoption by the state legislatures in Connecticut and New Hampshire which will afford the opportunity for extensive control of new construction, and changes in the nature and scope of hospital services. Existing health care planning laws are being amended in Illinois and Maryland for example, to strengthen the states' present capacity to control the expansion of health care facilities [Neely et al., 1970: 68-69].

In other states, the voluntary hospitals operating through their agent, Blue Cross, have employed additional techniques in an effort to control for-profit chains:

In some states, limitations on the development of propriety hospitals have resulted from agreements with, and policies adopted by third-party purchasers of care. In Michigan, for example, Blue Cross has been able to restrict its payments to "participating" hospitals, defining the category of "participating" providers of care in a manner equivalent to hospitals incorporated on a nonprofit basis. In Kansas, Blue Cross determines its cost on a formula which denies providers any margin of "profit" (wages or capital). The reimbursement formula can thus also serve to inhibit the development of for-profit hospitals [Neely et al., 1970: 69].

How successful these efforts will be to contain the growth of for-profit chains remains to be seen. On the other hand, the new health entrepreneurs have been quick to defend the role they are playing and their right to be on the American medical scene. For example, on February 25, 1970, Jack C. Massey, chairman of the board of the Hospital Corporation of America, told a U.S. Senate subcommittee:

We at the Hospital Corporation, and I am sure those in management of the other hospital proprietary groups, are convinced that free enterprise, using private capital in investor-owned hospitals, with physicians participating in management, can provide superior patient care while helping to halt the operating costs of health care in this country.

We believe that there is a need for participation of the private sector in the construction and operation of hospitals for the benefit of the people of this great Nation. . . .

With all the increased public expenditures on health care, there still remains a large number of communities which need additional or replacement hospitals, and which have been totally unable to finance them.

Hospital Corporation was organized to help fill some of this great need. . . Our company was formed to build a nationwide group of high-quality medical hospitals, with private capital, with the efficiency of business management. . . [Senate Antitrust and Monopoly Subcommittee, 1970: 132-133].

In the course of his testimony, Mr. Massey also alluded to the manner in which the Hospital Corporation of America coordinates some of the services of its member hospitals:

Our satellite concept ... makes sophisticated professional services available from one large metropolitan hospital to a group of smaller hospitals surrounding, at a very low cost to the small hospital and to the patient. Electro-cardiograms are transmitted by telephone from the smaller hospitals to Nashville, read by experts, and a report returned by phone within minutes. Laboratory specimens are picked up daily at the small hospitals and brought to Nashville for more elaborate tests than can be handled locally.

Our home office provides a central personnel resources pool which makes available the services of A.D.A. dietary personnel, pathological and radiological specialists, inhalation therapists, medical librarians, specialists in coronary care and other fields – to all hospitals. Centralized utilization of such personnel not only holds down costs but provides types of consultants which would otherwise be completely out of reach of the smaller hospitals.

We are achieving major cost savings in centralized purchasing of equipment and supplies. . . Group purchasing of standard items for 23 hospitals results in substantial saving. Buying insurance coverage for the hospitals as a group saves many thousands of dollars a year.

Support services which would otherwise have to be bought locally, at considerable expense are provided from headquarter at great savings: such services as legal, audit, public relations, personnel, employee communications, data processing and architectural [U.S. Senate, 1970: 135-136] .

The Hospital Corporation of America not only claims to coordinate services among its members, but also that it and its affiliated hospitals coordinate activities with local hospitals not under corporate control. For example, Massey told the Senate subcommittee that his corporation was planning a centralized laundry service with the other hospitals in Nashville. He also described an even more salient pattern of coordination:

We went to Selma, Alabama, and we bought a hospital. There were three hospitals, and we bought one. And they have an obstetrics department and a pediatrics department, and we sat down and worked out a situation where one could be obstetrical and pediatrics, and the other put in a new coronary care unit, and inhalation therapy, something they had never had in the city, and we took the coronary care unit and the inhalation because we were more familiar with it, and the other one took obstetrics and the other one took pediatrics.

They tell me it takes 2,000 obstetric patients a year to break even in a hospital. There are only 1,500 total in that town — or were last year, and now if three hospitals divided it, that would be 500 each, and it is going to cost somebody a lot of money; somebody has to pay for it. To me, that is a sensible approach, and the doctors love it. They have all their obstetrical patients together and all their coronary patients together and this is a sensible approach [U.S. Senate, 1970: 151].

Naturally, the critics of for-profit chains dispute this picture of ubiquitous benign effects painted by the chairman of the board of HCA. Their principal criticisms focus on the range of services offered and the types of clients served, as well as the degree of cooperation with other hospitals in the community. First, the critics charge that chains offer "stripped-down" service. That is, they do not provide the full complement of patient services associated with nonprofit community hospitals. It is especially alleged that they drop those services that are most costly and that other hospitals tend to run at a loss. In testimony before the same Senate subcommittee, John R. Gadd, executive director of the Lee Memorial Hospital, a nonprofit organization in Fort Myers, Florida, said:

Private hospitals cannot be compared with public community general hospitals because the corporate hospitals provide a stripped-down, simple-type service for simple type bread-and-butter illnesses. If the patients going to the profit hospitals were as sick as those in the public hospitals, requiring much more care and many more facilities, they probably would stay just as many days as patients do in nonprofit hospitals.

These fast-buck promoters would have the public believe that they operate a more efficient hospital; the truth is some of their operations are not much more complex than high-grade nursing homes. No reasonable person should attempt to compare the efficiency and cost of their operations with a much more complex community general hospital offering all the lifesaving and emergency services required in the care of senior citizens and the poor [U.S. Senate, 1970: 69].

These charges are somewhat exaggerated, although not wholly without foundation, according to data from Bernard Ferber's study, which compared selected characteristics of for-profit chains with those of unaffiliated profit hospitals and nonprofit hospitals. Among the factors Ferber examined was the availability of selected services that entail high cost: organized outpatient departments, emergency departments, home care programs, premature nurseries, inhalation therapy departments, and intensive care units. From his data (see Table 5-1), Ferber concludes (1971: 55):

> A higher proportion of nonprofit hospitals than of either group of for-profit hospitals had outpatient departments, emergency departments, home care programs, and premature nurseries. On the other hand, relatively more chain-operated than nonprofit hospitals had inhalation therapy departments and intensive care units; these services were proportionately least common among the other for-profit hospitals.

Ferber's data do not include any assessment of the relative quality or relative cost of these not-self-supporting programs. Hence, it is possible that for-profit chains come off looking as good as they do because of the "grossness" of the indicators available. Moreover, by focusing on the services one-at-a-time, Ferber is not able to tell us whether for-profit chains offer more, the same, or fewer overall services than do other hospitals.

The October 2, 1971, issue of *Business Week,* in an article titled "A Profit Boost for Hospitals," reports a study of 200 Southern California hospitals by Samuel J. Tibbitts, president of the Lutheran Hospital Society of California. The non-profit hospitals in Tibbitts' sample average 13.1 services as compared to 8.9 for for-profit hospitals. Indeed, the nonprofits had lower average per patient day costs – $112.96 versus $128.05. Of course, Tibbitts' sample apparently includes both chain and nonchain for-profit hospitals.

Nevertheless, the data in Table 5-1, with all their limitations, do suggest that while for-profit chains are slightly more deficient than nonprofit hospitals in certain key respects (notably outpatient service), the differences are not of the magnitude one might surmise from the preceding statement by Mr. Gadd. In fairness to the latter, however, the Ferber study focuses on only some of the services he feels are most neglected by for-profit chains. Gadd's list includes "emergency or outpatient facilities, care of children, care of pregnant mothers and their babies, psychiatric facilities, isotope and cancer treatment, facilities for special x-ray and laboratory equipment, and many, many others" (U.S. Senate, 1970: 158). In this regard, it may be worth noting that the Senate investigation brought out that three of the Hospital Corporation of America's units in Tennessee fail to provide the "full range of services" prescribed by state law and were required to obtain a waiver from the state health department in order to operate.

Gadd's testimony also contains allegations about the neglect of indigent patients by for-profit chains:

> An in-depth study of corporations masquerading as benevolent competitors would show that the hospitals in their chains that are showing the biggest profits are built in communities where there is an existing community hospital on which they and their doctors can dump the poor patients, the Medicare patients, the money-losing cases, and the real sick people [U.S. Senate, 1970: 150].

The chairman of the board must have anticipated a criticism of this kind because, earlier, he had told the subcommittee:

> Certainly, we do not encourage the so-called indigent patient to come to HCA hospitals if other, more appropriate, facilities are available. We pay large amounts of taxes to the Federal Government, and to the States and counties and cities in which we operate. These taxes help to support the tax-supported hospitals which are in the business to care for the nonpaying patient, and were established for this purpose. We think this is where they should go [U.S. Senate, 1970: 134].

When Senator Philip A. Hart of Michigan, subcommittee chairman, later read this statement to Mr. Gadd in order to obtain his response, the latter said:

> Well, this sounds like a legitimate argument, but I must say again that we get no more of the taxes from these fast-buck hospital corporations to pay for the discounters and the charity loads of our hospitals than we get from the Texaco filling station down at the corner. If they would, in our town, take their corporate tax dollar, and if you would permit them, sir, to allow us to send an armored car to their door and take it from their till and put it in our till, I might buy

part of that argument [U.S. Senate, 1970: 177].

A final charge against the for-profit chains is that rather than cooperating with other hospitals in the community, they are in direct conflict with them. In this regard, Mr. Gadd stated that the Hospital Corporation of America was attempting to build a hospital in Ft. Meyers, although Lee Memorial, his hospital, had only a 70 percent annual average census. If HCA succeeded, Gadd argued, the ensuing competition for private patients, physicians, nursing staff, and so on would ultimately force Lee Memorial to close. He suggested that the behavior of HCA in Ft. Meyers belied its claim that it sought to expand only into areas where there was an acute shortage of hospital beds (see U.S. Senate, 1970: especially 158-161).

It has also been alleged that for-profit chains fail to cooperate in comprehensive planning among hospitals. (See Gadd's full statement to the subcommittee, U.S. Senate, 1970: 152-165). The study of for-profit chains by the American Hospital Association provides some corroboration for these allegations. Questionnaires were sent to 114 areawide planning agencies established under section 314 (b) of the Comprehensive Health Planning Act of 1966. The A.H.A. researchers report that about 75 percent of the nonprofit hospitals, 47 percent of the chain-operated for-profit hospitals, and 71 percent of the other for-profit hospitals contacted the planning agency prior to the implementation of renovation, construction, or other major capital outlays completed in 1969 (Table 5-2). (If the nonprofit and nonchain for-profit hospitals that implemented capital expenditures prior to the existence of the planning agency are included, the relevant percentages of contacting hospitals are 85 percent and 79 percent, respectively.) "Although the number of chains is small," the report concludes, "the fact still remains that somewhat less than half of these hospitals were involved in officially organized community planning" (Neely et al., 1970: 72). It continues:

> The planning agency indicated that . . . it was able to exert control and/or influence over about 88 percent of the nonprofit hospitals, 71 percent of the chain-operated for-profit hospitals, and 67 percent of the other for-profit hospitals. Thus it appears that there is some willingness

on the part of for-profit hospitals to adhere to planning guidelines once
they are involved in the planning process [Neely et al., 1970: 72].

In sum, the spirit of corporate rationalism has brought would-be,
medical entrepreneurs from the business-sector into the health
field. The rapid growth of for-profit corporations attests to the
feeling that "business know-how" cannot only resolve the crisis in
American medicine, but also can return handsome profits for the
promoters. We hope that our summary of some of the testimony
before Senator Hart's subcommittee has given the reader a flavor
of the type and intensity of the opposition to for-profit chains.
Before further heat is generated, however, it is useful to see this
struggle in its true perspective. After all, 87 percent of all
community hospitals are nonprofit and for-profit chains control
only 3 percent of all community hospitals. Hence, even if all the
claims of the chains, or all the charges against them, were true,
these networks constitute such a small segment of the U.S. health
system that they are unlikely to affect appreciably the overall
delivery of services. Moreover, given the opposition they have
engendered, chains seem unable to alter significantly the 29 to 1
ratio in favor of nonprofit hospitals. Awareness of these facts
makes us realize that whether we extol for-profit chains or
condemn them, these enterprises play at best a marginal role either
as alleged causes of, or potential cures for, our health delivery
crisis.

THE KAISER-PERMANENTE SYSTEM

The same clearly cannot be said for the Kaiser-Permanente
program with its more than two million subscribers who are served
by 2,000 doctors, 21 hospitals with 4,200 beds, and 54 clinics in
six regions: Northern California, Southern California, Oregon
(including northern Oregon and southern Washington), Hawaii,
Colorado, and Ohio.[2] The Kaiser program is the single largest
private provider of health services in the United States, and it is
unselfconsciously expansionist in its designs. Moreover, because it
purports to provide comprehensive health services (in contrast to
the generally fragmented pattern found in the rest of the United

States) and because it claims to do so with considerable economy, the Kaiser-Permanente system is pointed to by many, including the president of the United States, as a panacea for our faltering delivery of health services. Hence, compared to other hospital chains, the Kaiser program is more than another strategic interorganizational specimen — it represents a potential paradigm for health care in the decades that lie ahead.

Although the program represents the pinnacle of corporate rationalism in the private sector, its inception and early development were the ad hoc responses to particular problems more than the unfolding of some grand design. It began in the late 1930s as a series of on-the-job medical centers devised by the late Henry J. Kaiser, the founder of Kaiser Industries, for 5,000 employees working on the giant Hoover, Grand Coulee, and Bonneville Dams project. Kaiser quickly decided that these centers would only pay for themselves if, instead of fee-for-services, deductions were made from the paychecks of those employees wishing to participate. In this way, Kaiser's prepaid medical plan was born.

With the coming of World War II, Kaiser Industries expanded into steel and ship-building, especially in California, Oregon, and Washington. During the war years, the workforce grew to over 200,000 employees. Work in shipyards and steel mills is especially prone to industrial accidents and thus Henry Kaiser called upon Dr. Sidney Garfield, who had set up the earlier health facilities, to organize a new, much larger Kaiser medical plan. By the end of the war, the program was providing health services to Kaiser workers at shipyards on San Francisco Bay, on the Columbia River, and at a steel mill near Los Angeles. To finance the new health care enterprise, Kaiser company stock had been donated to a nonprofit foundation called Permanente.

As the war drew to an end in mid-1945, and the shipyards began to close, the program's membership dwindled from more than 100,000 to less than 50,000. The program faced the first of its several organizational crises: Should it disband and thus give up its rather substantial investment in personnel and plant or should it strike out in new directions to enhance its viability? True to the dictum that human groupings seldom dissolve themselves voluntarily, Kaiser decided to continue, and in July 1945, the plan was thrown open to the general public with "an aggressive national campaign for his new type of health-care insurance" (Carnoy, 1970: 29). Today Kaiser Industry workers and their dependents represent only 3 percent of the total membership.

At the moment, the Kaiser health system has two key branches: one nonprofit, the other for-profit. The nonprofit segment consists basically of the Kaiser Foundation Health Plan, Inc., Kaiser Foundation Hospitals and their subsidiaries. The for-profit is composed of the Permanente Medical Groups.

The Health Plan forms the hub of the entire system, although formally it is primarily a health insurance company. However, it apparently has a far more extensive guidance capacity than the average third-party payer. According to Judith Carnoy (1970: 29), it has "powers that Blue Cross only dreams of." This power derives in large part from its close link to Kaiser Industries: seven of the nine board members "directly or indirectly represent Kaiser interests." Moreover, the Henry J. Kaiser Family Foundation, owner of about 15 percent of Kaiser Industry stock, provides the financial backbone for the Health Plans.

Kaiser Foundation Hospitals are economically controlled by the Health Plan. In 1969, $99 million of the $129 million of the hospitals' revenue came from the Health Plan. (The information is from the 1969 *Annual Report.*) Not only is it the cardinal economic provider for these hospitals, but it also buys all their major equipment and drugs, owns their physical facilities, pays their taxes, pays for all liability insurance premiums, and arranges and pays for the settlement of all claims. The Health Plan provides comparable services for the Permanente Medical Groups (which are discussed later). The Health Plan and Kaiser Hospitals have a common board of directors and officers.

Kaiser Foundation Hospitals, Inc., is a California-based, nonprofit corporation that owns and operates hospitals in California, Hawaii, Oregon, and Ohio. (The Kaiser enterprise in the Colorado region consists of one clinic in Denver.) Foundation hospitals range in size from 412 (in Los Angeles) to 56 beds (in Parma, Ohio). Kaiser Foundation Rehabilitation Center, located at the Kaiser-owned, 222-bed Vallejo Hospital in Vallejo, California, is a division of the hospital corporation that operates a program for persons with neuromuscular handicaps. The hospital corporation also runs a research institute and a school of nursing that offers a three-year course leading to a R.N. degree.

The structure of today's Permanente Medical Groups is an outgrowth of what the Program's *Annual Report* (1970: 3) called "a crisis of organization and management" in the mid-1950s. In its infancy, the program had operated as a single entity. However, as early as 1948, the physicians in Northern California had organized themselves into a partnership for the sharing of revenues, which was to become the prototype for the current medical groups. While the formation of this partnership probably indicated physician discontent with managerial practices, the latter, in turn, increasingly grew restive over physicians' "day-to-day operating decisions . . . which were idealistic, but undercapitalized and loosely-structured. . ." (1970: 6). As a result, efforts at long-range financial planning as well as greater economic and administrative rationality were undertaken. The Annual Report (1970: 6) tells us:

> Many physicians in the Program were wary of the rapid growth that was taking place in both Northern and Southern California Health Regions. New Health Plan members were flocking into clinics and medical centers at such a rate that staffing became an uncomfortable problem. More important, the physicians saw the increased involvement of the sponsor in the Program's management as a threat to their independence. Fear of lay domination became a factor.
>
> From 1952 to 1955 in a series of disagreements Permanente physicians and Kaiser managers groped for ways to solve the problem.

The agreement of 1955 created the framework for the modern Kaiser-Permanente system. It formalized the legal separation of Permanente Medical Groups from Health Plan and Hospitals corporations. In 1956, the first contract between Health Plan and a Medical Group was concluded in Southern California. The Annual Report (1969: 9) quotes the following excerpt:

> As independent contracting parties, Health Plan and Medical Group maintain separate and independent management, and each has full and complete authority and responsibility regarding its organization and operations.
>
> However, the nature of . . . the program is such that efficient

operation . . . requires continuing an effective liaison and close cooperation between Health Plan and Medical Group.

There are now six Permanente Medical Groups, one for each of the program's geographical regions. PMG represents an effort at group practice in which the participating physicians pool and share the profits. Members of the group are expected to treat their involvement in PMG as full-time and to eschew solo practice. Ordinarily, a physician joins a group for a trial period (usually three years), after which he becomes eligible for partnership and during which his income is a straight salary. Carnoy (1970: 29) describes the reimbursement of partners in the following way:

> The Kaiser Plan pays physicians salaries which are equal to the national average. Doctors who are partners in Permanente make from $26,000 to 100,000 a year, depending on the specialty. To keep the profit incentive in medical care, the Plan offers a profit-sharing program to "partners." (A "partner" is voted into the physician group after three years at a Kaiser facility.) The "incentive compensation," as it is called, consists of division of five percent of the net Health Plan revenue. Thus, during 1969, when PMG made extra profits of over $3 Million, they were divided among the physicians.

PMG practice is hospital based; that is, medical group facilities are located within a Kaiser Foundation hospital. In addition, services are reportedly coordinated with neighborhood primary-care clinics situated in peripheral areas. The formal expectation is that all facilities use a single medical record and all administrative services are unified. The degree to which this precept is carried out in the real world awaits empirical investigation. Nonetheless, it seems certain that Kaiser provides the formal structural conditions that make implementation more likely than in most other U.S. health systems.

The policy of the medical groups also calls for each subscriber to choose his own personal physician within PMG. A primary benefit of group practice for the physician is that his patient always has access to some physician at any time, although he himself is not available. This practice gives doctors more leisure time by allowing them to rotate weekends and nights. It affords the added benefit of permitting a physician to refer a patient to one or more specialists within a single organizational context, thus increasing the prospects for greater coordination in diagnosis and in treatment programs.

The same 1955 agreement that formalized the division between Kaiser Foundation Health Fund and Hospitals, on the one hand, and Permanente Medical Groups, on the other, also spelled out rules for the decentralization of program decision-making on a regional basis. Although the basic principles are the same in all regions, the regions differ in Health Plan rates, in Health Plan benefits (for example, South California includes psychiatric care, the others do not), in "community services" undertaken, and so on. Under the agreement, internal policy decisions for each area were to be made bilaterally between the heads of the local PMG and the Foundation Health Plan and Hospitals. At the time of the agreement, the program existed in three regions, Northern and Southern California and Oregon. Subsequently, three other regions (Hawaii, Colorado, and Ohio) were added. Further, pressure has grown within Health Plan, as well as among interested outside groups, for additional expansion of the program. In the face of decentralization, effective policy-making on this matter was found to be difficult. Decentralization also was viewed as a stumbling-block for the adequate consideration of matters that cross-cut regional lines and are likely to affect the entire program.

Therefore, in September 1967, the trend toward decentralization was reversed with the formation of the 16-man Kaiser-Permanente Committee. It is composed of the medical directors of each PMG, the regional managers for each region, the president of the Kaiser Foundation Hospitals and Health Plan and members of his central staff. The members decided that the committee would focus on such issues as expansion, consultation with other organizations, method of financing new regions, and so on. Formally, the committee is purely advisory in nature. According to the *Annual Report* (1969: 10) ". . . it recognized that its recommendations could not constitute decisions for any Medical Group, nor for the Board of Directors of Health Plan and Hospitals."

The foregoing makes us aware of the fact that the precise nature of the corporate guidance exercised in the Kaiser system has not been specified. Nevertheless, it seems safe to surmise that ultimate guidance responsibility lies somewhere in the Health Plan. Certainly, Health Plan staff dominate the Kaiser-Permanente Committee. On the other hand, it will require empirical research to determine the relative leverage of the board of directors, of the officers (singly, in subsets, or taken collectively), of the Kaiser Family Foundation, and so on.

Regardless of the fine points of its organizational structure, the Kaiser program is seen by many as making significant contributions to the formulation of an adequate health delivery system. The program itself summarizes its primary contributions (its functions, in sociological parlance) under four headings:

1. comprehensive coverage
2. continuity of service
3. economy
4. quality

The Annual Report (1970: 9-11) describes each of these as follows:

Comprehensive coverage

Health Plan members are entitled to visit Permanente physicians in their offices in Kaiser-Permanente facilities for general, emergency and specialized care without limit on the number of visits. Benefits are not limited to patients admitted to a hospital bed, or who have had their X-rays, laboratory tests, or other examinations as hospitalized patients. Nurses visit the home (if needed) without charge and, in some instances, physicians may make house calls at specified charges.

Depending upon the region and the type of coverage, members requiring hospital care are generally entitled to 150 or more days per year without charge. In most regions there is a moderate all-inclusive charge in maternity cases. Ambulance service is provided without . charge.

There are limits. No dental benefit is provided. Prescribed drugs are completely covered only during hospitalization, though they can be partially covered under supplementary plans as an outpatient service in some regions. Short-term psychiatric care is also available under some coverage. Eye refractions are covered, but eyeglasses are not.

The Health Plan reimburses members to a maximum of $3,000 for medical expenses incurred for emergency care due to illness or accident occurring outside the Plan's service areas.

Members who become eligible for Medicare are encouraged to continue their Health Plan membership under a comprehensive supplementary plan.

The Health Plan, where possible, will arrange coverages to suit special requirements of a consumer group.

Kaiser-Permanente offers seven-days-a-week, twenty-four-hours-a-day service. At each medical center, doctors' offices are combined with hospital facilities to provide a complete range of outpatient and inpatient services, obtainable by the member through one identified point of entry. Where the member is in an area served by a satellite clinic manned by general practitioners or primary-care specialists, the clinical staff is in close communications with the staff of the nearby medical center, the clinic and center being a part of the same system.

Continuity of Service

The Health Plan member is encouraged to choose his own doctor from the staff of the nearest Kaiser-Permanente facility — usually a pediatrician for children and an internist or general practicioner for adults. This primary physician will take care of the member's immediate needs, and refer him to specialists as necessary.

The member can see his doctor by appointment during regular office hours, or the doctor on duty if the patient comes to the daytime walk-in clinic or to the emergency clinic at night.

Where practical, the patient's medical record is maintained as a single unit. All doctors attending him contribute to the same record, and this record is available to any staff member attending him. This contrasts with the usual situation of having examination records, X-ray films, laboratory tests, orders and progress notes scattered throughout different offices and departments.

Economy

Prepaid group practice programs have demonstrated several measureable cost savings when compared with traditional systems of health care — particularly in the area of hospital utilization. An economic analysis conducted by the National Advisory Commission on Health Manpower based on 1965 data and reported in 1967 showed a 20-30 percent economic advantage in favor of the Program after appropriate adjustments for differences in the populations being compared.

Quality

One of the best assurances of good quality care is the training, experience and motivation of the physician. Permanente physicians are screened as they are accepted into the group and once in the group are continually exposed to evaluation by other members of the group.

A significant number of Permanente physicians have either teaching or research affiliations with local medical schools. Continuing education and clinical research are encouraged and supported.

In addition to the assurance of quality that rises out of a well-managed hospital-based group practice program, Kaiser-Permanente has adopted policies of adherence to all accepted licensing or accrediting procedures. For example, all Kaiser Foundation Hospitals, except those too new to have the necessary inspections, are accredited by the Joint Commission on Hospital Accreditation, representing the American Medical Association, the American Hospital Association and the American College of Surgeons.

Kaiser's claims of success must be balanced by some rather harsh criticisms levelled at the system. Even Kaiser's vaunted economic advantages do not escape attack from some of its more radical critics. Carnoy, (1970: 30) for example, says:

Like all successful businesses, Kaiser can put together a good "record." Compared to the California averages, Kaiser has significantly fewer hospital beds and physicians per member served; and for roughly comparable medical services, Kaiser expenses per member are about 30 to 40 percent less than the expenses of the average Californian, although its prices are rising. An increase of 18 percent occurred last winter and another seven percent increase is expected this fall. The most striking relative economy of Kaiser is in its number of hospital beds and its per-member cost of hospitalization. Lower hospital admission rates are the primary source of Kaiser's lower costs. Fewer days of hospital care per member explain three-fourths of the savings of Kaiser relative to the State with respect to the number of hospital beds required per person. Higher occupancy rates in Kaiser account for the other one-fourth of the savings in beds. Not all of this difference represents a true economy of Kaiser. Many members obtain part of their medical care outside the Plan, thus reducing the Kaiser expense per member. Also, by calculated plan, indigents and old persons — those most likely to require prolonged and expensive treatment, are underrepresented in Kaiser, compared to California's population.

The Kaiser program sounds relatively efficient, with medical care at fairly low costs. But in reality problems abound.

Kaiser Health Plan members don't always find it easy to obtain fast medical care. Usually when a patient calls for an appointment he will have to wait from two to three months to see his own physician — or, for that matter, any Kaiser physician. Frustrated, many patients go out of the system, preferring to see private doctors who give them fairly prompt service. Statistics show that Kaiser subscribers in the past have obtained about one-sixth of their physician and hospital care outside of the Kaiser Plan.

Of course, a close reading of this paragraph demonstrates that Carnoy only charges that some of Kaiser's lower expenses are accounted for by insensitive care or the exclusion of high risk populations. Other writers (for example, Richard Lyons in the February 19, 1971, *New York Times*) suggest that the economics are largely the result of the program's emphasis on preventive medicine through periodic examinations and immunizations that seek either to prevent illness or to treat it before it requires costly hospitalization.

In fairness it should be stressed that the central thrust of Carnoy's critique is not aimed at which factors account for what portion of the variance in Kaiser's lower expenses, but rather at the Kaiser system for breeding, what we shall call here, "insensitivity." An insensitive health system is one that treats a patient mechanically, that is, solely as an object, with no consideration of his or her psychosocial needs. (The issue of insensitivity is closely linked to that of unresponsiveness — already treated in the last chapter — but the two seem to be analytically, if not empirically, distinct. The differences between the two are discussed later.) What Carnoy suggests is that at the core of the pressures toward insensitivity in the Kaiser system is the profit-motive that is built into the medical groups. The Health Plan reimburses a medical group through "capitation" payments, that is, on the basis of the number of patients enrolled with the group. The magnitude of a physician's profit comes from having numbers in the program, rather than repeated visits by old patients. This has led to allegations that it sometimes takes two or three months to gain access to some Kaiser clinics and several hours wait once there. Dr. Sidney Garfield (the founder of the program) cites patient "abuse" as the cause of this long delay. In an article in the *Scientific American* (1970: 19) he says:

> Elimination of the fee has always been a must in our thinking, since it is
> a barrier to early entry into sick care. Early entry is essential for early
> treatment and for preventing serious illness and complications. Only
> after years of costly experience did we discover that the elimination of
> the fee is practically as much of a barrier to early sick care as the fee
> itself. The reason is that when we removed the fee, we removed the
> regulator of flow into the system and put nothing in its place. The
> result is an uncontrolled flood of well, worried-well, early-sick, and sick
> people into our point of entry — the doctor's appointment — on a
> first-come first-served basis that has little relation to priority of need.
> The impact of this demand overloads the system, and, since the well
> and worried-well people are a considerable proportion of our entry mix,
> the usurping of available doctors' time by the healthy people actually
> interferes with the care of the sick.

Economically prudent and administratively rational as this
statement is, it still demonstrates a psychosocial naivete; it ignores
those emotional and group influences in a society such as ours that
propel people who have nothing organically wrong with them to
seek medical assistance. Nor does it recognize the health
profession's responsibility for listening to such complaints.
Indeed, the Kaiser system's latest response to these client pressures
has an even stronger corporate rationalist thrust. Kaiser is
experimenting with a three-hour multiphasic screening procedure
— a battery of tests administered by machines and
paraprofessionals and interpreted by a computer — to separate the
sick from the healthy. In an article in the *Saturday Review*
(August 14, 1971), Harry Schwartz succinctly suggests how such
corporate rationalist procedures only further exacerbate the
insensitive tendencies of the system. He argues (1971: 55) that a
mass multiphasic screening system:

> is hardly the kind of warm, humane, intimate medical care most people
> want. On the contrary, the impersonality of such care, the lack of any
> long-term continued contact with one physician, is likely to repel many
> people. Moreover, the possibilities that a national system of pre-paid
> group practice will turn into a bureaucratic monster are enormous.

In essence, Schwartz suggests that the human costs of comprehensive care and continuity of care are too high, that the bureaucratic (corporately rational) response to fragmentation actually fragments the patient in another way: it radically divides physical need and psychic well-being. The critical question that only added research can finally answer concerns the degree to which patients are "willing" to adapt to this insensitivity.[3] Is the linking of psychic comfort with good medical care an aberration of the middle class with its tradition of treatment within the nexus of solo practice? Or is dealing with the "whole patient" an indispensible requisite for the efficacious delivery of health services? Of course, the issue is more multifaceted than this. The question also must be turned around; rather than asking about the malleability of the patient, we also must ask about the malleability of the system: To what degree can the strains toward insensitivity in a corporately rational system be reversed without losing some of the benefits of centralized coordination? (We return to some of these issues in the final chapter.)

The corporate rationalism of the Kaiser system also has led to charges that it is unresponsive. A health system is insensitive when it fails to consider psychosocial needs of the patient as an integral part of the medical treatment. It is unresponsive when it contains no mechanisms for incorporating the desires and demands of lower ranking participants into the decision-making apparatus. Critics of the Kaiser system argue that neither the patients, the public, nor the rank-and-file professionals have any say on what policies are proposed or carried out. Carnoy (1970: 31) says:

> There is no consumer representation on the Kaiser Board of Directors or even within the Kaiser hospitals. At the San Francisco hospital, a woman hired by management and representing Kaiser interests hears patients' complaints. Kaiser does not want consumer representation. As far back as 1957, Henry J. summed up company policy, stating, "You don't ask your corner grocer to share his ownership with people who buy at the store."

This statement is not completely accurate. In 1971, the Kaiser Foundation Hospitals and Health Plan had two "public representatives" on their board of trustees: Art Linkletter, the television personality, and Mary I. Bunting, then President of Radcliffe College. Nonetheless, although factually amiss, Carnoy probably is accurate insofar as it is difficult to conceive of these two individuals playing more than symbolic roles on a board of trustees. (Linkletter tends to be associated with conservative political causes. Mrs. Bunting was located 3,000 miles from Kaiser headquarters.)

Carnoy also asserts that Kaiser doctors and nurses have little influence on policy. To illustrate this point, she reports (1970: 31):

> At Kaiser's Santa Clara hospital facility, "partners" in the Ob-Gyn Department carried on heated negotiations with the administration, asking for more physicians, more personnel and more control in decision-making. But the Kaiser hierarchy was unresponsive to their demands, and five of the doctors quit. Similar walkouts have recently occurred at the Redwood City hospital. . .
>
> Nurses at the San Francisco hospital have said they need at least 30 more nurses to function effectively. But management says they only need 15. One nurse summed up the problem: "There is a great gap in the relationship between the Nursing Office and nurses because, unlike other area hospitals, the Nursing Office represents the Kaiser management. Errors occur constantly because of lack of nurses: intravenous injection bottles go dry and patients' arms begin to swell; patients' calls sometimes go unanswered for an hour; drugs are given to the wrong patients. During the night shift at the San Francisco surgery ward with 30 rooms, there is only one nurse and one orderly on duty. Patients cannot receive good care under these circumstances."

The Kaiser Foundation seems to be sensitive to the charge that professionals are not involved in planning. In response its *Annual Report* (1970: 17) concludes with this statement:

> The Program is a financially self-sustaining private enterprise. Therefore, it must maintain a balance between revenues and expenditures, and among members, personnel and facilities, requiring a sophisticated level of planning — both short-term and long-term. The need for achieving financial stability is as vital to the success of the Program as are service commitments to accessibility, quality and economy.
>
> The chief planning instrument in the Program is the budget — a

participatory phenomenon involving all levels of Medical Group, Health Plan and Hospitals supervision. While this "grass-roots" planning process is time-consuming, the resultant plans have a higher degree of relevance than would be the case if the budgeting was done by a staff division with no direct responsibility for seeing that the plans work out in actual practice.

Since the people who do the planning have the responsibility for carrying out their plans, there is a commitment on the part of the physicians and managers at every level of operation to achieve the agreed-upon financial goals. And because the impact of planning decisions is felt almost immediately, there is also the unusual personal satisfaction to be found in swift and constant testing of the validity of the planning process.

In a total system of health care, such as the Kaiser-Permanente Program, comprehensive health planning is necessary for success. The key is in the interrelationships among all resources: staff, equipment, and facilities. There is an increasing demand for broad spectrum planning to insure wise use of appropriate resources in the delivery of health care.

This statement does not refute the allegation of nonresponsiveness but rather handles it in a public relations manner. It remains to be seen whether Kaiser, or any other system of health care, inspired by corporate rationalism, can adequately deal with the responsiveness issue. This is not to say that we uncritically accept the picture drawn by Judith Carnoy. Nonetheless, we fully expect that in systems for whom control-from-the-top represents salvation, the question of whether and how to deal with the upward flow of demand remains acutely problematic. In the extreme, such demands may be viewed as downright subversive.

THE NEW YORK CITY HEALTH AND HOSPITALS CORPORATION

The Health and Hospitals Corporation in New York City represents a major effort to fuse the purported advantages of corporate rationalism with a concern for responsiveness. Because the corporation is still in a highly formative phase (that is, it is still subject to what Stinchcombe calls the "liabilities of newness;" see Stinchcombe, 1965: 148-153), it is impossible to make an assessment of its ultimate success or failure. However, a brief review of the factors leading to its founding, as well as some of the preliminary claims made for it and charges levelled at it, suggests that the corporation has by no means surmounted some of the critical pitfalls of corporate rationalism. (The following discussion relies heavily on Wielgus, 1970.)

On July 1, 1970, the New York City Health and Hospitals Corporation, a public, nonprofit body, took control of the municipal hospitals from the Department of Hospitals of the Health Services Administration. The formation of this corporation has its roots in proposals and debates over the city's endemic hospital crisis, which seemed especially acute in 1967. The renewed urgency was largely the result of the advent of Medicaid and Medicare, which for the first time gave indigent patients the economic opportunity to choose between municipal and private hospitals. The survival of the city-owned hospitals was once more regarded as questionable. The idea of a public benefit corporation to run these hospitals is usually attributed to the Piel Commission Report. However, while that commission played a decisive role on the road to implementation, other forces also were important.

The underlying problem that all proposals attempted to resolve from 1967 on was: How can an efficient health delivery system be established and still preserve accountability to the "public"? Can business efficiency and public control be combined? Can the medical services be detached from the traditional checks-and-balance system of city government?

Six investigating committees representing public and private interests have called attention to the inefficiency, inadequacy, and inflexibility of the hospital system of New York. The 16,000-bed system was outmoded and unresponsive to public needs. It had developed as an adjunct to city government, which forced hospital directors to work through bureaucratic channels of city government to obtain equipment or personnel. (It sometimes took nine or ten months to get a new x-ray technician. A new building for Bellevue, first proposed in 1947, was later slated for completion in 1974.)

State officials demanded that city officials improve things, medical committees proposed the city "get out of the hospital business," and others suggested that more autonomy be given to hospital directors. From this deluge of suggestions one idea emerged as basic to reform: the need for a change in the structure of responsibility for health services.

One of the first proposals came from Dr. Martin Cherkasky, the director of Montefiore Hospital in the Bronx. (See chapter 4 on the Einstein-Montefiore empire.) He suggested that hospital directors needed more autonomy, that medical needs should be detached from the red-tape of city bureaucracy. His experience with the operation of the affiliation system, he claimed, had made it clear that as long as hospitals were a part of the municipal government, health services always would be poor. He repeated this idea, with various refinements, throughout 1966 and 1967.

Mayor John Lindsay attempted to give hospital directors greater autonomy for buying equipment, repairing facilities, and hiring staff, but the bill was stymied in the State legislature. Pressure from contractors, building unions, and other lobbies were reported to have blocked this reform. The first attempt to modify the authority structure of the municipal hospitals had thus failed even though it required only minimal change in the pattern of city government.

The New York Academy of Medicine, in February of 1967, suggested that the city create an independent hospital authority to supervise operation of hospitals by community boards, a pattern based on the voluntary hospital system. This would have meant that the city would give up its municipal hospitals. Although some officials saw this plan as a way out from under the burden of running a hospital system, the lack of public accountability in the plan was considered a serious political weakness. Health officials repeatedly assured the public that the city was not "going out of the hospital business."

The Institute for Policy Studies offered another plan, the Burlage Report, in April 1967. For Burlage, the keystone of hospital-reform was community control. A central, representative commission would appoint and supervise a financing unit and a planning unit, with advice from community representatives. These neighborhood units would handle the day-to-day operation of the hospitals. The central unit would be appointed by the Mayor and the City Council would review the budget, thus assuring its public accountability. A major political liability in this plan was the detachment of planning from city supervision. The scope of community responsibility also was greater than city officials were willing to grant. In effect, what the Burlage Report did was to convert the responsiveness issue from one of public accountability to one of community control.

Dr. Howard Brown, Health Services Administrator, suggested in May 1967 that the city create a public service corporation to direct local community boards, operate the hospitals, and supervise health care. He based his proposal on the structure of the health care of the Catholic Archdiocese of Brooklyn. It is difficult to say what role this suggestion played in the final formation. Later that month, Dr. Lewis Thomas of New York University Medical School suggested the creation of a public corporation to Dr. Brown and Hospitals Commissioner Joseph Terenzio. This corporation would handle all public funds for health care, control internal hospital operations, and exert budget controls. Although not discussed publicly, this suggestion seems to be the core of the later corporation, which added a greater control by the city.

That same year, a study group in the Mayor's Office summarized the various proposals on hospital reform and concluded that of all plans, the formation of a public corporation, accountable to city government, with community advisory groups, offered the best balance of efficiency and accountability. Thus two-thirds of the corporation's governing board was to be composed of representatives from medical, civic, and philanthropic groups; the other one-third was to be composed of public officials, all subject to the Mayor's approval.

The most extensive and systematic proposals were presented in December 1967 by a commission headed by Gerald Piel. In the past few years the Piel Commission has come under heavy attack from the critics of the Health and Hospitals Corporation. In a letter appearing in the March/April 1971 issue of *Social Policy,* Piel went to great lengths to differentiate his commission's proposals from what was finally enacted by the state legislature. The letter serves as both a vehicle for emphasizing the differences in philosophy between the commission report and the corporation it spawned, as well as a useful summary statement of the report's key recommendations:

TO THE EDITOR:

The members of the so-called "Piel Commission" are not as ready to accept paternity for the Health and Hospitals Corporation as certain politicians, publicists, reports, and critics have been eager to bestow this distinction on them.

In our three recommendations we sought above all the abolition of the double-standard, two-caste system in the health services of New York City. These recommendations embodied a novel political and economic strategy. This called for (a) placing the reponsibility for the delivery of health services in the hands – or, if you prefer, on the back – of the private-voluntary, medical economy; and (b) evoking the political authority to secure the availability and delivery of health services to all, equitably and in response to need.

Our first recommendation urged the city government to promote the merging of the assets of the private and public sectors into a single, economically desegregated and rationally organized, regionalized, and decentralized service system. Although we did not attempt to spell out in detail how this desirable end was to be accomplished, we did set out the essentials of the political and economic strategy.

Our second recommendation set the political strategy. We urged the city – the political authority – to capacitate itself to represent the public interest by making the Health Services Administration (HSA) into an entirely new kind of public health agency. The HSA would be legally charged and intellectually and otherwise equipped to (a) monitor the health needs of the people; (b) plan the allocation of resources for the entire local medical community to serve those needs; (c) finance the provision of those resources; (d) contract with the private-voluntary, medical economy to secure the use of those resources in the public interest; and (e) make the delivery system publicly accountable for its performance under the contract and for its use of resources so largely created by public funds. No such agency now exists in any governmental unit. . .

Our third recommendation set the economic strategy. We urged the city to place its health services delivery system outside the city government in a health services corporation under the operating responsibility of the private-voluntary system and subject to the legal, contractual and financial powers exercised by the city through the HSA. We had three motives and objectives here. The first was to eliminate the legal and other caste distinction between the private-voluntary (e.g., Presbyterian) and municipal (e.g., Harlem) hospitals, so anachronistic now in view of their common and increasingly equal dependence upon public funds. The second was to free the deployment of public assets (existing municipal hospitals, etc., plus the capital and current operating funds) from the constraint and paralysis exerted by the "overhead" agencies (Bureau of the Budget, Comptroller's Office, etc.) and by federal and state as well as city statutes. The third was to make a clean, arms-length separation between the political and policy-making authority vested in the HSA and the managerial and professional responsibility to be lodged in the health services corporation.

In time, we expected the health services corporation to delegate its operating responsibilities to subsidiary corporations under local, voluntary trusteeships that would take over the hospitals and other facilities. In doing so, the corporation was to play a principal role in promoting the rational structuring of the health services in regional and community systems.

We deplore the fact that the public/private composition of the corporation's board of directors blurs the distribution of authority and responsibility between the public and private sectors, which tends to contribute to the perpetuation of the invidious, second-class distinction that still attaches to the municipal hospitals.

The city government should stop walking in circles around the planning power and funds made available to it by federal (Hill-Staggers) and state (Folsom) legislation. As we said in our report, the planning power is the decisive power; it should be vested in the government, not dissipated, as it now is, between public and private-voluntary agencies.

GERALD PIEL
Chairman, Mayor's Committee to Evaluate the Work of the Health Research Council of the City of New York.[4]

In 1969, the New York City Health and Hospitals Corporation was proposed by the Mayor's office, based on the various proposals discussed, especially the Piel Report. Originally, there were to be 13 trustees: seven city health officials, five private citizens appointed by the Mayor, and an executive director elected by the others. It was to implement the plans of the Health Services Administration, and its budget would be reviewed periodically by the Comptroller and the City Council. It would delegate more authority to hospital directors, manage all sources of revenue for health services, set employee working conditions and wages, purchase materials and equipment, and contract to repair and construct facilities.

From February to April, debate about this proposal, which required approval by the City Council and the State legislature, modified it somewhat. Community advisory boards were to be established for each hospital and were to function as the counterpart of trustees in the private sector to advise the corporation. However, the State legislature gave the corporation at least two years after its inception to set up these community boards. As a result of pressure from the City Council, the composition of the trustees was changed. There were to be 16: five city health officials, ten citizens appointed by the Mayor (five of whom were to be approved by the City Council), and a director elected by the others.

After one year of operation, John Sibley of the *New York Times* (July 26, 1971) reported conflicting claims for and against the new unit. In his article, he tells us that Dr. Joseph T. English, president of the corporation, listed three major achievements. First, the new system was able to recruit 1,000 new registered nurses in a single year, bringing the total to 5,500. Second, English cited the corporation's success in handling the abortion program (which began on July 1, 1970). "You remember the predictions," English is quoted as saying. "It was going to be a disaster . . . Well, those dire predictions didn't come true. Every woman eligible for an abortion in a municipal hospital got one." At the end of the corporation's first year, its hospitals had performed almost 26,000 abortions. The third achievement, according to English, was an improved system of collecting payments from Blue Shield, Medicaid, and Medicare, as well as other third-party insurers. "By the end of the year," he told the *Times,* "we were making these collections at a rate two and a half times greater than had ever been done before."

Martin E. Segal, an investment banker and insurance expert who serves on the board of trustees, is reported as citing the establishment of separate budgets for each of the 18 hospitals as another important gain. This had not been necessary under the abandoned centralized mode of operation of the Department of Hospitals. Each hospital now is required to issue regular expenditure reports to the central office; hence, coordination is formally built into decentralization. This process is reportedly being computerized.

The essence of the ciriticism levelled against the corporation is neatly captured in a quotation by Dr. Marshall Brunner, the president of the Committee of Interns and Residents: "The central office," Sibley quotes him as saying, "seems to be interested only in computerization. Nothing has trickled down through the administrative maze into the hospital wards. We don't have any more bed sheets than we did a year ago." The statement, of course, strikes at the heart of the alleged abuses of corporate rationalism. The article in the *Times* (Sibley, 1971: 10) contains accusations by doctors and nurses that the corporation has not significantly altered the delivery of health services:

> Dr. Brunner is president of the Committee of Interns and Residents, which is the bargaining agent for all house staff doctors in the municipal hospitals. The committee is compiling a registry documenting instances of unnecessary deaths and suffering among patients in the city system.
>
> The doctors' complaints were echoed by Mrs. Mary Biris, a supervisory nurse at the City Hospital Center at Elmhurst, Queens. Mrs. Biris reported that the two wards under her supervision were meant for 42 patients, but the usual census was 50 to 55.
>
> "We're drastically short of supplies," she said. "We're lucky if we can change sheets once every two days.
>
> *The Overtime Funds*
>
> When she is short on staff and requests permission to keep nurses on duty for extra shifts, Mrs. Biris said, "We're told there's no money for overtime and we'll have to get along with the people we have."
>
> She added: "And while they're putting in new carpets at 125 Worth Street (the corporation headquarters), nothing is being done for the patients' comfort."
>
> She pointed out that patients in her wards had no tables on which to set their meal trays, and were forced to balance the trays on their laps.
>
> The New York State Nurses Association, which represents the nurses in the city system, has consistently complained that its members are forced to do non-nursing chores, including serving meals, housekeeping duties and wheeling patients to the X-ray departments.
>
> Mrs. Gloria Cappella of the nurses association, said that at Metropolitan Hospital, where she had worked, "If a patient misses the regular Wednesday X-rays, he waits until the next Wednesday — at a cost of $113 a day."

A somewhat brighter picture was painted by Dr. Saul J. Farber, chief of the Department of Medicine at Bellevue Hospital.

"The main improvement," Dr. Farber said, "has been relieving professional people of doing nonprofessional jobs."

Until recently, he said, it had been common for physicians to wheel patients to the X-ray rooms.

A More Severe View

"We still have a long way to go, though," Dr. Farber said. He noted, for instance, that Bellevue has no blood-taking team. Staff physicians have to take blood, a job that is done by technicians in virtually all private hospitals.

Dr. Farber is president of the Society of Urban Physicians, whose membership includes most chiefs of service in the city hospitals. His predecessor in the post was Dr. M. Henry Williams Jr., director of the chest service at the Bronx Municipal Hospital. Dr. Williams declared flatly:

"I can't think of anything that the corporation has contributed to patient care. The creature comforts of the patients, the niceties, are no better than ever."

As for the nurse recruitment program, Dr. Williams said, "We'd have gotten the same results from the old department."

Dr. Williams scoffed at the corporation's contention that it had speeded the purchasing of supplies..

"Almost a year ago," he said, "we asked for ultraviolet lights in the TB ward to help keep the place sterile. We not only didn't get the lights, we can't get a direct answer when we ask about them."[5]

In addition, like most enterprises generated by corporate rationalism, the Health and Hospitals Corporation, despite its professed ideology, has acted as slowly as law will permit to implement community boards. As of October 1971, only Goldwater Hospital, an institution dealing with a larger than average number of chronic patients, had a local board. Goldwater is located on Welfare Island in the East River, so that the community is in fact the patients themselves. Some community boards existed prior to the corporation (for example, at Lincoln Hospital). However, these boards do not have legal status under the enabling legislation because they were not set up within prescribed guidelines. Moreover, what role the community boards ultimately will play is extremely hazy. The formulation of the goals and duties of community boards in the (N.Y.C.H. & H.)

corporation's *Interim Policy and Guidelines* is in the broadest possible generalities and tells us very little.:

> Each Community Board shall participate in establishing policy at its hospital, and, as provided in the legislation forming the Corporation, each Community Board shall consider and advise the Corporation and the hospital upon matters concerning the development of plans and programs of the Corporation.
>
> Functions in which Community Boards shall participate will include, but not be limited to, the following:
> 1. The establishment of priorities in relationship to planning.
> 2. The allocation of funds within the hospital budget.
> 3. Judgment as to the acceptability of services rendered to patients.
> 4. Area-wide planning through appropriate agencies and mechanisms.
>
> Members of the Community Board shall participate in the recruitment, screening, and interviewing of applicants for the position of Chief Executive Officer shall require the concurrence of the Community Board.
>
> As the Corporation's role in providing health services and facilities broadens, the Corporation shall seek to create additional Community Boards or have those broadened interests represented in existing Community Boards.
>
> Each Community Board may establish rules and regulations that will enable it to function effectively.
>
> Support for staff assistance, technical guidance, training, and consultation will be made available to Community Boards.
>
> The Board of Directors charges the President of the Corporation with the development of guidelines consistent with the above policy and with the development of a process through which each hospital will devise and implement plans for the establishment of Community Boards consistent with the policy.

Hence, what role community participation ultimately will play in a more responsive health system has yet to be determined. As of this writing, responsiveness is a factor in the system solely in terms of accountability to city government. It need hardly be emphasized that this government has not been notably successful in transforming the municipal health system in the past.

In sum, the New York City Health and Hospitals Corporation's early experiences have been much the same as the other corporate patterns previously discussed. The initial thrust has been at reform-from-above. It has aimed at putting the municipal hospitals on a sounder administrative and economic footing. The hope remains that these reforms will trickle down to the units directly responsible for the delivery of health services, but the charges of insensitivity are frequent and often seem to be well substantiated. Finally, corporate rationalism has as yet failed to deal adequately with the issue of responsiveness, either within the Hospitals Corporation or elsewhere. However, unlike the preceding cases cited in this chapter, the Hospitals Corporation is formally committed to responding to demands from consumers. What becomes of this potential remains to be seen.

FEDERAL EFFORTS

The federal government, in the spirit of corporate rationalism, has tried to promote the coordination of health services within circumscribed regions. Compared to the Health and Hospitals Corporation, the Department of Health, Education and Welfare (H.E.W.) is acting as sort of supracorporation that provides the incentive for guidance and coordination within distinct clusters of health care units, rather than in a single one. However, the federal efforts have been subject to false-starts and programs that are at cross-purposes. They are certainly not even so far along as the Health and Hospitals Corporation; hence, no definitive evaluation of them can as yet be put forward. Here, we briefly consider two of the past decade's more ambitious instances of corporate rationalism on the federal level: (1) the Regional Medical Program and (2) the Comprehensive Health Planning Program.

THE REGIONAL MEDICAL PROGRAM

The Regional Medical Programs (RMP) grew out of the Johnson Administration's effort to control the "killer diseases," that is, heart disease, stroke, and cancer, which are responsible for over 70 percent of the annual deaths in the United States. Accordingly, in March 1964, President Johnson appointed a commission to recommend steps to reduce illnesses and deaths from these diseases through the better utilization of medical manpower and facilities. (The following discussion of the Regional Medical Programs was written prior to the efforts by the Nixon administration in 1973 to dismantle them.) Dr. Michael DeBakey, the noted heart surgeon, was its chairman. The commission recommended a rudimentary national medical system to fight the three diseases through regional research centers, diagnostic and treatment stations in teaching hospitals, and regional networks to link these centers, including stations as well as community hospitals. However, because of intense opposition, especially from the American Medical Association, the RMP, in the form in which Congress finally created it, is considerably more ill-defined and loosely coordinated.

The legislation, signed on October 6, 1965, stipulated that the program was to accomplish its ends "without interfering with the patterns, or the methods of financing, of patient care or professional practice, or with the administration of hospitals, and in cooperation with practicing physicians, medical center officials, hospital administrators, and representatives from appropriate voluntary health agencies." In short, pressure from medical interest groups guaranteed from the outset that the RMP would not be used as a vehicle to transform the existing health system with its prevailing patterns of priorities, power, and privilege.

Thus, rather than create a new system, RMP deliberately was designed to serve as an extension of existing programs. If any single activity was especially encouraged, it was planning. Overall, the bill authorized funds for grants to "public or nonprofit private universities, medical schools, research institutions and other public or nonprofit institutions and agencies for (1) planning, (2) conducting feasibility studies, and (3) operating pilot projects for the regionalization of research, training, and demonstration activities dealing with heart disease, cancer, and stroke."

The law defined a regional medical program as a "cooperative arrangement among a group of public or nonprofit private institutions or agencies engaged in research, training, diagnosis and treatment related to heart disease, cancer or stroke, and . . . related disease or diseases. . ." According to the law, the group thus formed can only qualify as an RMP if: (1) it is in a geographic location that the Surgeon General approves as appropriate; (2) it consists of one or more medical centers, one or more clinical research centers, and one or more hospitals; and (3) it has arrangements for cooperation that the Surgeon General finds adequate to the purposes of the title.

RMP legislation requires advisory units on the national and regional levels. The law authorized the Surgeon General to appoint a 12-man National Advisory Council. Each appointed member's term is for four years and no member may serve more than two consecutive terms. The purpose of this committee is to advise the Surgeon General on matters of national policy for the Regional Programs. The Regional Advisory Groups are not intended to have direct administrative responsibility for their respective Regional Programs. Rather, the intention of the legislation was that the Advisory Group ensure that the RMP "is planned and developed with the advice and assistance of a group which is broadly representative of the health interests of the Region" (Regional Medical Programs, 1969: 13). Each Regional Advisory Group has two official duties: (1) to stimulate and approve all proposals for operational activities and (2) to provide H.E.W. with annual progress reports.

A 1969 study by the Office of Planning and Evaluation in the Division of Regional Medical Programs found the Advisory Groups generally not succeeding in their prescribed duties because: (1) Group members have full-time outside commitments and meet infrequently; hence, (2) they had adopted a passive, reviewing role rather than an active advisory one; and (3) the executive committees of most Groups are controlled by medical center officials and, consequently, a committee's decision "often represent a fait accompli for the Regional Advisory Group which has little option but to endorse" (Report of Planning Study, 1969: 10).

In addition to the Advisory Group and its executive committee, most local RMPs, according to this study, are characterized by two additional administrative levels: a core staff and a "superstructure." The core staff would seem to be the logical hub of planning since it consists of the full-time employees of the RMP headed by the Program Coordinator. The "superstructure" often includes (1) planning committees or task forces with an overall regional orientation and, less frequently, (2) local advisory or action groups with a community orientation. The 1969 study concludes: "There is every indication that in most Regions the real planning focus is the planning committees and task forces and not the core staff." Several reasons are offered (Report of the Planning Study, 1969: 10) for the deficient planning posture of most core staffs:

There seems to be a tendency to reorganize the Regional Program core staff after an initial phase, usually 18-24 months. This has happened already in Northlands, New Jersey, and Washington/Alaska, and is being contemplated in Wisconsin. This seems to result because initially Regions were under a great deal of pressure to "go operational." Thus a great deal of effort was usually spent in project stimulation and development and preparing an operational application for submission. During this period relatively little progress was made in the creation of a planning process. The programs realize this and in taking a long-range point of view with a better understanding of what is required in RMP, they reorganize their efforts considering the increased variables they must deal with. Other programs seem not to have fully grasped the need for creating a structure for continuous regional planning or are just now beginning to do so.

A Study of the Regional Medical Program issued by Arthur D. Little, Inc., and the Organization for Social and Technical Innovation, in November 1970 focuses heavily on the fiscal dilemmas of the RMP. Although 54 of 55 approved programs had moved from the planning stage to "full operational status," the report (1969: 1-3) noted that:

... the past two years have been marked by increasing fiscal constraint, manifest in many ways including a personnel freeze... During the early stages of the program more money was available than could be usefully spent considering the amount of time needed for the regions to get organized and plan before "going operational." But as more regions came on stream and built needs for more funding, the financial situation tightened to the point where there were, as of June 30, 1970, about $30 million in approved but unfunded projects. In other words, a reasonably clear balance between funds available and the need for funds has never really been achieved and maintained. The current deficiency of funds to support even completely approved (and therefore presumably worthwile) projects has added a substantial element of uncertainty to the confusion of newness and its accompanying lack of positive program definition.

In short, this report suggests that RMP is foundering because it was vaguely formulated to begin with and because subsequently authorized funds were not allocated. Consequently, insofar as RMP represents a manifestation of corporate rationalism, it has nevertheless failed to display the efficiency and muscle at the top that is the hallmark of this perspective.

Indeed, it is generally agreed that, until now, the major participants in RMP, as well as its major beneficiaries, have been university medical centers. The Health Policy Advisory Center (Health-PAC) has argued that in New York City, RMP has functioned largely to strengthen the hands of the existing medical empires (see Health-PAC *Bulletin,* July/August 1969). According to Health-PAC, the medical schools originally showed no interest in RMP. Subsequently, Cornell University Medical College and Downstate applied for separate grants to plan a RMP. Washington turned down both because New York was a "natural region" and should not be fragmented. In time, the seven medical schools and the New York Academy of Medicine formed a corporation, the Associated Medical Schools of Greater New York, which was awarded a two-year planning grant to form New York Metropolitan Regional Medical Program (NYM-RMP).

Only the medical schools and the Academy of Medicine received seats on the NYM-RMP board of trustees. The Health and Hospital Planning Council of Southern New York, the Health Services Administration, and local medical societies, however, were included in representation on the Regional Advisory Group. According to the Bulletin, the medical school deans retained the right to select the chairman of the Group and to change NYM-RMPs by-laws. Seventeen of the original 45 members of the Advisory Group were on the staff of the medical schools and their affiliates. Unaffiliated physicians and the smaller voluntary hospitals were not represented. The committee's public sector was "mostly Wall Street businessmen and philanthropists" (Report of the Planning Study, 1969: 3). Also included as a "public" representative was the vice-president of the Health and Hospital

Planning Council of Southern New York. (As we noted in chapter 3, many have charged this council with serving as a front for New York's medical empires.)

Health-PAC's description of the New York scene seems to confirm the other assessments of RMPs cited above. For instance, Health-PAC argues that the medical schools undermined the planning role of the NYM-RMP central staff. Local staffs were created and the deans gave the central director no say in the selection of local staff. Local coordinators, although nominally on the staff of the central director, turned out to serve largely as agents of their respective medical empires. Further, the schools and the New York Academy each took $45,000 per year for whatever RMP staff they needed. Each medical school assumed planning responsibility for a circumscribed area in its vicinity. "Actually . . .," Health-PAC says, "the medical schools did not develop borough-wide or regional responsibilities. . . The medical school RMP coordinators, whose function was supposedly to stimulate grant applications in their entire region, rarely bothered to look outside of their own institutions and affiliates" (Health-PAC *Bulletin,* July/August 1969: 4-5). Those grants that were available largely went to the medical schools and their affiliates.

A defender of NYM-RMP could point out, of course, that Health-PAC has a distinctive perspective in terms of which the accuracy of its reportage must be judged. Nonetheless, the mildness of the actual rebuttal offered by the Director of Regional Medical Program Services (printed in Health-PAC *Bulletin,* September 1969: 16) suggests considerable acceptance of the picture drawn by Health-PAC in official HEW circles:

Dear HEALTH-PAC:

I have read carefully your well written article in the Metropolitan New York Regional Medical Program published in the HEALTH-PAC BULLETIN. The article reflects a great deal of insight into the specific problems of that specific Region, as well as a good grasp of the historical developments of the national program. . .

In the final paragraph of your article you make a fairly sweeping indictment suggesting that medical schools "elsewhere" have "failed to use RMP for anything beyond their own narrow interests". . .

However, it is my opinion that the medical schools of this nation,

along with the hospitals and professional groups, have made a major
contribution to establishing effective Regional Medical Programs. . .

It would be surprising if a new concept such as Regional Medical
Programs was uniformly successful in its development in all areas of this
diverse country. You have commented on a single program operating in
a very complex metropolitan community. I think our entire track
record is somewhat better than you make it out to be.

STANLEY W. OLSON, M.D.
Director, Regional Medical Programs Service, U.S. Public Health Service,
HEW

COMPREHENSIVE HEALTH PLANNING

Whereas the Regional Medical Programs sprang from a specific
concern with three "killer diseases," Comprehensive Health
Planning (CHP) has focused on the fragmentation that previous
federal programs apparently promoted on the state and local
levels. Congressional testimony in 1966 established that there were
13 distinct categories of federal assistance in the health field (for
example, attacks on cancer and dental disease, support for schools
of public health, and so on) in which 16 different formulas for
grant awards were involved. Funds were restricted to each
category and could not be transferred to another even if real need
could be demonstrated. The Interstate and Foreign Commerce
Committee of the U.S. House of Representatives reported that
although new federal assistance programs had given more and
more responsibility to state and local health departments, there
had not been a commensurate increase in their capacities to
provide comprehensive health services within their jurisdictions.
That is, because they received funds from several different
agencies and departments (the Office of Economic Opportunity,
the Departments of Commerce, Agriculture, Housing and Urban
Development, as well as H.E.W.), each with its own unique strings
attached, these state and local units were unable to coordinate or
rationally allocate their resources. This, it was felt, led to
"fragmentation of services, duplication and the unwise use of
health resources that are in short supply. . ." [*89th Congress,
Second Session, U.S. Code Congressional and Administrative
News,* vol. 3, 1966: 3822].

In November 1966, Public Law 89-749, the Comprehensive Health Planning and Public Health Services Amendments of 1966, were passed by Congress and signed by the president. In December 1967, the so-called Partnership for Health Amendments (P.L. 90-174) were added to clarify the program and to increase appropriations. Both laws called for each state to provide comprehensive health planning and to select a council made up of providers and consumers of services to advise the agency. Consumers were guaranteed a minimum of 51 percent of the seats on each advisory council. The state CHP programs were to be funded by federal formula grants. In addition, the statewide planning agency was given somewhat greater discretion in the use of already appropriated categorical grants.

Section 314(b) of the 1966 law provided for the establishment of even more localized planning units under the rubric of Areawide Health Planning. The Surgeon General, with the approval of the appropriate state agency, was authorized to allocate project grants to any public or nonprofit private agency or organization, to cover up to three-quarters of the costs for projects to develop "comprehensive regional, metropolitan area, or other local area plans for coordination of existing and planned health services. . ."

As of July 1, 1969, there were 93 314(b) (Areawide Planning grants) funded agencies located in 37 states (Stone, 1969). However, in most of these, the activities involved planning for the establishment of an areawide planning agency, rather than actually running one. Thus, in New York City, the Mayor's Organizational Task Force (MOTF) labored for two years before a planning unit was finally established on October 1, 1971. The bulk of this planning for planning seems to have consisted of negotiating with various health interest groups and working out jurisdictional disputes with existing agencies; for example, the Health and Hospital Council of Southern New York, NYM-RMP. (For a concise summary of MOTFs blueprint, see the January 1971 issue of its pamphlet, *Health Planning.*)

As we mentioned above, the entire statewide and areawide planning program is too new to allow for a definitive assessment. Indeed, many state and local programs are still on or just off the drawing boards. Even the statewide comprehensive planning programs, although officially set up, still appear to be highly fluid, in reality. Perhaps the most graphic illustration of the degree to which these programs exist only inside somebody's head is the variability in how they are described. Thus, the November 16, 1968, issue of *Hospitals* contained a Special Report of a symposium held the previous month marking the second year since the enactment of P.L. 89-749. The symposium included a discussion by George A. Bell, director of research of the Council of State Governments, regarding the types of comprehensive planning agencies set up in the various states. The figures that Bell offers perceptibly vary from those put forward in a report by Nancy N. Anderson of the Institute for Interdisciplinary Studies of the American Rehabilitation Foundation and dated December 1968. First, Bell (*Hospitals,* 1968: 26d) tells us:

> Ten states have vested the health planning function in central planning agencies. Thirty have placed it within the state health agencies, six have set up interdepartmental committees, three have located the planning function within their governors' office, and one has vested the responsibility in a combination of the planning and health agencies.

Then Anderson (1968: 5) reports:

> In 29 states and the District of Columbia, governors placed the comprehensive health planning function in their state health department. In 16 states, they placed it in a unit of the executive office of the governor — generally, the state planning agency, or in some states, the department of administration or the budget office. In five, the comprehensive health planning agency is an interdepartmental commission.

Further, the Anderson report says 45 states have now set up advisory councils, while the *Hospitals* Special Report places the figure at 46. No doubt, a statistician might argue that the differences between the two sets of figures are not statistically significant. Nonetheless, they are sociologically significant, insofar as they suggest the general vagueness surrounding the implementation of the program. As a matter of fact, the symposium reported in *Hospitals* indicated there was considerable lack of clarity about such issues as the nature of the planning to be undertaken by the planning agency, what constituted a consumer, and what the nature of consumer input was to be. Almost two years later, an article by Avery M. Colt in the *American Journal of Public Health* (1970: 1194-1204) continued to raise many of the same questions.

While some are still raising questions about the intent of the CHP legislation, others have become progressively more outspoken in their denunciation. Professor Cyril Roseman of Berkeley has taken an extremely dim view of CHP. In October 1970, at the meeting of the American Public Health Association, he (1970: 2) said the "failings" of CHP are largely a result of:

> a "scientistic" charade, in which the normal processes of political conflict and consensus formation are considered a "prostitution" of the pure planning process and are rationalized by participants (especially board members representing major health provider groups) as evidence of the immaturity of the CHP process not yet arrived at the "science" of planning. The implicit model of a science of planning envisioned is the rather mechanistic calculus employed by traditional health facilities planners — adding, subtracting, multiplying and dividing to arrive at conclusions regarding gaps, duplication, cost-reduction and efficient allocation of resources. The nature of the CHP process, however, makes such a model misguided at best and pernicious at worst. Comprehensive health planning could better proceed at this point in time if a charade were discarded and in its place were inserted an overtly political model of planning — involving multiple conflicting interests, limited resources, ambivalence toward innovation/status quo maintenance, and overwhelming manifest needs throughout the health field in the light of quite restricted potential means for solution through CHP.
>
> In short, CHP at both the state and area-wide levels too often has involved a plodding effort to inventory resource allocations made yesterday, using statistics, needs-estimating procedures, and computers to pretend to a planning sophistication that is misdirecting energies from the real issues of health planning for the future.

Hence, for Roseman the failings of CHP flow from an excessive zeal for the trappings of corporate rationalism with no appreciation for the political vortex within which intra- as well as interorganizational decisions are forged. "Relying heavily on personal field observation in the western states, records of comprehensive health planning bodies in states throughout the nation, and the result of field interviews in forty comprehensive health planning agencies. . ." he identifies (1970: abstract) four principal problems of CHP as:

1. a pattern of conflict avoidance in policy formulation and goal establishment
2. a failure to deal with root causes of health problems
3. a lack of political influence, leadership, or expertise, coupled in some states with a naive supportive clientele inside and outside of the health field
4. grossly inadequate funding to provide plans for comprehensive health care delivery in the light of anticipated universal health insurance.

In sum, the federal government's ventures into the realm of corporate rationalism (via RMP and CHP) have been relatively unsuccessful to date, even in terms of the canons of corporate rationalism itself. There is no indication that the massive infusion of governmental funds has significantly transformed the health delivery systems of regions, states, or areas in more economically or administratively rational directions. Rather, the advisory groupings that have been set up seem, for the most part, to reflect the existing organization of local health vested interests. Hence, federal funds have, at best, established more comprehensive mediating units, rather than real guiding ones. In the final analysis, of course, guidance reasonably cannot be expected to come from a Regional Advisory Group or from a state or areawide planning council. Rather, guidance, if it is to be effective, must come from the provider of the funds themselves; that is to say, the federal government. Until now, the government has not offered the guidance. It has, instead, under the exigencies of crises, political pressures, and health fads, developed a myriad of ad hoc programs that often function at cross-purposes. This view is supported by Dr. James A. Shannon, the former director of the National Institutes of Health. According to Dr. Shannon, the major thrust of the CHP concept has been blunted by HEW programs that are in direct conflict. Among the programs he cited are:

1. Programs for the mentally ill and mentally retarded administered by the National Institute of Mental Health (NIMH) and the Health Services and Mental Health Administration

2. Regional medical programs (RMP) aimed at developing medical service arrangements for victims of heart disease, cancer, stroke, and related illnesses
3. Maternal and child health programs which contain both research and service-oriented programs managed by the Children's Bureau of the Social and Rehabilitation Service (SRS)
4. An array of other programs with "some measure" of biomedical research, medical manpower, and medical service functions included in SRS.

Dr. Shannon said other examples could be cited, but that these were "sufficient to emphasize the diffusion and functional ambiguity of the DHEW health organization."

In this context, Dr. Shannon's comments about the regional medical program should be noted:

> This program is conducted under authorities that are considered by many to be in direct conflict with the concepts which underpin the programs of "Comprehensive Health-Partnership for Health," even though they are contained in the same operating unit of HSMHA. It is interesting to note that the legislative consideration of the regional medical programs antedated by some months the enactment of the Comprehensive Health legislation. Nonetheless, in the congressional presentation of the comprehensive health programs little note was taken of then recently enacted RMP legislation. Avoidance of what would be inevitable program conflicts was not considered.[6]

Perhaps the most promising aspect of RMP and CHP has been their efforts to build in mechanisms for participation by the public, consumers, and so on. Much needs to be done in this area: who the consumers and the public are, who their representatives ought to be, and how they are best plugged into the decision-making process are still being debated. Nonetheless, while effective control-from-the top has eluded these programs so far, these efforts suggest to the observer that corporate rationalism may not be always necessarily unresponsive to demands from below. Further, insofar as planning has become officially politicized, because governors, mayors, and so on play a crucial role in CHP, these federal programs are creating other conditions favorable to a more responsive health system. This is especially the case for CHP because ultimate accountability is with elected officials, whose decisions are subject to review by legislators and also by citizens through the electoral process.

SUMMARY AND CONCLUSIONS

In this chapter, we examined corporate control configurations, that is, interorganizational fields in which guidance is provided by an administrative supraagency rather than by a member unit. Corporate patterns are eminently contemporary insofar as they represent a very prevalent strategy for overcoming the current health crisis. Corporate rationalism regards administrative and economic reform and coordination at the top as the prime prerequisites for a better health delivery system.

We have seen that the corporate rationalist impulse is present throughout the health field: It is focused on small aggregations of units, as well as on large ones; it covers small geographic areas, as well as immense ones; it is found in the private sector, as well as in the public; it exists among nonprofit, as well as for-profit, units; and the local, state, and federal governments all have shown interest in it. Despite the diversity of its manifestations, corporate rationalism seems to raise many of the same issues wherever it is found. To its credit, it has pointed to the archaic administration of individual hospitals, as well as to the almost total absence of a system of coordination among health care units. This lack of operating efficiency (especially when compared to America's business sector) undoubtedly has contributed to the continued fragmentation of health care, as well as to its prohibitive expense. However, the question still remains whether corporate rationalism represents the panacea some of its adherents claim it to be.

At the core of the critique of corporate rationalism is the fact that it is a health philosophy that focuses on the less salient (less goal-relevant) aspects of an effective delivery system. True, until recently, the administrative nuts-and-bolts of the system have been too neglected. On the other hand, corporate rationalism, with its single-minded focus on reform-from-above, seems sometimes to ignore that health delivery units exist to service people and that, hence, consumer satisfaction is an essential ingredient of successful goal attainment. The charges against corporate rationalism reported in this chapter, for the most part, suggest a failure in this regard. It has been noted that corporations rely on the "trickle down" approach; that is, a belief that tightening the reins of the administrative overlayer inevitably will lead to greater and more satisfactory modes of defining, diagnosing, and treating illnesses. To date, the evidence for such a hope has not yet been produced. Further, corporate systems tend to be insensitive, that is, in the name of comprehensive care, they often ignore the patients' psychosocial needs. Finally, health corporations are struggling with charges of unresponsiveness. Although some accountability to governmental agencies exists for some corporations, most corporations have not been successful in institutionalizing access to decision-making by consumers, the public, and the staff.

The problem, of course, is not to "throw the baby out with the bathwater." We must preserve the insights of corporate rationalism, while realizing that no single approach will satisfactorily transform the American health system.

NOTES

1. See "A Profit Boost for Hospitals," Business Week, October 2, 1971, pp. 96-102. The article contains statistics on for-profit chains that are slightly up-dated from the 1970 A.H.A. report.

2. Our discussion of the Kaiser-Permanente Plan was written prior to the appearance of the depth analyses contained in Somers (1971).

3. In a private communication, Eliot Freidson has noted that the corporate rationalizer's primary aim is to produce a "record." Now in an industry that manufactures standardized items – for example, toasters – there probably is some intrinsic relationship between the record and the product. However, where the raw material being processed is something as unstandardized as "sick" human beings, the relationship between record and product is considerably more problematic. The great danger, of course, is when the corporate rationalizer succeeds in making the record the organizational product – that is, when social reality is constructed in terms of a record as opposed to the real needs of the patient.

4. © 1971 by Social Policy. Reprinted by permission from Social Policy Corporation, New York, New York 10010.

5. © 1971 by The New York Times Company. Reprinted by permission.

6. Dr. Shannon's statements are taken from *Federal Role in Health: Report of the Committee on Government Operations, United States Senate, Made by its Subcommittee on Executive Reorganization and Government Research* (pursuant to S. Res. 320, 91st Cong.) April 30, 1970. His testimony is summarized on pp. 17-23. All of the material we have presented is found on p. 19.

REFERENCES

ADAMS, L. A. (1963) "The central purchasing division." Hospital Progress 44 (October): 135-138.

——— (1968) "Group purchasing and automated inventory control." Hospitals 42 (December): 65-68.

ALFORD, R. R. (1972) "The political economy of the American health system." Politics and Society, 2, no. 2 (Winter): 127-164.

ANDERSON, N. N. (1968) "Comprehensive health planning in the states: a study and critical analysis." Minneapolis: Institute for Interdisciplinary Studies, American Rehabilitation Foundation.

BORCZON, R. S. (1965) "In-depth organization chart of the Franciscan Sisters of the Poor." Hospital Progress 46 (November): 86-91.

BUSINESS WEEK (1971) "A profit boost for hospitals." (October): 96-102.

CANNON, N. L. (1968) "Three years after a merger: an appraisal and a 'look ahead.' " Hospitals 42 (September): 55-59.

CARNOY, J. M. (1970) "Kaiser: you pay your money and you take your chances." Ramparts 8 (November): 28-31.

COLT, A. M. (1970) "Elements of comprehensive health planning." Amer. J. of Public Health 60 (July): 1194-1204.

EIGHTY-NINTH CONGRESS, Second Session (1966) U.S. Code Congressional and Administrative News. Volume 3. Brooklyn: Edward Thompson.

FERBER, B. (1971) "An analysis of chain-operated for-profit hospitals." Health Services Research 46 (Spring): 49-60.

GARFIELD, S. R. (1970) "The delivery of medical care." Scientific American (April): 15-23.

HEALTH POLICY ADVISORY CENTER, [Health-PAC] (1969a) "Regional medical program: the anatomy of a muddle." Bulletin (July/August): 3-5.

——— (1969b) "Letters to editor (from Stanley W. Olson, M.D.)". Bulletin (September): 16.

HOSPITALS (1968) "Special report." (November): 16.

HUFF, W. S. Jr., (1964) "Computer handles total financial workload for 12-unit hospital system." Hospitals 38 (January): 81-86.

KAISER FOUNDATION MEDICAL CARE PROGRAM (1969) Annual Report, Oakland, Calif.

——— (1970) Annual Report, Oakland, Calif.

LITTLE, A. D., Inc. (1970) A Study of the Regional Medical Program, New York: Organization for Social and Technical Innovation.

LYONS, R. D. (1971) "Nixon's health care plan proposes employees pay $2.5 billion more a year." New York Times (February 19).

MAYOR'S ORGANIZATIONAL TASK FORCE FOR COMPREHENSIVE HEALTH PLANNING (1971) Health Planning (January). MOTF Pamphlet. New York.

NEELY, J. R., et al. (1970) Study of For-Profit Hospital Chains, unpublished study. Chicago: American Hospital Association.

NEW YORK CITY HEALTH AND HOSPITALS CORPORATION (1971) Interim Policy and Guidelines, New York.

OFFICE OF PLANNING AND EVALUATION, DIVISION OF REGIONAL MEDICAL PROGRAMS. (1969) Report of Planning Study of Office of Planning and Evaluation, Division of Regional Medical Programs, Washington, D.C.: U.S. Government Printing Office.

PIEL, G. (1971) "To the editor." Social Policy 1 (March/April): 71-72.

REGIONAL MEDICAL PROGRAMS SERVICE, U.S. DEPARTMENT OF HEALTH, EDUCATION AND WELFARE (1969) Progress Report: Regional Medical Programs. Bethesda Md. Regional Programs Service, U.S. Department of Health, Education and Welfare.

ROSEMAN, C. (1970) "Problem and prospects for comprehensive health planning." Paper presented at the Comprehensive Health Planning Section of the 98th Annual Meeting of the American Public Health Association, Houston: (October).

SCHWARTZ, H. (1971) "Health care in America: a heretical diagnosis." Saturday Review (August).

SENATE ANTITRUST AND MONOPOLY SUBCOMMITTEE, 91ST CONGRESS, SECOND SESSION (1970) The High Cost of Hospitalization. Washington, D.C.: U.S. Government Printing Office.

SHORTLIFFE, E. C. "Program organization following corporate merger of community hospitals." J. of the Amer. Medical Assn. 206 (September): 109-111.

SIBLEY, J. (1971) "Year-old hospital unit is praised and assailed." New York Times (July 26).

SOMERS, A. R. (ed.) (1971) The Kaiser-Permanente Medical Care Program: A Symposium. New York: Commonwealth Fund.

STARKWEATHER, D. B. (1970) "Health facility merger and integration: a typology and some hypotheses," pp. 4-44 in Paul E. White and George J. Vlasak (eds.) Inter-Organizational Research in Health: Proceedings of the Conference on Inter-Organizational Relationships in Health. Washington, D.C.: U.S. Department of Health, Education and Welfare.

STINCHCOMBE, A. L. (1965) "Social structure and organization," pp. 124-193 in James G. March (ed.) Handbook of Organizations, Chicago: Rand-McNally.

STONE, L. B. (1969) "From organization to operation: the evolving areawide comprehensive health planning scene." Minneapolis: Health Research Center, Institute for Interdisciplinary Studies, American Rehabilitation Foundation.

STUART, R. B. (1970) A Study of the Effects of Corporate Merger on Selected Clinical Services in Three Phoenix Area Hospitals. Waco, Texas: Baylor Univ.

SUBCOMMITTEE ON EXECUTIVE REORGANIZATION AND GOVERNMENT RESEARCH. (1970) Federal Role in Health: Report of the Committee on Government Operations, United States Senate. Washington, D.C.: U.S. Government Printing Office.

WIELGUS, K. (1970) The Development of a Public Health and Hospitals Corporation. Unpublished report. New York: Center for Policy Research.

TABLE 5-1

PERCENT DISTRIBUTION OF HOSPITALS WITH SELECTED SERVICES, BY SIZE AND TYPE

Size (number of beds)	All types	Nonprofit	For-Profit All for-profit	For-Profit Chain-operated	For-Profit Other
ORGANIZED OUTPATIENT DEPARTMENT[a]					
All sizes	33.1	34.6	21.5	11.1	24.2
Less than 50	24.5	23.7	27.9	7.1	28.9
50-99	20.9	21.7	15.8	8.6	19.0
100-199	26.7	27.9	14.3	13.6	14.8
200 or more	62.2	63.1	16.7	20.0	14.3
EMERGENCY DEPARTMENT[b]					
All sizes	85.7	88.2	66.0	84.9	61.2
Less than 50	72.8	76.7	56.7	85.7	55.3
50-99	84.5	86.2	73.4	79.3	70.6
100-199	91.7	93.2	75.2	88.6	65.6
200 or more	96.5	96.6	87.5	100.0	78.6
HOME CARE					
All sizes	7.2	7.9	1.8	3.2	1.4
Less than 50	2.1	2.5	0.7	0.0	0.7
50-99	3.0	3.3	0.5	1.7	0.0
100-199	7.5	7.7	5.7	6.8	4.9
200 or more	17.4	17.6	8.3	0.0	14.3
PREMATURE NURSERY					
All sizes	47.1	49.9	24.8	36.5	21.7
Less than 50	23.3	19.3	16.7	14.3	16.8
50-99	39.8	41.8	26.1	31.0	23.8
100-199	55.1	56.2	42.9	43.2	42.6
200 or more	80.8	81.6	37.5	70.0	14.3
INHALATION THERAPY DEPARTMENT					
All sizes	52.6	53.5	44.8	77.8	36.4
Less than 50	19.1	17.5	25.6	57.1	24.1
50-99	39.1	36.7	54.9	74.1	46.0
100-199	68.8	68.3	74.3	84.1	67.2
200 or more	91.1	91.3	83.3	100.0	71.4
INTENSIVE CARE UNIT					
All sizes	44.2	46.0	29.6	68.3	19.7
Less than 50	9.3	9.2	9.5	42.9	7.9
50-99	25.0	23.7	33.7	53.4	24.6
100-199	58.5	57.7	67.6	88.6	52.5
200 or more	92.4	92.5	87.5	100.0	78.6

a Excludes hospitals which have special outpatient services only (e.g., renal dialysis, psychiatric, and rehabilitation).
b Excludes hospitals with emergency psychiatric services only.

SOURCE: Ferber (1971) "An analysis of chain operated for-profit Hospitals." Health Service Research 46 (Spring): 54.

TABLE 5-2

HOSPITALS REPORTED AS COMPLETING MAJOR CAPITAL EXPENDITURES DURING 1969 AND EXTENT OF CONTACT WITH 314(b) PLANNING AGENCIES, 1970

	Nonprofit Hospitals		For-Profit Chains		Other Profit Hospitals	
	No.	%	No.	%	No.	%
Hospitals completing major capital expenditures[a]	251	100.0	15	100.0	21	100.0
Hospitals contacting planning agency[b]	188	74.9	7	46.7	15	71.4
Hospitals not contacting planning agency[c]	63	25.1	8	53.3	6	28.6
Hospitals contacting planning agency	188	100.0	7	100.0	15	100.0
Indicated control effected	165	87.8	5	71.4	10	66.7
Indicated control not effected	23	12.2	2	28.6	5	33.3

NOTE: Data are from 314(b) Planning Agencies within the Continental U.S. that completed all items on the questionnaire.

[a] Includes hospitals which completed renovation and construction.

[b] Prior to implementation.

[c] 31 non-profit hospitals and 2 non-chain (other) profit hospitals did not contact the 314(b) Planning Agency because such agency was not in existence at the time of major capital expenditure planning.

SOURCE: Neely et al., (1970) Study of For Profit Hospital Chains. Unpublished study. Chicago: American Hospital Association.

CHAPTER 6

SUMMARY, CONCLUSIONS, AND
RECOMMENDATIONS

In the introduction, the reader was warned not to expect an unduly optimistic portrait of coordination among America's health care organizations. Therefore, in this one respect, at least, the last five chapters should not have been a disappointment. Feudalism, mediation, empires, and corporate rationalism, taken singly, raise serious problems for the policy researcher interested in more effective, efficient, responsive, and sensitive health delivery systems. None, by itself, seems to offer a sure-fire solution.

Our study has no way of determining the frequency of the various types of control configurations. Nevertheless, in terms of sheer number of instances, feudalism is undoubtedly the most common interorganizational pattern. In other words, contacts among health care units are far more likely to be direct, informal, and focused overwhelmingly on mutual consultation than they are to be mediated or guided. However, feudalism is a "central tendency" not only because it represents the most frequent control configuration, but because it is basic to all our theoretical constructs.

The fact that feudal networks are embedded in each of the other fields suggests that the more complex control configurations frequently represent efforts to overcome some inherent deficiencies of feudalism.[1] What, then, are these deficiencies; that is, why is there a push to move beyond feudalism? A field with only feudal coordination probably is the closest empirical manifestation of social entropy (Etzioni, 1968: 95-96) in the interorganizational realm. While it is certainly not an instance in which there is no intermember contact or where each unit fends entirely for itself, it is, by definition, a state of minimal actualization of a multimember network. The absence of a common focus of identification and integration makes it probable that the members will have little motivation for acting in concert and that the maintenance of any existing collaborative bonds is acutely problematic. In such a setting, other organizations are viewed primarily as external constraints upon what one would like to do or can realistically accomplish. Hence, the "implicit utilitarian-pluralist" perspective against which we cautioned in chapter 1, although theoretically overly narrow, probably very closely mirrors what administrators have most wanted to know about interorganizational bonds: How can my organization master the multiunit labyrinth in which it is located so that it can pursue its goals in the most "satisficing" manner? Obversely, the popularity of this particular perspective serves as testimony for the likely prevalence of feudal fields.

THE PUSH BEYOND FEUDALISM

In the health sector today, there is a rough consensus that individual units acting alone can no longer obtain satisficing solutions over any sustained period of time. The rising public expectations about what constitutes an adequate array of health services, along with a concern for the costs involved, have led to a broad agreement that comprehensive and economical medical care can flow only from pluralities of units coordinating their activities. If, indeed, social entropy is an especially acute problem in feudal settings (in the sense that collaborative bonds are not maintained or extended unless continual conscious social effort is added), then the desire to preserve and institutionalize the gains of collaboration is a likely impetus for the growth of coordinating agencies specializing in such tasks. Mediated fields appear to be efforts to protect feudal accomodations, that is, to formalize previously informal, often ad hoc, arrangements, and to guarantee third-party supervision and adjudication. However, because the resources and responsibility for wielding systemic power are still dispersed to a considerable degree among the member units, the emergence of a mediating agency more represents a move to maintain and to streamline existing arrangements than to transform radically the interorganizational field in more effective and efficient directions. As we argued in chapter 3, efforts at guidance in fundamentally mediated fields commonly founder either on the rocks of crises of confidence or crises of legitimacy. In brief, a mediated field provides guarantees for more permanent lateral coordination among members, but the feudal-base upon which it is built still gives such a field its overall flavor.

Consequently, mediating agencies may provide some minor, incremental improvement in the effectiveness (more comprehensive care) within fields of health-related units; but we would not expect a systematic upgrading of the field's overall capacities. Imperial fields have a greater potential for transformation of the feudal-base, because the allocation of resources is shaped to reflect the power and interests of an elite-member. An interorganizational empire contains the rudiments of a more rational division of labor for the field. Not all the units must have the same resources or vie for the most prestigious goals. Two critical concomitants are: (1) imperial fields seem to be (as compared to feudal ones) rather successful in coaxing additional resources from the relevant environment (for example, the federal government), and (2) therefore they are able to deliver more health services. In addition, imperial fields presumably are less vulnerable to the purported pitfalls of overbureaucratization, because coordination is provided primarily by a member unit rather than by a specialized administrative agency external to the routine give-and-take of the field (as is the case with both mediated and corporate settings).

Nevertheless, as we suggested in chapter 4, interorganizational empires are liable to many of the same dysfunctions incurred by historical bureaucratic empires. The absence of an administrative entity acting for the field as a whole, (while it may forestall overbureaucratization) curtails the potential scope both of the rational division of labor and of rational decision-making, leaves the internal organization and outlook of the member units essentially unaltered, and makes the empire-builders (rather than the field as a whole) the prime beneficiaries of increased coordination. Moreover, the rise of empires in the health sector exacerbates the strains stemming from the alleged lack of responsiveness in organizational life. Individual hospitals, as discrete entities, are open to the charge that they fail to include adequately the demands of the community and their staffs in the decision-making processes. However, it is only with the advent of permanent, identifiable interorganizational fields (in which the fate of some units is shaped significantly by others) that responsiveness, as a political issue, becomes optimally visible and arouses extensive public concern. This is the result, in no small way, of the fact that the constituencies for intraorganizational responsiveness are relatively small, isolated groups confronting a purely local elite, whereas the advocates of interorganizational responsiveness are larger units, facing elites who set policy affecting a multiplicity of organizations extending over several communities.

A corporate field apparently has a greater potential for introducing rationality into its feudal-core than do empires, because its guiding unit is not a competitor for the strategic resources and also because it tends to have far greater administrative capabilities. However, because the elite-unit is to some degree outside the "action space" of the health care units it controls, the disaffections over responsiveness found in empires become even more acute here. When we add to this that: (1) the key personnel in the corporate agency are overwhelmingly in administrative rather than in professional roles;[2] and (2) corporate rationalism is the prevailing ethos, we begin to see why there is such a ubiquitous feeling that these agencies do not listen to demands of the local communities or even to the professional and nonprofessional staffs in hospitals. Further, the bureaucratic character of the corporation brings the charge of insensitivity most vividly to the foreground. Other kinds of settings (simple health care units, as well as feudal, mediated, and imperial fields) may be equally indifferent to the psychosocial aspects of health, but the scope and impersonality of corporate control makes such fields particularly obvious foci of discontent.

THE TEMPTATIONS OF CORPORATE RATIONALISM

Of course, the advocates of corporate rationalism are trying to devise strategies to deal with the twin gremlins of unresponsiveness and insensitivity; but these efforts are only in their early stages, and it remains to be seen whether newer approaches, which are still fundamentally bureaucratic in nature, can cope with the alleged dysfunctions of previous bureaucratic procedures. Nevertheless, there is something inherently attractive in the corporate solution to the health care crisis, because a good case can be made for its enhanced effectiveness and efficiency, and it can be argued plausibly that the problems of unresponsiveness and insensitivity are transient "liabilities of newness" that will be overcome with more experience. In other words, there is a real temptation, in preparing a concluding chapter such as this, simply to recommend a national corporate health system (along the lines of a more rational and integrated version of Comprehensive Health Planning) that would be centralized and make all-encompassing health policy. Unfortunately (or, perhaps, fortunately, too) such a recommendation has practical, as well as theoretical, limitations.

We already have alluded to several of these limitations. First, in such settings, guidance is provided by a supraagency that remains, to some degree, external to the field that it coordinates. That is, the corporation is an administrative entity that tends to be at least partially outside the "action-space" of health care units making up the field's feudal-base. Consequently, external elites are less likely to respond reliably to the demands of the member units; that is, considerable conscious effort is required to devise mechanisms that will insure that these "outsiders" will be somewhat consistently responsive. It seems probable that when elites are external, effective guidance will be jeopardized insofar as resistance by the units in the feudal-base is likely to remain a more persistent problem.

The second limitation previously mentioned is that a corporate field, because of its administrative center, is more prone to the dysfunctions of overbureaucratization than other guided fields. For instance, bureaucracy generates a devotion to rational procedures and predictable behavior that tends to promote an "overconformity to means amid an ignoring of goals or to their actual displacement" (see Merton, 1968). Exclusive reliance on the corporate rationalist remedy to the health care crisis no doubt entails a not inconsiderable element of goal-displacement, insofar as primary concern shifts from the delivery of health services (the production of goals) to the streamlining of administrative procedures (the rationalization of means). It generally has been assumed by sociologists that excessive goal-displacement may interfere with a social system's adaptation because of a lessened ability to adjust to changing situations not envisaged in existing rules. Further, many social scientists have suggested that bureaucratization, with its systematic dissociation of means from ultimate goals, is a prime source of alienation both at work and in society as a whole.

The limitations imposed by being an external elite and the tendency toward overbureaucratization are analytically distinct. However, empirically we expect them to reinforce one another. The externality of a corporate agency from its feudal-base increases the intensity with which it will view health care problems in bureaucratic (corporately rational) terms, rather than professional ones. On the other hand, the degree to which the corporation relies on bureaucratic procedures reinforces its estrangement from the health care units it serves and hence solidifies its external status.

A third factor constraining us from simply recommending a rational corporate health system flows from the apparent obstacles to effective guidance faced by an external elite. Correlative to the fact that corporate agencies tend to have a difficult time maintaining responsiveness is that their downward cybernetic capabilities also are often impaired. In other words, not only are there impediments to the upward transmission of perspectives from the member units, but similarly, the external position of the controlling-unit hinders the successful transmission of perspectives downward in a way that reduces differences in outlook among the members. Obviously, deficiencies in the ability to mobilize consensus make it improbable that the corporation significantly can transform the character of the feudal-base through persuasion alone. In turn, this suggests that a corporation, to have any real impact on the field that it guides, must apply its power to coincide with the structure of power among the member units, in order to neutralize the potential centers of resistance. That is, corporations that seek more immediate tangible results more readily will attain these if their decisions favor those health care units that are already the most powerful ones in the field. Certainly, the early track-records of CHP and RMP, reviewed in the previous chapter, strongly support such a proposition.

In short, paradoxical as it may seem, corporate control configurations seem to have an innate tendency to drift away from comprehensive planning geared to overall transformation of the system, toward more incremental planning that fosters the prevailing distribution of power and privilege. This tendency serves to remind us that we ought never facilely to equate the existence of a centralized (corporate) guiding overlayer with the capacity for comprehensive planning. According to Rudolf Klein, the history of the National Health Service (NHS) in Great Britain provides a prime example of a guiding overlayer minus any substantial capacity for comprehensive guidance. He reports (1972: 119-121):

> . . . The extension of the government's area of activity in Britain since the War, while apparently greatly strengthening the power of the central bureaucracy, has in fact increased its dependence on the advice, health and cooperation of outside bodies. Every advance into a new field has meant involving a profession or pressure group whose support is needed both to obtain information and to execute policies. Nowhere is this more true than in the NHS. To think of the medical and health professions as pressure groups working from outside the system is to miss much of the point. The relationship between the central bureaucracy and the health professions is symbiotic. The latter are strongly represented not only on the staff of the Department of Health and Social Security (DHSS) but on countless advisory committees, as well as on the regional and local boards responsible for hospitals. Thus, in the context of the NHS it would probably be fairer to talk about the professionalization of the bureaucracy than the bureaucratisation of the medical services . . .
>
> . . . As a machinery for allocating resources on a rational, equitable basis, the NHS has disappointed hopes and given new fuel to the arguments of the market economy school. Indeed, when one tries to analyse the planning process, to delineate who makes which decisions about what resources to allocate to whom, the evidence tends to slip through the fingers like so much sand. The experience of the NHS's first 20 years at any rate — for now there are signs of change — is that planning was

conspicuous by its absence: Government policy has been made largely by a series of accommodations to cases and events and by the projection to the future of past trends.

The most conspicuous example of this can be found in the geographical spread of resources. The 1971 distribution of resources follows exactly the 1948 distribution, which in turn was largely determined by the Victorian pattern of disease and philanthropy. The Treasury's tradition of financial supervision, the Health Department's passive administrative style and professional conservatism have between them meant that the NHS budget has been planned on a predominantly incremental basis. Those regions which had a great many hospital beds and doctors in 1948 have been given proportionately more money, while those with fewer resources have been given less. The result has been to perpetuate geographical inequalities which have little if any relationship to "need" for medical care, however that may be defined . . .

Less well-documented, but perhaps more important than the matter of geographical inequalities, is the performance of the NHS in allocating resources to the different secrots within the health service. Yet this is crucial. For perhaps the central weakness of the market economy model health service is its inability to provide for the needs of the non-earning, dependent members of the community: the young, the old, the mentally sick or handicapped, and the chronically ill . . .

The performance of the British NHS on this score has been disappointing. Provision for the old and the mentally ill or handicapped was poor in quality in 1948 and remains poor in quality today. This sector, with its unsuitable 19-century buildings, has not only suffered badly from lack of capital which has afflicted the NHS as a whole. It is also underprivileged, undernursed, underdoctored and underequipped. Only now, following a number of public scandals involving the maltreatment of patients in such institutions, has a political decision been made to divert more resources to this neglected sector.[3]

MIXED CONTROL PATTERNS

In short, corporate fields, which at first glance appear to be the panacea for all the problems of the health system, actually are subject to incompatible pressures that make their success extremely problematic. On the one hand, to be truly transforming, a corporate agency ultimately must penetrate and (to a degree) reshape the power constellations and vested interests found in the feudal-base. On the other hand, corporations needing tangible results can most effectively obtain these when their policies coincide with the prevailing configurations of power. Concretely, this means, for example, that if a regional planning agency began to allocate resources in a way that favored the less powerful units (for example, municipal hospitals, small non-university-linked voluntary hospitals, nonchain proprietary hospitals) at the expense of the more powerful ones (for example, university medical centers), the latter could be expected to generate sufficient opposition to undermine the successful implementation of that policy. Their rationale for this, of course, would be that they have far greater capabilities (human and material, professional and administrative) for the effective and economical utilization of newly dispersed resources than do their less powerful confreres. In other words, resistance on their part, they would argue, is justified because they are advocating a more productive utilization of assets.

Such an argument is not without merit. However, if a policy-maker were to accept it totally, it would guarantee the perpetual second-rate status of the weaker units. As things now stand, such a status serves as a drain on the overall effectiveness and efficiency of the health delivery system. For example, despite the efforts of the Affiliation Program (chapter 4) and the Health and Hospitals Corporation (chapter 5), the conditions of New York City's municipal hospitals continues to diminish the overall quality of the medical services already available to the citizens, while stoking the flames of ineconomy smoldering within New York's public and private health sectors. We are not campaigning for complete equality among health care units, but it is impossible to legitimate the present system of inequality on functional grounds.

Hence a cardinal issue is: How can the excessive slanting of power within a health care field be rectified while one is simultaneously promoting increased comprehensive planning? Empires would seem to be no more successful in this regard than corporations. We have just finished arguing that corporations are more fortunate in planning efforts where they take the power-structure as a given. Our analysis of empires (in chapter 4) suggested that, in this instance, the guiding unit (the imperial center) has a profound vested interest in perpetuating the present profile of power and privilege because it is the primary beneficiary in such a system. Therefore, we are faced with the fact that exclusive reliance on centralized guidance (whether corporate or imperial), while it represents an improvement in coordination over feudalism and mediation, nevertheless tends to result in incremental changes at best. In other words, even if the establishment of a comprehensive national health corporation were politically feasible (which is unlikely), the overall potential of such a system to transform significantly the delivery of health services in this country is extremely doubtful.

The trick, as we see it, is to try to maintain and to expand the coordinating capacity of centralized control, while preserving the strengths inherent in the pluralistic health system. It might be noted at the outset that we use the term "pluralistic" quite broadly to suggest settings in which there are multiple centers of health care power, while recognizing fully that not all these may have equal leverage. Hence, imperial fields are indeed pluralistic, although one of the units has special access to the responsibility and resources of systemic power. Further, in arguing for the preservation of "inherent strengths" of the pluralistic system, we are not calling for the passive acceptance of existing gross inequities. Indeed, we shall suggest that the inherent strengths cannot be adequately realized until radically skewed power differentials are modified.

Any program for continuing the beneficial features of corporate control and interorganizational pluralism must come to grips with at least three broad problems: (1) What form and scope should the new corporatism take in a mixed corporate-pluralist system? (2) What should be the nature of the pluralist-base (for example, more imperial or more feudal)? (3) What role should community groups and professional and nonprofessional staff play in formulating policy? We consider each of these questions in turn. However, the reader is cautioned beforehand to expect the raising of questions and the posing of alternatives more than the presentation of a definitive model for the reconstruction of the health system.

THE PARAMETERS OF CORPORATISM

In trying to circumscribe the parameters of corporatism in any mixed corporate-pluralist field, two questions immediately present themselves. First, of the four major problem areas of multiunit health delivery systems discussed in this book — effectiveness (comprehensiveness), efficiency (economy), responsiveness, and sensitivity — to which is the corporate mode best suited and least suited? Second, regardless of the substantive areas of decison-making, what kinds of decisions, formally speaking, are corporations best able to make?

PROBLEM AREAS

We have dealt at some length, in this and in the preceding chapter, with the problem areas to which the corporate style is most and least appropriate. Clearly, underpinning the philosophy of corporate rationalism is the assumption that upgrading the operating efficiency of health delivery networks also will enhance their effectiveness (the delivery and coordination of services) and ultimately neutralize complaints about such issues as alleged unresponsiveness and insensitivity. Corporate entities have a plethora of administrative and economic manpower and skills. Moreover, because they can provide the units they serve with centralized accounting, billing, purchasing, and data processing, they not only increase the efficiency of the entire field, but lift off the shoulders of the health care units burdensome and unwanted tasks.

However, corporate control, if it is extended, can help promote economy in another way. Health care units, either singly, in isolated clusters, or through their mediating agencies (for example, hospital associations), lack the overall capacity to control significant segments of rising health care costs.[4] Such factors as the price of drugs and the ever more elaborate medical technologies are beyond the control of these groupings. At the moment, prices are set largely in response to the exigencies faced by the national (and international) profit-oriented industries that produce these items; no degree of cost-consciousness within hospitals is likely to affect them significantly. Another contributing factor to spiralling health care costs is the relative availability of personnel (professional, semiprofessional, and nonprofessional) and the costs of this labor. For example, individual hospitals cannot increase the supply of nurses or have an appreciable impact on their salary-scales. By contrast, a health care corporation, if its base is large enough, may have some clout in these areas. For instance, a large and powerful corporation through the manipulation of purchasing presumably could have an impact on the prices of drug and medical equipment. Indeed, insofar as a corporate system would be, to some degree, under federal sponsorship, it could use governmental regulation or the threat of it to "jawbone" into line those sectors of the pharmaceutical and medical technology industries whose prices were deemed exorbitant. A more powerful health corporation also might undertake programs to relieve the shortage of health personnel, either through training programs or through inducements to work in hospitals, communities, or regions that were chronically understaffed. Further, some hospital corporations already are serving as the bargaining agent for the hospitals under their jurisdiction. If this pattern is extended, it might well increase rationality and predictability in the realm of hospital salary and wage scales. It also could have the added benefit of deflecting antipathy generated by collective bargaining away from the member-hospitals (and onto itself), thus reducing staff alienation within hospitals.

It might be added that the corporate model also can directly enhance the effectiveness of health delivery systems, insofar as it can guarantee a more steady and higher-level flow of monetary and goal-relevant resources. Of course, the ability to accomplish this is, in large part, determined by the links a corporation has to the government. Thus arises the question of what the national organization of a corporate system ought to be. At one extreme is a monocratic corporate model, which would organize the health system into a rigid hierarchy of control emanating from Washington, D.C. Under such a system, there would indeed be regional corporations, but they would be subject to a kind of control that would leave them with an extremely narrow band within which their conduct could legitimately vary. In short, the mode would be a kind of medical autocracy that would have practically all the power and most of the decision-making at the apex of the hierarchy and little or none below. It has been pointed out, on the political-economic level, that this is essentially the Stalinist model for economic planning.

At the other extreme, there is what, for want of a better phrase, we call the feudal-corporatist model. Under such a system, there would be local or regional health corporations (such as a local CHP or New York City's Health and Hospitals Corporation), but there would be little or no provision for coordination among them. Hence, such a system would eliminate feudalism on the local (intracorporate) level but promote feudalism on a national (intercorporate) one. Under such a model, the destructive rivalries that have existed among health providers merely would be transferred upward to the intercorporate level. Clearly, a successful national corporate system must operate somewhere between these two extremes, thus providing some centralized coordination with a relatively broad capacity for local flexibility in planning. No detailed plan for such a system exists at this time. However, the so-called Ameriplan of the American Hospital Association sketches the bare outlines of such a system. In the 1970 Report of a Special Committee on the Provision of Health Services (1970: 6-8) the AHA recommends the following:

> The basic innovation of AMERIPLAN is an organization called a Health Care Corporation having the resources necessary to provide truly comprehensive health care to a defined population. The establishment of Health Care Corporations would allow the health field to move from what some have called a cottage industry to a modern, coordinated and comprehensive system for the delivery of health care.
>
> To permit the establishment and growth of Health Care Corporations, and to assure uniform availability of adequate health services throughout the country, legislation would be enacted by the federal government which would require the adoption of federal regulations defining the scope, standards of quality, and comprehensiveness of health services and stating the benefits to be provided for all of the people. These regulations would be administered at the state level with care being provided locally by Health Care Corporations.
>
> Health Care Corporations would have the following characteristics:
> (1) Each Health Care Corporation would synthesize management, personnel, and facilities into a corporate structure with the capacity

and responsibility to deliver the five components of comprehensive health care to the community: health maintenance, primary care, specialty care, restorative care, and health-related custodial care.

(2) Health Care Corporations would cover the comprehensive health needs of every geographic area and of all of the population, with some Health Care Corporations spanning geographic and political boundaries where necessary to assure that all persons have access to care. All persons would have the opportunity and be encouraged to join Health Care Corporations.

(3) The Health Care Corporations would assure optimum service to the community by physicians. Every practicing physician would have the opportunity to be affiliated with a Health Care Corporation, and physicians would have the opportunity and could accept the responsibility of participating in the management of Health Care Corporations.

Various forms of medical practice, including group practice, would be permitted within the Health Care Corporation.

(4) The Health Care Corporation would be responsible for providing professional peer review and other mechanisms to evaluate the quality of all health care on a continuing basis. Such evaluation of quality would be an integral part of AMERIPLAN and a basic responsibility of the Health Care Corporation.

(5) The Health Care Corporation would identify its manpower needs, and be responsible for the inservice education and training of its health manpower and the recruitment of all health personnel for its providers.

(6) The proper growth of Health Care Corporations would only occur through the most appropriate, economical use of all resources. Enforceable regulatory controls would be established by legislation in each state to assure that needs would be met without unnecessary construction or duplication of facilities and services.

(7) Each Health Care Corporation would develop a suitable mechanism by which the community could express its health needs and through which the Corporation could actively respond. All persons in the community would have a role in identifying how health services would be provided, in determining how care could be made more accessible, and how the delivery of care could best support the dignity of the individual and his family.

The A.H.A. is somewhat vague about how the approximately 400 regional corporations would be structured and run, but it subscribes to the general principal of community and professional staff participation in the decision-making process (Special Committee, 1970: 15-18).

Moreover, it clearly advocates that all the health care units in a given area, irrespective of ownership and sponsorship, fall under the aegis of the corporation, insofar as the latter "would be directly responsible for the delivery of health services" (Special Committee, 1970: 17). However, the fine-detail of how the public and private sectors are to be coordinated by the corporation still needs to be spelled out. Nevertheless, Ameriplan seems to meet our specification for a viable corporate system quite well at several points:

1. it recognizes the importance of the corporate dimension in adequate health delivery;
2. it sees implicitly that the corporate style is particularly useful in providing incentives and in overcoming fragmentation (improved effectiveness), as well as promoting fiscal and administrative economies (improved efficiency);
3. it recognizes that intercorporate feudalism is no more desirable than interorganizational feudalism; but, at the same time . . .
4. it realizes that federal coordination through a National Health Board should set only the broad limits of policy and that specific directives should derive from, or within, the local health care corporation.[5]

FORMS OF DECISIONS

This brings us logically to the question of the kinds of formal decisions that corporations are best able to make. In a sense, we have just been speaking of the formal aspect of decisions, because we have suggested that decisions from a governmental supracorporation should remain highly unprescriptive. Such a supracorporation should be confined to formulating general policies, broad guidelines, orienting directives, and so on. The testimony of Dr. Shannon cited in the preceding chapter provides ample evidence that, to date, HEW has been deficient in this capacity; that is, it presides over a maze of contradictory and overlapping programs that do not formally acknowledge one another's existence. Nonprescriptive decision-making is in no way to be equated with this scatter-gun approach. Indeed, if the government is to render adequate guidlines for health delivery systems, it must cease the proliferation of conflicting and contradictory programs. This will require not only that the officials at HEW present something approximating a united front vis-a-vis health interest groups, but also that they encourage Congress to do the same. As long as senators and congressmen continue to push "pet" health programs (for example, in kidney dialysis, cancer, and mental health) that establish brand-new administrative structures and ignore earlier arrangements, the federal government will be unable to exercise effective nonprescriptive control. Proposals for decategorization and block grants to improve flexibility are a heartening first step in such a direction but only that.

Once we acknowledge the largely nonprescriptive role of the federal government in decision-making, we still must deal with what forms of decisions are left to the corporate overlayer as a whole, as opposed to the pluralistic-core. Talcott Parsons (1960), in an analysis of intraorganizational structure, suggests there are three levels of activity and decision-making in all organizations: the technical, the managerial, and the fiduciary or institutional. These categories apply equally to business enterprises and to hospitals and, we here suggest, to the relations among health care facilities as well as within them.

The technical level is concerned with the direct production of the organization's goals. In the case of hospitals, this means the issues focus on the actual process of healing; that is, the application of the existing health services to the individual patient either to obtain a cure or to ease his or her suffering. The managerial level is concerned with the administration of the production process; that is, with the questions of effectively allocating human and nonhuman resources so as to facilitate goal attainment. In hospitals, planning on the managerial level focuses on the exigencies raised by dealing with aggregations of patients as something more than isolated actors. Planning on this level entails not only such profound decisions as how to acquire and use a hyperbaric chamber, but also with much more pedestrian concerns, such as the posting and collection of bills, the managing of queues in the OPD, and the preparation of menus. The highest level, the fiduciary, serves to articulate the organization with the larger society, so that its rules conform to acceptable standards of "good practice" and it is on good terms with regulative agencies whose approval it needs in order to continue operations. Moreover, Parsons implies that the boards of trustees, which usually carry on the fiduciary functions, tend to be responsible for much of the long-range, strategic planning (as compared to the more short-range, operational planning that occurs on the managerial level). For medical organizations, this dimension points to the capacity to anticipate future demands that external units (both individuals and collectivities) are expected to make on health facilities, as well as how to acquire those resources which will be required to meet these demands.

As just indicated, we believe that this three-level imagery is also useful for the analysis of pluralities of organizations — in the present instance, for the understanding of health delivery systems. Collaborative systems of health care units, as do single hospitals, have treatment goals. The critical addition on the technical level of such interorganizational fields is that treatment not only must be applied to the patient, but it must be comprehensive in the sense that specialized services available in disparate facilities are applied in such a way as to promote his or her general well being. The technical issue here is what services are appropriate, given the patient's needs. The problem of acquiring the requisite resources and personnel, and coordinating their utiliziation is, on the other hand, largely a managerial question. Finally, the fiduciary level is more concerned with the projected future state of the interorganizational field, as well as the "certification" and good-will of strategic societal and governmental agencies.

Clearly, the corporate model is almost totally unsuited to technical decisions. The defining of illness, diagnosis, and the planning of a course of treatment require professional decisions; that is, judgments based on the technical competence of the personnel involved. As Parsons points out: "For no matter how far removed these professionals may be from certain levels of concrete 'operations,' they must necessarily have the last word in planning and evaluating these operations (that is, setting the criteria of effective operation in technical terms), simply because their managerial superiors are seldom, if at all, equally competent in the technical field" (1960: 66). In short, the primacy of technical competence is not well served by the corporate rationalist style.

Further, we should not be deluded in pinning our hopes for corporate rationalism on the technical level simply because, in the interorganizational realm, the treatment process ordinarily requires considerably more coordination than in a single organization. The criteria for adequate courses of treatment are still most appropriately professional. To be sure, administrative acumen can greatly assist the professional staff in this regard, but administrative skills entail largely ancillary or staff functions on the technical level.

Advocating professional primacy on the interorganizational technical level does not resolve all the decision-making problems. Some of these are not even specifically interorganizational in content. For instance, one ought to examine how interprofessional relations are best coordinated (that is, bonds between physicians of different specialties and between physicians and other health professionals). Is a hierarchic pattern in which physicians (or one category of physicians) are clearly dominant desirable, or is some effort at collegiality (as in some forms of milieu therapy) a preferable style? Other questions that await resolution are distinctly interorganizational in character. For example, to insure that the patient is not needlessly transformed into a commodity on an assembly line, a totally "rational" (in terms of operating efficiency) division of labor is not desirable. That is, some overlap in specialty and equipment must be tolerated among linked health care facilities in a way that it would or ought not to be among business organizations that coordinate their activities. Hence, in fields of health care units, there always ought to be a discrepancy between how personnel and resources are allocated in purely cost-benefit terms and how they are allocated in reality. Ideally, the most significant portion of this variation should be accounted for by the operative professional norms on the technical level.

While the corporate model makes only a minimal contribution to decision-making on the technical level, it is, conversely, well suited to the needs of the fiduciary level. Fluency in administrative, budgetary, and legal language greatly facilitates the articulation of a health delivery system with the strategic units in its environment. Insofar as most of the health systems in all societies are unlikely to become self-supporting, skill in enticing resources, especially financial, from the governmental and business sectors is a critical asset. These latter units tend to impose their own ethnocentric criteria of effectiveness and efficiency on people-processing organizations such as hospitals and schools, and not unexpectedly, tend to find them extremely wasteful.

An endemic strain is likely to develop as a result. The grantor of funds periodically may become exasperated by the inefficient professional organizations and curtail its contributions. In turn, those working on the technical level may come to view these recurrent complaints as unwarranted instrusions on their professional competence. The role of the fiduciary level, then, is to serve as a buffer between the operating-efficiency oriented grantors and the professional practitioners in order to insulate the latter and to cool out the former. In this way, those operating on the fiduciary level, if successful, have the capacity to smooth out strategic financial inputs to health systems and make them less subject to short-term fluctuations. This capability becomes all the more indispensable when large numbers of organizations are involved. For example, if the Health and Hospitals Corporation cannot provide a relatively consistent input to New York's city hospitals, then it is not a single unit that is threatened, but all of the municipal hospitals and possibly some of the voluntary facilities with affiliation contracts, as well.

Corporate rationalism seems to be appropriate to the fiduciary level not only because it is a useful style for appeasing outside powers, but also because it lends itself quite readily to long-range planning. We are not suggesting that professional considerations do not play an important role in determining a health system's future needs and how to meet them. However, it seems to us that such activities also entail a considerable measure of decisions of a cost-benefit variety. Long ago, Thomas Hobbes alerted us to the fact that human wants are potentially infinite, and this is no less true if the desired goals are health services. The demands put upon a health system in modern society are, in large part, a result of the services presently available or projected. In other words, to a large extent, health planning is going to shape further wants. Hence, an assessment of the relative desirability of future goals, as well as the relative cost of different amounts of them, is precisely the kind of question that profits from some use of a corporate rationalist perspective. For example, the decision to assign a priority to programs for adolescent schizophrenics over improved medical care for the aged does not flow solely from the relative "nobility" of one goal over the other, but from the relative "payoff" of one in dollars and cents terms.

Between the technical and fiduciary levels lies the managerial domain; its intermediate status makes judgments of the relative value of corporate control on this level more difficult. Clearly, insofar as the managerial sector deals with such problems as the day-to-day procurement of personnel and material, a cost-benefit perspective is extremely useful. However, there is also an allocative dimension to the managerial problem; that is, a key question that the administrator on this level must ask concerns how best to deploy the people and the resources at hand. The question is especially pressing when human and nonhuman assets must be dispersed, not only among competing subunits within the same organization, but also among different organizations. Although corporate rationalism is certainly helpful in answering this problem, it does so more effectively in collaboration with professional criteria. The prevalent mechanism of making physicians (professionals) the chief executive officers of hospitals probably represents a useful administrative device for ameliorating the dilemma on the intraorganizational level. However, the degree to which such a mechanism is at all successful is probably based partly on the relative proximity of the physician-administrator to the technical level. After all, medical care is usually going on in the same physical plant in which he presides. On the other hand, many of those on the managerial level of an interorganizational field are far more distant (ecologically, socially, and in the matter of day-to-day decisions) from units primarily charged with health care. Hence, while these managers also may be physicians by original training, their professional status is not likely to be nearly so salient in their ongoing role performances.

What is needed, then, is a device (or devices) for blending corporate and professional criteria for the smoothest possible solution to managerial problems. One general principle, in our opinion, should inform the detailed formulation of such procedures: All other things being equal, in fields of health care units, managerial decisions should be made as close to the pluralist-core as possible. In other words, whenever feasible, operational policy ought to be made by an elite unit in a field (an imperial center) or by some consortium of leaders. In the sense that managerial decisions tend to be more prescriptive than fiduciary ones (because they are more specific, immediate, short-term, and concrete), they should be made closer to the local level actually delivering services and further away from some ultimate center of corporate control. (The rationale for this position has been discussed in the preceding subsection.) There is no need for concern that issues of operating efficiency will be unduly slighted on the more local level, because the leadership positions in the individual health care units are, after all, administrative. Moreover, as we have just argued, these local administrators, because of prior training and proximity to the technical level, are more likely to temper their corporate rationalist perspectives with professional orientations.

In essence, we are suggesting that in the matter of managerial decisions (as contrasted especially to fiduciary decisions), the locus of responsibility, wherever appropriate, should be clusters of health care units — in a word, it should be decentralized as much as possible. Further, our foregoing discussion suggests that this level ideally should be as unencumbered as possible by distinctive administrative entities; that is, where feasible, the managerial decisions should be made by the health care units themselves and, if that is not possible, that they should be aided by a mediating agency rather than by a corporation. We suggest that corporations are more appropriately used to coordinate among clusters of health care units than to coordinate within particular fields. Of course, some of the decisions may indeed be managerial, but certainly they would be a "higher order" managerial (and probably bordering on the fiduciary), than those made within the individual pluralist-cores.

THE NATURE OF THE PLURALIST CORE: EMPIRES WITHOUT IMPERIALISM

Granted then that the more concrete day-to-day managerial decisions are best made within a pluralist-core (by the health units in a field), the question of how such a core ought to be organized still remains to be considered. A central point made earlier in this chapter — and, indeed, one which pervades our entire monograph — is that feudalism in isolation represents the least desirable mode of interorganizational articulation because the capabilities for joint action and autonomous transformation are extremely minimal. However, the other type of field not associated with a coordinating agency, the empire, while more effective and efficient than the feudal, also tends to be more alienating. Hence, *empires, too, seem to be burdened by inherent constraints on their transformation-potential.*

The problem, in other words, is to find a way of organizing the plurality of health care units in such a way as to avoid the drift toward social entropy springing from feudalism, as well as to steer clear of the disruptive effects of skewed power that stem from empires. What we need, to put it succinctly, are empires without imperialism. Empires are valuable because systemic power becomes crystallized in one or a few units, while the pitfalls of overbureaucratization are minimized. What is required are mechanisms of checks-and-balances that set limits on the power of the imperial center and open it up to the input of demands from other units. In this way, empires will become what Health-PAC has called "health commonwealths."

It seems unlikely that health empires will transform themselves in this direction through natural processes of development. Rather, the paring-down of imperial power necessarily entails conscious intervention. The forces urging community control, of course, have such a goal in mind. (We will speak more about what community-participation can and cannot accomplish in the following section.) However, given the relative concentration of power currently found in most imperial centers, the reliance on internal forces to reshape the pluralist-core will most likely lead to protracted and highly alienating conflict and to a most uncertain outcome. Indeed, the net result of a full-blown "colonial revolution" is the diminished transformation-potential of the field and, perhaps, schism, if not total fragmentation.

Thus, it is imperative that forces external to empires intervene to assist in their transformation in more egalitarian directions. A variety of mechanisms is available in this regard. For instance, federal and state grants to pluralities of health care units could contain restrictions on how the funds, or the personnel and equipment they purchase, are to be allocated within a given field. Such controls should remain nonprescriptive; they should merely circumscribe the outer-limits beyond which the distribution of resources is deemed unjust. Another mechanism is already operative in the case of the New York Health and Hospitals Corporation. Each succeeding wave of affiliation contracts seeks to increase the accountability of the imperial center and to promote the independent leverage of the municipal hospitals. Short of abrogating some or all existing contracts, the corporation cannot eliminate the superordinate position of the medical centers. But, then, this is probably not desirable. Certainly, with periodic intervention, the corporation can correct gross inequities and monitor the fields for the emergence of new ones.

Obviously, the foregoing is but a broad outline that awaits a detailed blueprint. However, it hopefully is specific enough to make clear that we view *empires without imperialism* as a crucial desideratum to be pursued. The delineation of such a goal and an active commitment to it by health policy makers will, we think, preserve the gains of differentiation of power and skills within a plural field, while avoiding the most corrosive effects of excessive power concentrations.

PARTICIPATORY DEMOCRACY AND HEALTH SYSTEMS

Finally, any program advocating a mixed system of centralized-corporate and more local-pluralist control also must come to grips with the issue raised most eloquently by health radicals: the argument that the American health system can become truly responsive only if the interests of the consumers are formally built into it, along with the interests of those professionals and nonprofessionals who participate in the delivery of health care.

Indicative of the rapidity with which new ideas are incorporated into the American mainstream (and often rendered banal) is the speed with which "community-staff participation" has become an empty shibboleth evoked by almost the entire spectrum of health interest groups. The apparent consensus around this slogan flows in no small way from the fact that few really know what it means or have a clear program for its implementation. The phrase, community control, for instance, specifies neither *who* is the community nor *what* is controlled.

As to the latter question: we have suggested that there are three broad levels of decision-making: technical, managerial, and fiduciary. Does the notion of community (and staff) control require involvement on all three of these levels, or are some more amenable to participatory democracy than others? The incidents at Lincoln Hospital (recounted in chapter 4) seem to suggest that militants, initially at least, make the technical level the prime target of their assaults. Of the five major crises of 1970, four (demands for a preventive medicine program, and attacks on the organization of the departments of pediatrics, psychiatry, and obstetrics and gynecology) were concerned with issues on this level. Divorced from the specific context of Lincoln, these confrontations can be seen as efforts to redefine the operating criteria dominating the technical level. That is, they can be interpreted as efforts to play down (if not replace as in the psychiatric case) the dominance of professional criteria.

Here, of course, the distinctions between the community and the staff, and between the professional and nonprofessional staffs, become critical. The involvement of the professional staff in technical decision-making is, at the most general level, nonproblematic. Nonetheless, the precise form of professional decision-making is hotly contested. Nurses, social workers, clinical psychologists, and so on bridle increasingly under physician dominance. Hence, although we prescind from a deeper analysis of the question of professional decision-making, we recognize that major changes are undoubtedly overdue in this realm. In passing, it may be worth noting that given the variation of performance requirements in the specialties, it is probably more efficient to deal with the exigencies of professional reorganization on a department by department basis (that is, one plan for psychiatry, another for radiotherapy, another for internal medicine, and so on).

If we presume, then, that professional reorganization is in order, we must still deal with the participation of the community and the nonprofessional staff. In a recent striking about-face, Health-PAC, perhaps the leading advocate of "medical power to the people," has given up on community control and has shifted its line to "worker control." In a sense, this represents the abandonment of the New Left strategy for revolution-from-the ghetto, in favor of the Old Left position of revolution-from-the-factory (at least as far as the health system is concerned). The *Bulletin* (1972: 1) explains Health-PAC's shift as follows:

> Initially many at Lincoln felt that control of the hospital on behalf of the community was the key goal. Time and practice have shown, however, that the workers at the hospital are in fact pivotal. Their actions have made the greatest inroads and have had the most continuity. This arises in part out of the differences in the relation of workers and community residents to a hospital. Workers are at the hospital everyday. A major part of their lives is spent there. Far more than outsiders, they know how it actually runs. Community people visit the hospital infrequently and when they do, it is often under conditions of great personal stress — the worst condition for focusing attention of the institution. Furthermore, workers at the hospital are concentrated in one place and are relatively accessible to each other. Thus it has happened at Lincoln that the slogan of "community-worker control" has to some degree shifted toward "worker control," even as those involved have attempted to develop creative tactics to unite workers and patients.

What we should learn from Health-PAC's admission of defeat is not that community participation should be given up in toto, but that community control of the technical level (at least as envisioned by Health-PAC during its more utopian moments) is an unrealistic goal. As the quotation makes all too clear, maintaining community interest in health facilities is quite a different matter from maintaining involvement in the educational process. Most healthy adults have only occasional encounters with hospitals and when free from symptoms, they do not want to contemplate the possibility of their own ill-health. Parents, by contrast, especially when they have several children, tend to be more committed to a sustained involvement in the local school.

However, there is some value for a community presence on the technical level. Such a presence ought not to be focused primarily on the issues of effectiveness (that is, how successfully the array of health services is applied to the patient). Rather, it should be more concerned with the tendencies toward insensitivity which are the frequent outcomes of health care in large, complex organizations. Mechanisms must be developed that insure that such systems regularly take into account the needs of the "whole patient" and do not treat him as a mere medical commodity.

Traditionally, the issue of insensitivity has been treated under the rubric of medical ethics. Devices such as tissue committees, peer review committees, and so on represent efforts to guarantee high levels of ethical practice within health facilities. We do not disparage either these mechanisms or efforts among professionals to elaborate them and to add new ones. However, the more the patient is viewed as the passive recipient of the medical ethics process, the greater will be his feeling that he is being handled purely as an object.

On the other hand, the alternative is not to have a community representative peek over each doctor's shoulder as he makes his or her rounds (or each nurse's or social worker's, and so on). In short, what needs to be developed is a community *presence* to whom the patient can appeal comfortably, if necessary. Yet this presence should be unobtrusive, that is, it should not seek to replace criteria of technical competence in the direct application of health services. What kinds of individuals, statuses, or groups can play such a role is unclear at the moment. Such questions as whether the selection of these "sensitivity ombudsmen" should be left to the community, whether they should have a formal occupational position in the delivery system, and how their effectiveness is to be judged also need to be studied further. Certainly, some elements in the health professions, such as social workers, aspire to such a role. But if a social worker is to become a health ombudsman, he or she must develop stronger ties to the community and lessen his or her involvement with the official health system.

By implication, at least, Health-PAC is suggesting that hospital workers can play this kind of a role (while of course, arguing that their control of decision-making should be expanded to other sectors as well). Such a role for the nonprofessional staff seems plausible when they and the patients have racial, religious, or class attributes in common, as distinct from those of the professional staff. That is, it is premised on the assumption that a Black or Puerto Rican maintenance worker understands better the needs of Black or Puerto Rican patients or is more naturally sympathetic to them than a white, middle-class physician. While this may be true under some circumstances, it is not universally true. Nor is it true in settings where the patient's status-set looks more like the doctor's than the nonprofessional staff's (for example, as in an elite mental hospital). Moreover, to rely on the strata of the staff with the lowest skills and lowest education as the guarantors of sensitivity is asking more from these groups than they may be able to provide in some regular, systematic way.

A clearer role for community and staff participation in decision-making emerges when we move from the technical level up to the managerial and fiduciary rungs. It is on these levels that administrative factors become increasingly important. Certainly both the community and the staff have a legitimate interest in how the resources available are allocated among the member units. A given cluster of health delivery units (an empire minus imperialism) ought to contain mechanisms for developing these inputs. As we pointed out in our chapter on empires, this means that interest groups must cease to be purely local in nature and be sufficiently empirewide to cut across parochial perspectives. For example, consumer groups must be developed that see themselves as part of the total Einstein-Montefiore empire. In this way, they can make evaluations on what contributes to the overall effectiveness and efficiency of the system and not just the operation of, let us say, Lincoln Hospital. The same is true of hospital workers. In their case, labor unions serve as an obvious mechanism for promoting collectivity-orientation. Given the diversity of populations, it will not be nearly so easy to organize community groups on an empirewide basis. Community groups have tended to focus on local, ethnic, and religious considerations and to treat the larger system as the adversary.

Just as the community and health workers deserve a vital impact on how local clusters of health care units allocate their resources, so, too, they can make an important contribution to long-range health planning (associated with the fiduciary level). Such planning should begin within the regional corporation that supervises several of these pluralist clusters. The areawide planning agencies being set up under CHP may serve as one model here. First, by being a public benefit corporation, and, hence, partly in and partly outside of the governmental sector, they have the potentiality for being free of daily, routine political pressures, while retaining the element of public accountability, which is a major benefit of governmental involvement. Hence, groups such as consumers and workers should campaign to have public officials appoint members of their constituencies to these agencies. Further, they should serve notice that the performances of local CHPs are fair game as issues in local electoral politics and that governors, mayors, and legislators will be judged by the electorate, in part, on how the corporations in their jurisdictions "deliver." Much the same philosophy would seem to apply to the national health system. Direct penetration of NIH seems to be a less feasible step than political mobilization to put pressure on the executive and legislative branches. Once again, this presupposes a capacity to organize health consumers above and beyond purely local interests; and, in this case, also above and beyond regional interests and toward authentically national interests.

In sum, we are arguing that the goals implicit in such slogans as "community control" and "participatory democracy" are best served on the managerial and fiduciary levels of the health system by mechanisms enhancing public accountability. More "direct" mechanisms such as community boards, seem more applicable for the operation of single hospitals, rather than for networks of health care organizations. While we find such local boards commendable, we must caution that they have a possible negative valence insofar as they undermine commitment to the larger system. However, local boards can serve as the health ombudsmen within the hospital, as well as contribute to its internal managerial and fiduciary decisions.

The question of *who* is the community is even more complex than the one regarding what it is trying to control. The community obviously is more than the patients (past or present) and their families. Whom else, then, do we include? If we speak of the community as including the entire population served by a given unit or set of units, then we must ask: how is their will expressed? A system of health plebiscites seems totally unworkable. Should we allow groups who claim to speak for the community to act as its agent? Or should local boards be elected, even though the experience from antipoverty programs and education suggest that electoral participation is likely to be extremely low?

All of these questions require far more extensive treatment than is available in a chapter such as this. However, let us make one suggestion. As we see it, part of the difficulty of organizing groups for local planning is that it has been done on a segmental basis. Several cities are now experimenting with community planning boards. These tend to deal with problems of housing and urban development. There are separate community boards for schools, health, and so on. We suggest that the community would be more willing to participate in local planning if there were only one community board, that dealt with all of these issues. This would require that arbitrary boundaries such as health districts, school districts, and so on which now do not necessarily coincide, be made to coincide.

Since we are counselling direct participation by community groups only on the individual hospital and empire levels, the question of representation is not nearly so unwieldy as if we were suggesting similar mechanisms for regional and national corporations. In these realms, any health interest group has a right to exist and to advocate its positions. The acid test of its representativeness here will be its ability to secure the enactment of legislation, the appointment of officials, and the election of preferred candidates. The only knotty problem is how health interest groups that will speak for the most underprivileged segments of society are to be mobilized and how to maintain their mobilization. At the moment, insofar as the less privileged are more readily activated by particularistic appeals, regional and national interest groups are more successfully created from a federation of local groups than by trying to create organizations from the top down.

CONCLUSIONS

In this chapter, we have advocated a mixed health system. It is mixed because although we argue for more corporatism, more governmental intervention, and more centralization, we have noted the limits and pitfalls of an overreliance on these strategies. Totally centralized planning cannot work in a health system as complex as ours. We must make use of local insight and initiative. Moreover, to debate endlessly about this point is futile, because total centralization could not be enacted reasonably soon in America even if it could be proven to work. Thus, it seems both prudent and efficacious to utilize the capabilities existing in the private-pluralist sector. This does not mean that the private sector ought not to be transformed, but that the transformation should be a reasonable one based upon a rational and humane division of labor that does not make each facility just like every other one.

The "fit" between the corporate superstructure and the pluralist-base will not be a "snug" one. There will be numerous areas of friction, strain, controversy, and conflict. However, the health policy maker ought not to look at these contradictions merely as "dysfunctions" to be overcome. Rather, they are also signs of vitality in the health delivery system, and they point to sectors of indeterminacy that are areas of opportunity for meaningful social change.

NOTES

1. In our study, by definition, feudalism has been immersed in mediated and guided fields. However, in the American case, at least, it is probably true to say that, historically, feudalism has been empirically *prior,* as well. Nevertheless, one must not conclude that conceptual-priority and empirical-priority inevitable go hand-in-hand. It is clearly conceivable that in contemporary modernizing societies, agencies for potential mediation or for potential guidance are designated prior to the development of lateral bonds among the units to be coordinated. Indeed, it may well be that these latter units (for example, hospital, clinics) do not even exist at the time the agencies are designated. In these settings, among the most problematic issues are the creation of a feudal-base and what concrete directions such a base might take. From this, it follows that many of the specific policy problems modernizing societies face in coordinating their health services are substantively different from those of "postmodern" ones (for example, the United States). Nonetheless, the formal language of feudalism, mediation, empires, and corporate rationalism developed in this monograph may still be usefully applied to the "premodern" setting.

2. Of course, they may very well be professional in terms of their formal training, but this is not the auspices under which they are performing.

3. Reprinted by permission from The Public Interest 26 (Winter, 1972), pp. 112-125. ©National Affairs, Inc., 1972.

4. Harry Greenfield has very correctly pointed out that the costs incurred by hospitals are not identical with the costs (that is, price or charge) to the purchaser of hospital services. However, he demonstrates that they tend to move in the same direction and at the same rate. See Greenfield, 1972: Chapter 2.

5. In preparing for the publication of this monograph, we were informed by the American Hospital Association that their revised version of AMERIPLAN is found in *Policy Statement on the Provision of Health Services* (1971). Their model for the Health Care Corporations remains fundamentally the same in this publication. The contextuating role of government via the National Health Board and State Health Commissions is spelled-out in a bit more detail than in the 1970 report. Anyone interested in the official position of the A.H.A. on the organization of American Health Care is referred to the 1971 statement.

REFERENCES

AMERICAN HOSPITAL ASSOCIATION (1970) Special Committee on the Provision of Health Services: AMERIPLAN — A Proposal for the Delivery of Health Services in the United States. Chicago: American Hospital Association.

––– (1971) Policy Statement on the Provision of Health Services. Chicago: American Hospital Association.

ETZIONI, A. (1968) The Active Society. New York: Free Press.

GREENFIELD, H. (1972) Hospital Efficiency and Public Policy. New York: Center for Policy Research.

HEALTH POLICY ADVISORY CENTER [Health-PAC] (1972) "Editorial: institutional organizing." Bulletin 37 (January): 1-2.

KLEIN, R. (1972) "The political economy of national health." Public Interest 26 (Winter): 112-125.

MERTON, R. K. (1968) "Bureaucratic structure and personality," pp. 249-260 in Social Theory and Social Structure. New York: Free Press.

PARSONS, T. (1960) "Some ingredients of a general theory of formal organization," pp. 16-96 in Structure and Process in Modern Societies. New York: Free Press.

INDEXES

NAME INDEX

SUBJECT INDEX

Health care crisis: Ineffectiveness, 15-16, 22, 193, 205, 206, 211, 212, 213, 215, 219, 221-225, 226-231, 235-236; Inefficiency, 15, 16-17, 22, 148, 178-179, 184, 193, 206, 211, 212, 213, 215, 219, 221-225, 226-231; Insensitivity, 22n, 179, 180-181, 206, 211, 215, 216, 221, 236-239; Unresponsiveness, 15, 17, 22, 179, 181-184, 191-193, 204, 206, 211, 214-216, 221, 233-239
Health care crisis, New York City. *See* Affiliation Plan
Health care, bureaucratization or over-bureaucratization of, 17, 213, 214, 215-216, 232
Health care, traditional values of, 18-19
Health delivery systems: effectiveness, efficiency, responsiveness and sensitivity. *See* Health care crisis: Ineffectiveness; Inefficiency; Insensitivity; Unresponsiveness
Health, Education and Welfare (H.E.W.), Department of, 193 *passim*, 226 *passim*
Health and Hospital Planning Council of Southern New York, 92-95, 99, 104, 132, 197-198, 200; *list of members,* 92-93
Health and Hospitals Corporation of New York City, 93, 115-116, 134, 140, 146, 149, 183-193, 207, 219, 223, 229, 233
Health Policy Advisory Center (Health-PAC), 17, 23, 95, 106-108, 109, 118-124, 125, 127-128, 137, 142, 144n, 145, 197-199, 234-236
Health Services Administration (HSA) of New York City, 184, 187-188, 197
Health Services and Mental Health Administration, 203
Hillside Hospital (N.Y.), 146
Hospital Corporation of America (HCA), 161, 164-166, 168-169
Houston State Psychiatric Institute Medical Empire, 141-142; *Connery, et al.'s list of members,* 142

Imperial fields. *See* Control configurations, interorganizational: Empire
Independent Staffing, in mediating agencies, 83, 84-88, 101
Institute for Policy Studies, 185
Intercorporate feudalism, 223, 225. *See also:* Control configurations, interorganizational: Corporations
Intermittent versus sustained interorganizational relations, 28, 46, 48-49
Interorganizational relations, basic ingredients, 36-37. *See also:* Control configurations, interorganizational and Content of interorganizational relations
Intricacy, of interorganizational relations, 47, 48-49

James Ewing Hospital (N.Y.), 111
Jefferson Medical School, 153
Jewish Hospital of Brooklyn (N.Y.), 85, 113, 146
Jewish welfare federations: comparison of Cincinnati, Detroit, Philadelphia, Toronto, St. Louis, San Francisco, 96-101
Johns Hopkins Medical Empire (Md.), 109
Joint Commission on Hospital Accreditation, 178
Joint policy formation, range of. *See* Comprehensive planning, degree of

Kaiser Foundation Health Plan, Inc. *See* Kaiser-Permanente System
Kaiser Foundation Hospitals, Inc. *See* Kaiser-Permanente System
Kaiser Foundation Rehabilitation Center (Calif.), 172-173
Kaiser-Permanente System, 147, 149, 170-183, 206n, 207
Kings County Hospital Medical Center (N.Y.), 85, 111, 116, 118, 128, 146

Lasa fever virus, 42-44, 49, 53
Lee Memorial Hospital (Fla.), 166, 169

213; locus of responsibility 26-27, 36, 88-101, 107, 213. *See also:* Crisis of compretence; Crisis of legitimacy

Queens Hospital (N.Y.), 117, 146

Regional Medical Program (RMP), 149, 193-199, 203, 204, 207, 208, 217; New York Metropolitan Regional Medical Program (NYM-RMP), 197-199, 200

Resource-types (goal relevant versus ancillary), 25, 32-33, 36-37, 46, 48-49, 102, 144

Resources and responsibility for planning in mediating agencies, 83, 88-101. *See also:* Power, Systemic

Rockland State Hospital (N.Y.), 51-52, 65

Roosevelt Hospital (N.Y.), 12

St. Elizabeth of Hungary Clinic (Ariz.), 86-87

St. Francis Hospital (Colo.), 49-50, 52

St. Francis, Third Order of (Peoria, Ill.), 154-156, 158, 160

St. Luke's Hospital Center (N.Y.), 121, 124

St. Mary's Hospital (Ariz.), 86

St. Mary's Hospital (N.J.), 59

Salience, of interorganization relations, 25, 34, 36, 37, 46, 48-49, 102, 144, 205; relationship to goal-relevance, 34, 37

San Francisco Medical Society, 74-75

Satellites, health care, 143

Scope, interorganizational (broad versus narrow), 25, 36, 37, 46, 48-49, 72-73, 102, 144

"Sensitivity ombudsmen," 236

Social entropy, 212

Social and Rehabilitation Service (SRS), Children's Bureau of, 204

Society of Urban Physicians, 191

Staff control or participation. *See* Health care crisis: Unresponsiveness

Sydenham Hospital (N.Y.), 115

Symmetry, of interorganizational relations, 25, 35, 36, 37, 46, 48-49, 102-103, 144; relationship to dependence and power, 35, 52, 103

System-elite. *See* control configuration, interorganizational: Corporations

Technical level of interorganizational fields, 226-231, 234, 239

Tri-Hospital Plan (Passaic, N.J.), 58-59

Tucson Hospital Medical Educational Center (THMEP), 86-88

Tucson Medical Center (Ariz.), 86

U.S. Veterans Administration Hospitals, 62-64; Kansas City (Mo.), 63-64; New York City's, 110

University of Delaware Medical School, 153

University of Kansas School of Medicine, 63-64

University of Southern California Medical Empire, 109

Vallejo Hospital (Calif.), 172

Value-added typology, 26

Wilmington General Hospital (Del.), 150

Wilmington Medical Center (Del.), 149-153

Yale University Medical School, 42-44, 53

ABOUT THE AUTHOR

EDWARD W. LEHMAN is Associate Professor of Sociology and Director of Undergraduate Studies in Sociology at New York University. A Senior Research Associate at The Center for Policy Research, his fields of interest are political sociology, medical sociology, and complex organizations. Among the journals he has contributed to are *American Sociological Review, Social Forces, Science,* and the *Journal of Chronic Diseases.* He is currently completing a book on political sociology and conducting a nation-wide study on psychiatric manpower in community mental health centers.

SAGE LIBRARY OF SOCIAL RESEARCH

Also in this series:

NOTES